HAMMOND

WORLD ATLAS

COLLECTORS EDITION

HAMMOND
World Atlas Corporation
New Jersey

Collectors World Atlas

Library of Congress Cataloging-in-Publication Data

Hammond World Atlas Corporation.
    Hammond world atlas.–Collectors ed.

        p.   cm.
    Includes index.
    ISBN 0-8437-1604-5
    1. Atlases.   I. Title.   II. Title: World atlas.

G1021. H279   1997 <G&M>
912--dc20
                                        96-36318
                                            CIP
                                            MAP

Contents

5–15	Gazetteer—Index of the World
16–17	World—Languages
18–19	World—Occupations
20–21	World—Natural Vegetation
22–23	World—Climates
24–25	World—Time Zones
26–27	World—Air Distances
28–32	World—Statistics
33	Arctic Ocean
34–35	World—Political
36–37	World—Physical
38–39	World—Population
40–41	North America
42–43	Canada
44–45	United States
46–47	Mexico
48–49	Central America
50–51	West Indies
52–53	Cuba, Hispaniola & Jamaica
54–55	Puerto Rico & Lesser Antilles
56–57	South America—Northern Part
58–59	South America—Southern Part
60–61	Africa—Northern Part
62–63	Africa—Southern Part
64–65	Europe
66–67	United Kingdom & Ireland
68–69	Norway, Sweden, Finland & Denmark
70–71	Germany
72–73	Netherlands, Belgium & Luxembourg
74–75	France
76–77	Spain & Portugal

Contents

78–79	Italy
80–81	Switzerland
82–83	Austria, Czech Republic, Slovakia & Hungary
84–85	Balkan States
86–87	Poland
88–89	Eastern Europe
90–91	Russia and Neighboring Countries
92–93	Asia
94–95	Near & Middle East
96–97	Turkey, Syria, Lebanon & Cyprus
98–99	Israel & Jordan
100–101	Iran & Iraq
102–103	Southern Asia
104–105	China & Mongolia
106–107	Japan & Korea
108–109	Philippines
110–111	Burma, Thailand, Indochina & Malaya
112–113	Southeast Asia
114–115	Australia & New Zealand
116–117	Pacific Ocean
118	Antarctica
119–124	Flags of the World
125	Road Atlas—Contents, Symbols
126–180	Highway Maps—United States
181	Highway Map—Mexico
182–191	Highway Maps—Canada
192	Highway Mileage Table
193–224	Index

This alphabetical list of continents, countries, states, possessions, etc., gives the areas, populations, index references and page numbers on which they are shown on the largest scale. The index reference letter and number indicates the square on the respective map in which the named area is located.

*Member of the United Nations. †Does not appear on map.

Country	Area (Sq. Miles)	(Sq. Kilometers)	Population	Page No.	Index Ref.
*Afghanistan	250,000	647,500	23,738,085	102	A1
Africa	11,707,000	30,321,130	705,924,000	60-63	
Alabama, U.S.A.	51,705	133,916	4,040,587	128	
Alaska, U.S.A.	591,004	1,530,700	550,043	129	
*Albania	11,100	28,749	3,293,252	85	C3
Alberta, Canada	255,285	661,185	2,545,553	191	
*Algeria	919,591	2,381,740	29,830,370	60	C2
American Samoa	77	199	57,366	117	J7
*Andorra	174	450	74,839	77	G1
*Angola	481,351	1,246,700	10,623,994	62-63	D6
Anguilla, U.K.	35	91	7,099	51	F3
Antarctica	5,500,000	14,245,000	....	118	
*Antigua and Barbuda	170	440	66,175	51	G3
*Argentina	1,068,296	2,766,890	35,797,536	58-59	B-D5-8
Arizona, U.S.A.	114,000	295,260	3,665,228	130	
Arkansas, U.S.A.	53,187	137,754	2,350,725	131	
*Armenia	11,506	29,800	3,465,611	89	F6
Aruba, Netherlands	70	193	65,974	50 55	D4
Ascension Island, Saint Helena	34	88	719	62	A5
Ashmore and Cartier Islands, Australia†	61	159	939	114	B2
Asia	17,128,500	44,362,815	3,407,967,000	92-93	
*Australia	2,967,893	7,686,850	18,438,824	114-115	
Australian Capital Territory	927	2,400	280,132	115	D4
*Austria	32,375	83,851	8,054,078	82	B-C3
*Azerbaijan	33,436	86,600	7,735,918	89	G6
Azores, Portugal	902	2,335	237,000	35	J4
*Bahamas, The	5,382	13,939	262,034	50	C1
*Bahrain	240	622	603,318	95	G4
Baker Island, U.S.A.	1	2.6	....	117	J5
Balearic Islands, Spain	1,936	5,014	690,000	77	G3
*Bangladesh	55,598	144,000	125,340,261	103	E2
*Barbados	166	430	257,731	51 55	G4

Gazetteer–Index of the World

Country	Area (Sq. Miles)	Area (Sq. Kilometers)	Population	Page No.	Index Ref.
*Belarus	80,154	207,600	10,439,916	89	C4
*Belgium	11,780	30,510	10,203,683	73	
*Belize	8,865	22,960	224,663	48	B1
*Benin	43,483	112,620	5,902,178	60	C4
Bermuda, U.K.	21	54	61,629	41	M6
				51	H3
*Bhutan	18,147	47,000	1,865,191	103	D2
*Bolivia	424,163	1,098,582	7,669,868	56	C4
Bonaire, Neth. Antilles	112	291	8,087	51	E4
				55	
*Bosnia & Herzegovina	19,781	51,233	2,607,734	84	B2
*Botswana	231,803	600,370	1,500,765	63	E7
Bouvet Island, Norway	22	57	....	35	K8
*Brazil	3,286,470	8,511,965	164,511,366	56-57	
British Columbia, Canada	366,253	948,596	3,282,061	190	
British Indian Ocean Territory, U.K.	29	75	....	93	F6
*Brunei	2,228	5,770	307,616	112	E5
*Bulgaria	42,823	110,912	8,652,745	84	D3
*Burkina Faso	105,869	274,200	10,891,159	60	B3
*Burma (Myanmar)	261,969	678,500	46,821,943	110	A2
*Burundi	10,745	27,830	6,052,614	63	F5
California, U.S.A.	158,706	411,049	29,760,021	132-133	
*Cambodia	69,900	181,040	11,163,861	111	D4
*Cameroon	183,568	475,441	14,677,510	60	D4
*Canada	3,851,787	9,976,139	29,123,194	42-43	
Canary Islands, Spain	2,808	7,273	1,495,000	76	B4
				35	J4
*Cape Verde	1,556	4,030	393,843	35	J5
Cayman Islands, U.K.	100	259	33,192	50	B3
Celebes, Indonesia	72,986	189,034	12,520,711	113	G6
*Central African Republic	240,533	622,980	3,342,051	61	D-E4
Central America	197,480	511,475	29,201,000	48-49	
*Chad	495,752	1,283,998	7,166,023	60-61	D3
Channel Islands, U.K.	75	194	133,000	67	E6
*Chile	292,258	756,950	14,508,168	56	B4
				58	B-C5-8
*China, People's Rep. of	3,705,386	9,596,960	1,221,591,778	104-105	
China, Republic of (Taiwan)	13,892	35,980	21,655,515	105	F3

Country	Area (Sq. Miles)	(Sq. Kilometers)	Population	Page No.	Index Ref.
Christmas Island, Australia	52	135	889	93	H6
Clipperton Island, France	2	5.2	....	41	H8
Cocos (Keeling) Islands, Australia	5.4	14	604	93	G6
*Colombia	439,733	1,138,910	37,418,290	56	B2
Colorado, U.S.A.	104,091	269,596	3,294,394	134	
*Comoros	838	2,170	589,797	63	G6
*Congo, Dem. Rep. of the	905,563	2,345,410	47,440,362	63	E5
*Congo, Rep. of the	132,046	342,000	2,583,198	62	D5
Connecticut, U.S.A.	5,018	12,997	3,287,116	136	
Cook Islands, New Zealand	91	236	18,000	117	K7
Coral Sea Islands, Australia	8.5	22	....	116	E-F7
				115	D2
Corsica, France	3,352	8,682	249,737	75	B7
*Costa Rica	19,730	51,100	3,534,174	48	C3
*Côte d'Ivoire	124,502	322,460	14,986,218	60	B4
Crete, Greece	3,218	8,335	456,642	85	D5
*Croatia	22,050	57,110	5,026,995	84	A2
*Cuba	42,803	110,860	10,999,041	50	B2
				52-53	
Curaçao, Neth. Antilles	178	462	145,430	50	E4
				55	
*Cyprus	3,571	9,250	752,808	96	E5
*Czech Republic	30,387	78,703	10,318,958	82	C2
Delaware, U.S.A.	2,044	5,294	666,168	139	F2
*Denmark	16,629	43,069	5,268,775	69	B3
District of Columbia, U.S.A.	69	179	606,900	139	D1
*Djibouti	8,494	22,000	434,116	61	G3
*Dominica	290	751	83,226	51	G4
				54-55	
*Dominican Republic	18,815	48,730	8,228,151	50	D3
				52-53	Q-S7
*Ecuador	109,483	283,561	11,690,535	56	B3
*Egypt	386,659	1,001,447	64,791,891	61	F2
				94	B2
*El Salvador	8,124	21,040	5,661,827	48	B2
England, U.K.	50,516	130,836	48,068,400	66-67	
*Equatorial Guinea	10,831	28,052	442,516	60	C4
*Eritrea	46,842	121,320	3,589,687	61	F3

Country	Area (Sq. Miles)	(Sq. Kilometers)	Population	Page No.	Index Ref.
*Estonia	17,413	45,100	1,444,721	88	C3
*Ethiopia	435,184	1,127,127	58,732,577	61	F-G4
Europe	4,057,000	10,507,630	732,653,000	64-65	
Falkland Islands & Dependencies, U.K.	6,198	16,053	2,317	58-59	D8
*Faroe Islands, Denmark	540	1,399	48,871	64	D2
*Fiji	7,055	18,272	792,441	116	H7
*Finland	130,128	337,032	5,109,148	68-69	E2
Florida, U.S.A.	58,664	151,940	12,937,926	140-141	
*France	211,208	547,030	58,470,421	74-75	
French Guiana	35,135	91,000	145,270	57	D2
French Polynesia	1,544	4,000	219,999	117	M8
*Gabon	103,347	267,670	1,190,159	62	D5
*Gambia, The	4,363	11,300	1,248,085	60	A3
Gaza Strip	139	360	813,322	94	G3
*Georgia	26,911	69,700	5,174,642	89	F6
Georgia, U.S.A.	58,910	152,577	6,478,216	142	
*Germany	137,803	356,910	84,068,216	70-71	
*Ghana	92,100	238,540	18,100,703	60	B4
Gibraltar, U.K.	2.28	5.91	31,874	76	D4
*Great Britain & Northern Ireland (United Kingdom)	94,525	244,820	58,610,182	66-67	
*Greece	50,942	131,940	10,583,126	85	C4
Greenland, Denmark	840,000	2,175,600	57,611	40	P2
*Grenada	131	340	95,537	51 55	F4
Guadeloupe & Dependencies, France	687	1,779	402,815	51 54-55	F3
Guam, U.S.A.	209	541	153,307	116	E4
*Guatemala	42,042	108,889	11,558,407	48	B2
*Guinea	94,927	245,860	7,405,375	60	A3
*Guinea-Bissau	13,946	36,120	1,178,584	60	A3
*Guyana	83,000	214,970	706,116	56	D2
*Haiti	10,714	27,750	6,611,407	50 52	D3 P6
Hawaii, U.S.A.	6,471	16,760	1,108,229	129	
Heard & McDonald Islands, Australia	113	293	....	35	M8
*Honduras	43,277	112,087	5,751,384	48	C2

Country	Area (Sq. Miles)	(Sq. Kilometers)	Population	Page No.	Index Ref.
Hong Kong	403	1,044	5,542,869	105	E3
Howland Island, U.S.A.	1	2.6	....	117	J5
*Hungary	35,919	93,030	9,935,774	83	E-F3
*Iceland	39,768	103,000	272,550	64	C2
Idaho, U.S.A.	83,564	216,431	1,006,749	143	
Illinois, U.S.A.	56,345	145,934	11,430,602	144	
*India	1,269,339	3,287,588	967,612,804	102-103	
Indiana, U.S.A.	36,185	93,719	5,544,159	145	
*Indonesia	741,096	1,919,440	209,774,138	112-113	C-H6-7
Iowa, U.S.A.	56,275	145,752	2,776,755	146	
*Iran	636,293	1,648,000	67,540,002	100-101	
*Iraq	168,753	437,072	22,219,289	100	
*Ireland	27,136	70,282	3,555,500	67	B-C4
Ireland, Northern, U.K.	5,452	14,121	1,610,000	66	C3
Isle of Man, U.K.	227	588	72,751	67	D3
*Israel	8,019	20,770	5,534,672	98-99	
*Italy	116,305	301,230	57,534,088	78-79	
*Ivory Coast (Côte d'Ivoire)	124,502	322,460	14,986,218	60	B4
*Jamaica	4,243	10,990	2,615,582	50,53	
Jan Mayen Island, Norway	144	373	....	35	J2
*Japan	145,882	377,835	125,716,637	106-107	
Jarvis Island, U.S.A.	1	2.6	....	117	L6
Java, Indonesia	48,842	126,500	107,581,306	112	D-E7
Johnston Atoll, U.S.A.	0.91	2.4	327	117	K4
*Jordan	34,445	89,213	4,324,638	98-99	
Kalaallit Nunaat (Greenland), Denmark	840,000	2,175,600	57,611	40	P2
Kansas, U.S.A.	82,277	213,097	2,477,574	147	
*Kazakhstan	1,049,150	2,717,300	16,898,572	90	E-F3
Kentucky, U.S.A.	40,409	104,659	3,685,296	148-149	
*Kenya	224,960	582,646	28,803,085	63	F4
Kermadec Islands, New Zealand	13	33	5	117	J9
Kiribati	277	717	82,449	117	J6
*Korea, North	46,540	120,539	24,317,004	106	C2
*Korea, South	38,023	98,480	45,948,811	106	C3
*Kuwait	6,880	17,820	2,076,805	94	F4
*Kyrgyzstan	76,641	198,500	4,540,185	90	D3
*Laos	91,428	236,800	5,116,959	110	D3
*Latvia	24,749	64,100	2,437,649	88	C3

Gazetteer–Index of the World

Country	Area (Sq. Miles)	(Sq. Kilometers)	Population	Page No.	Index Ref.
*Lebanon	4,015	10,399	3,858,736	96	F6
*Lesotho	11,718	30,350	2,007,814	63	E7
*Liberia	43,000	111,370	2,602,068	60	B4
*Libya	679,358	1,759,537	5,648,359	60-61	D2
*Liechtenstein	62	160	31,461	81	E1
*Lithuania	25,174	65,200	3,635,932	88	B3
Louisiana, U.S.A.	47,752	123,678	4,219,973	150	
Loyalty Islands, New Caledonia	414	1,072	14,518	116	G8
*Luxembourg	999	2,587	422,474	73	H8
Macau, Portugal	6	16	490,901	105	E3
*Macedonia	9,781	25,333	2,113,866	85	C3
*Madagascar	226,657	587,041	14,061,627	63	G6-7
Madeira Islands, Portugal	307	796	262,800	76	A2
Maine, U.S.A.	33,265	86,156	1,227,928	151	
*Malawi	45,745	118,480	9,609,081	63	F6
Malaya, Malaysia	50,806	131,588	11,138,227	111	C7
*Malaysia	127,316	329,750	20,376,235	111	C6
				112	D5
*Maldives	116	300	280,391	93	F5
*Mali	478,764	1,240,000	9,945,383	60	B2
*Malta	124	320	379,365	79	E7
Man, Isle of, U.K.	227	588	69,788	67	D3
Manitoba, Canada	250,999	650,087	1,091,942	189	
Marquesas Islands, French Polynesia	492	1,274	5,419	117	N6
*Marshall Islands	70	181	60,652	116	G4
Martinique, France	425	1,101	394,787	50	G4
				54-55	
Maryland, U.S.A.	10,460	27,091	4,781,468	139	
Massachusetts, U.S.A.	8,284	21,456	6,016,425	136-137	
*Mauritania	397,953	1,030,700	2,411,317	60	A3
*Mauritius	718	1,860	1,154,272	35	M7
Mayotte, France	144	373	97,088	63	G6
McDonald Islands, Australia, see Heard & McDonald Islands					
*Mexico	761,601	1,972,546	97,563,374	46-47	
Michigan, U.S.A.	58,527	151,585	9,295,297	152	
*Micronesia, Fed. States of	271	702	122,950	116	F5

Country	Area (Sq. Miles)	(Sq. Kilometers)	Population	Page No.	Index Ref.
Midway Islands, U.S.A.	1.9	4.9	453	116	H3
Minnesota, U.S.A.	84,402	218,601	4,375,099	153	
Mississippi, U.S.A.	47,689	123,515	2,573,216	154	
Missouri, U.S.A.	69,697	180,515	5,117,073	155	
*Moldova	13,012	33,700	4,475,232	89	C5
*Monaco	0.7	1.9	31,892	75	G6
*Mongolia	606,163	1,569,962	2,538,211	104-105	C-E1
Montana, U.S.A.	147,046	380,849	799,065	156	
Montserrat, U.K.	40	104	12,738	51	G3
*Morocco	172,414	446,550	30,391,423	60	B1
*Mozambique	309,494	801,590	18,165,476	63	F6-7
Myanmar, see Burma					
*Namibia	318,694	825,418	1,727,183	62-63	D7
Nauru	8	21	10,390	116	G6
Navassa Island, U.S.A.	2	5	....	50	C3
Nebraska, U.S.A.	77,355	200,349	1,578,385	157	
*Nepal	54,363	140,800	22,641,061	102	D2
*Netherlands	14,413	37,330	15,653,091	72-73	
Netherlands Antilles	390	1,010	203,505	51	E4,F3
Nevada, U.S.A.	110,561	286,353	1,201,833	132-133	
New Brunswick, Canada	28,354	73,437	723,900	182	
New Caledonia & Dependencies, France	7,335	18,998	184,552	116	G8
Newfoundland, Canada	156,184	404,517	568,474	43	L5
New Hampshire, U.S.A.	9,279	24,033	1,109,252	158	
New Jersey, U.S.A.	7,787	20,168	7,730,188	159	
New Mexico, U.S.A.	121,593	314,926	1,515,069	135	
New South Wales, Australia	309,498	801,600	5,731,906	115	D4
New York, U.S.A.	49,108	127,190	17,990,455	160-161	
*New Zealand	103,736	268,676	3,587,275	115	F4
*Nicaragua	49,998	129,494	4,386,399	48	C2
*Niger	489,189	1,267,000	9,388,859	60	C3
*Nigeria	356,668	923,770	107,129,469	60	C4
Niue, New Zealand	100	259	1,837	117	K7
Norfolk Island, Australia	13.4	34.6	2,756	116	G8
North America	9,363,000	24,250,170	443,438,000	40-41	
North Carolina, U.S.A.	52,669	136,413	6,628,637	162-163	
North Dakota, U.S.A.	70,702	183,118	638,800	164	
Northern Ireland, U.K.	5,452	14,121	1,610,000	66	C3
Northern Marianas, U.S.A.	184	477	51,033	116	E4

Gazetteer–Index of the World

Country	Area (Sq. Miles)	(Sq. Kilometers)	Population	Page No.	Index Ref.
Northern Territory, Australia	519,768	1,346,200	175,876	114	C3
*North Korea	46,540	120,539	24,317,004	106	C2
Northwest Territories, Canada	1,304,896	3,379,683	57,649	42-43	E-J2
*Norway	125,181	324,220	4,404,456	68-69	
Nova Scotia, Canada	21,425	55,491	899,942	182-183	
Oceania	3,292,000	8,526,280	24,436,000	116-117	
Ohio, U.S.A.	41,330	107,045	10,847,115	166-167	
Oklahoma, U.S.A.	69,956	181,186	3,145,585	168	
*Oman	82,031	212,460	2,264,590	95	H6
Ontario, Canada	412,580	1,068,582	10,084,885	186-187	
Oregon, U.S.A.	97,073	251,419	2,842,321	167	
Orkney Islands, Scotland	376	974	19,700	66	E1
*Pakistan	310,403	803,944	132,185,299	102	B-C1-2
*Palau	177	458	17,240	116	D5
Palmyra Atoll, U.S.A.	3.85	10	....	117	K5
*Panama	30,193	78,200	2,693,417	49	D-E3
*Papua New Guinea	178,259	461,690	4,496,221	116	E6
Paracel Islands, China	....	....	....	112	E2
*Paraguay	157,047	406,752	5,651,634	58-59	D5
Pennsylvania, U.S.A.	45,308	117,348	11,881,643	170-171	
*Peru	496,223	1,285,220	24,949,512	56	B3-4
*Philippines	115,830	300,000	76,103,564	108-109	
Pitcairn Islands, U.K.	18	47	73	117	O8
*Poland	120,725	312,678	38,700,291	86-87	
*Portugal	35,552	92,080	9,867,654	76	
Prince Edward Island, Canada	2,184	5,657	129,765	183	D2
Puerto Rico, U.S.A.	3,515	9,104	3,812,569	51	E3
				54	D2
*Qatar	4,247	11,000	665,485	95	G4
Québec, Canada	594,857	1,540,680	6,895,963	184-185	
Queensland, Australia	666,872	1,727,200	2,977,813	115	D3
Réunion, France	969	2,510	666,067	35	L7
Rhode Island, U.S.A.	1,212	3,139	1,003,464	137	D3
*Romania	91,699	237,500	21,399,114	84	C-D2
*Russia	6,592,735	17,075,200	147,987,101	88-91	
*Rwanda	10,169	26,337	7,737,537	63	F5
Sabah, Malaysia	29,300	75,887	1,790,000	112	F4

Country	Area (Sq. Miles)	(Sq. Kilometers)	Population	Page No.	Index Ref.
Saint Helena & Dependencies, U.K.	162	420	6,762	35	J6
*Saint Kitts and Nevis	104	269	41,803	51	F3
*Saint Lucia	239	620	159,639	51	G4
Saint Pierre & Miquelon, France	93.5	242	6,757	43	L6
*Saint Vincent & the Grenadines	131	340	119,092	51	G4
				55	P
Sakhalin, Russia	29,500	76,405	655,000	91	H3
*Samoa	1,104	2,860	219,509	117	J7
*San Marino	23.4	60.6	24,714	78	D3
*São Tomé & Príncipe	371	960	147,865	62	C4
Sarawak, Malaysia	48,202	124,843	1,648,217	112	E5
Sardinia, Italy	9,301	24,090	1,650,000	79	B4-5
Saskatchewan, Canada	251,699	651,900	988,928	188-189	
*Saudi Arabia	756,981	1,960,582	20,087,965	94	E-F4-5
Scotland, U.K.	30,414	78,772	5,111,200	66	D-E2-3
*Senegal	75,749	196,190	9,403,546	60	A3
*Seychelles	176	455	78,142	93	E6
Shetland Islands, Scotland	552	1,430	22,600	66	G1
Sicily, Italy	9,926	25,708	4,990,000	79	D-E6
*Sierra Leone	27,699	71,740	4,891,546	60	A4
*Singapore	244	632.6	3,461,929	111	E6
*Slovakia	18,859	48,845	5,393,016	83	E2
*Slovenia	7,836	20,296	1,945,998	84	A2
Society Islands, French Polynesia	677	1,753	117,703	117	L7
*Solomon Islands	10,985	28,450	462,855	116	G6
*Somalia	246,200	637,658	9,940,232	61	G4
*South Africa	471,008	1,219,912	42,327,458	63	E7-8
South America	6,875,000	17,806,250	314,335,000	56-59	
South Australia, Australia	379,922	984,000	1,400,630	114	C3
South Carolina, U.S.A.	31,113	80,583	3,486,703	162-163	
South Dakota, U.S.A.	77,116	199,730	696,004	165	
*South Korea	38,023	98,480	45,948,811	106	C3
*Spain	194,884	504,750	39,244,195	76-77	
Spratly Islands	....	....	....	112	E4
*Sri Lanka	25,332	65,610	18,762,075	104	D4
*Sudan	967,494	2,505,809	32,594,128	61	E-F5

Gazetteer–Index of the World

Country	Area (Sq. Miles)	Area (Sq. Kilometers)	Population	Page No.	Index Ref.
Sulawesi (Celebes), Indonesia	72,986	189,034	12,520,711	113	G6
Sumatra, Indonesia	164,000	424,760	36,505,703	112	B-C5-6
*Suriname	63,039	163,270	443,446	57	D2
Svalbard, Norway	23,957	62,049	2,914	68	A1
*Swaziland	6,703	17,360	1,031,600	63	F7
*Sweden	173,731	449,964	8,946,193	68-69	
Switzerland	15,943	41,292	7,248,984	80-81	
*Syria	71,498	185,180	16,137,899	97	G-H5
Tahiti, French Polynesia	402	1,041	95,604	117	L7
Taiwan	13,892	35,980	21,655,515	105	F3
*Tajikistan	55,251	143,100	6,013,855	90	D4
*Tanzania	364,699	945,090	29,460,753	63	F5
Tasmania, Australia	26,178	67,800	452,851	115	D5
Tennessee, U.S.A.	42,144	109,153	4,877,185	148-149	
Texas, U.S.A.	266,807	691,030	16,986,510	172-173	
*Thailand	198,455	513,998	59,450,818	110	C3
Tibet, China	463,320	1,200,000	2,196,029	104	B2
*Togo	21,927	56,790	4,735,610	60	C4
Tokelau, New Zealand	3.9	10	1,503	116	J6
Tonga	289	748	107,335	117	J8
*Trinidad and Tobago	1,980	5,128	1,273,141	51	G5
Tristan da Cunha, Saint Helena	38	98	251	35	J7
Tuamotu Archipelago, French Polynesia	341	883	9,052	117	M7
*Tunisia	63,170	163,610	9,183,097	60	C1
*Turkey	301,382	780,580	63,528,225	96-97	
*Turkmenistan	188,455	488,100	4,225,351	90	C4
Turks and Caicos Islands, U.K.	166	430	13,941	50-51	D-E2
Tuvalu	10	26	10,297	116	H6
*Uganda	91,135	236,040	20,604,874	61	F4
*Ukraine	233,089	603,700	50,684,635	89	C-E5
*United Arab Emirates	29,182	75,581	2,262,309	95	G5
*United Kingdom	94,525	244,820	58,610,182	66-67	
*United States of America	3,618,765	9,372,610	267,954,767	44-45 126-127	
*Uruguay	68,039	176,220	3,261,707	59	D6
Utah, U.S.A.	84,899	219,888	1,722,850	174	
*Uzbekistan	172,741	447,400	23,860,452	90	D3

Country	Area (Sq. Miles)	(Sq. Kilometers)	Population	Page No.	Index Ref.
*Vanuatu	5,699	14,760	181,358	116	G7
Vatican City	0.17	0.44	830	78	D4
*Venezuela	352,143	912,050	22,396,407	56	C2
Vermont, U.S.A.	9,614	24,900	562,758	158	
Victoria, Australia	87,876	227,600	4,244,282	115	D4
*Vietnam	127,243	329,560	75,123,880	110	D3
Virginia, U.S.A.	40,767	105,587	6,187,358	138-139	
Virgin Islands, British	59	153	12,000	51	H1
				54	F
Virgin Islands, U.S.A.	132	342	97,229	51	H1
				54	F-G
Wake Island, U.S.A.	2.5	6.5	302	116	G4
Wales, U.K.	8,017	20,764	2,886,400	67	E4
Wallis and Futuna, France	106	275	14,499	117	J7
Washington, U.S.A.	68,139	176,480	4,866,692	175	
West Bank	2,100	5,439	1,319,991	98-99	
Western Australia, Australia	975,096	2,525,500	1,587,050	114	B3
Western Sahara	102,703	266,000	217,211	60	A2
West Virginia, U.S.A.	24,231	62,758	1,793,477	138-139	
Wisconsin, U.S.A.	56,153	145,436	4,891,769	176	
World (land)	57,970,000	150,142,300	5,733,687,096	34-35	
Wyoming, U.S.A.	97,809	253,325	453,588	177	
*Yemen	203,849	527,970	13,972,477	94	D6
*Yugoslavia	39,517	102,350	10,655,317	84	B2
Yukon Territory, Canada	207,075	536,324	27,797	42	C3
*Zambia	290,583	752,610	9,349,975	63	E6
*Zimbabwe	150,803	390,580	11,423,175	63	E-F6

Eckert Projection (equal-area)

LANGUAGES. *Several hundred different languages are spoken in t*
World, and in many places two or more languages are spoken, sometimes
the same people. The map above shows the dominant languages in ea

Samoyede · Yakut Chukch Eskimo

Bogul Ostyak · Lamut Lamut

Bashkirs · U · S · S · I · A · Tungus · Aleut

Tatar

Kazakh (Kirghiz) · Mongol

Caucas · Nogai · North Chinese

Kurd · Uzbek · Turki · Tajik · Turki

Persian · Afghan · Tibetan · Chinese · Japanese

Baluchi · Urdu · Sindhi · Hindi · Bengali · Lolo Miao · S.Chinese

Marathi · Munda · Burmese · Shan · dialects

Tamil · Oriya · Telugu · Mon · Annamite

Somali · Khmer · Tagalog

Micronesian

Swahili · Malayan · Melanesia

Malagasy · Polynesia

English · E · English

| | Russian |
| | other Indo-European languages |

Hamitic Languages

Copyright by C. S. HAMMOND & CO., N. Y.

lity. **English, French, Spanish, Russian, Arabic** and **Swahili** are spoken by
y people as a second language for commerce or travel.

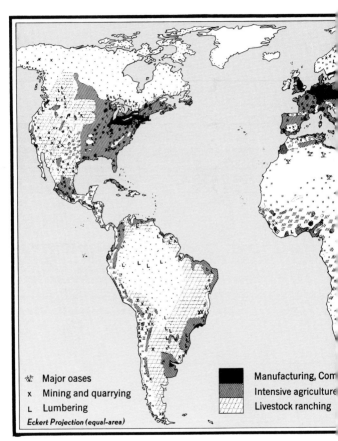

<table>
<tr><td>✿</td><td>Major oases</td><td rowspan="3">■ Manufacturing, Com</td></tr>
</table>

✿	Major oases	■ Manufacturing, Com
x	Mining and quarrying	▨ Intensive agriculture
L	Lumbering	▨ Livestock ranching

Eckert Projection (equal-area)

OCCUPATIONS. Correlation with the density of population shows ▪
the most densely populated areas fall into the regions of manufacturing ▪
intensive farming. All other economies require considerable space. The r▪

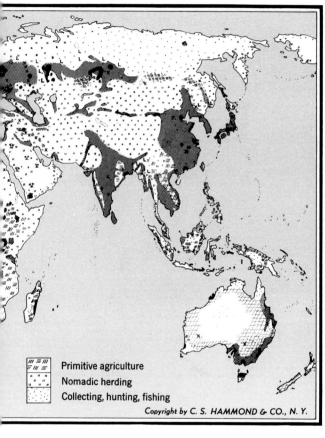

≡ ⫴	Primitive agriculture
	Nomadic herding
⋰ ⋰	Collecting, hunting, fishing

Copyright by C. S. HAMMOND & CO., N. Y.

...arsely inhabited areas are those of collecting, hunting and fishing. Areas ...th practically no habitation are left blank.

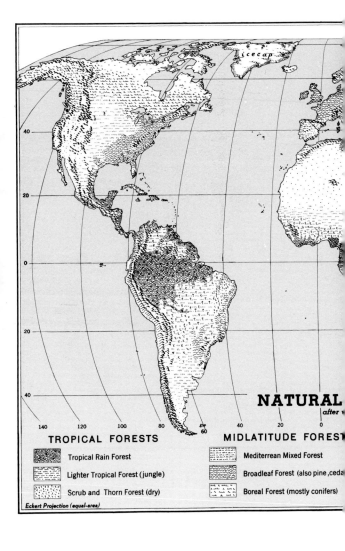

icecap

NATURAL

after

TROPICAL FORESTS

Tropical Rain Forest

Lighter Tropical Forest (jungle)

Scrub and Thorn Forest (dry)

MIDLATITUDE FOREST

Mediterrean Mixed Forest

Broadleaf Forest (also pine, ceda

Boreal Forest (mostly conifers)

Eckert Projection (equal-area)

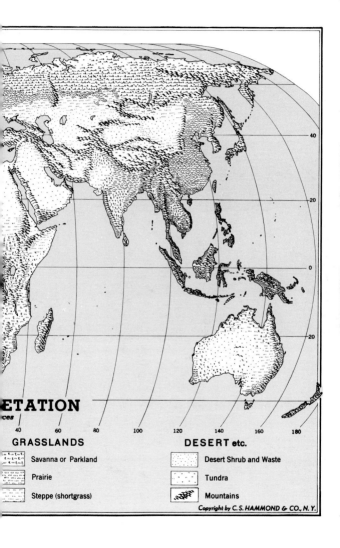

ETATION
ces

GRASSLANDS

Savanna or Parkland

Prairie

Steppe (shortgrass)

DESERT etc.

Desert Shrub and Waste

Tundra

Mountains

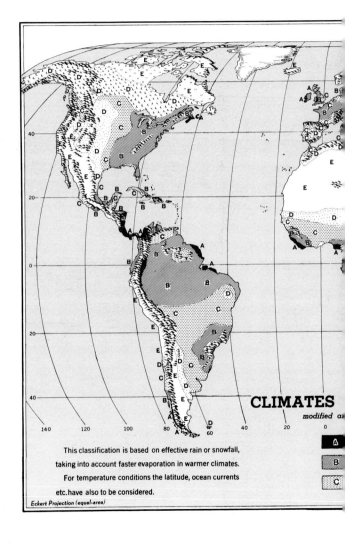

CLIMATES

modified a

This classification is based on effective rain or snowfall,
taking into account faster evaporation in warmer climates.
For temperature conditions the latitude, ocean currents
etc. have also to be considered.

Eckert Projection (equal-area)

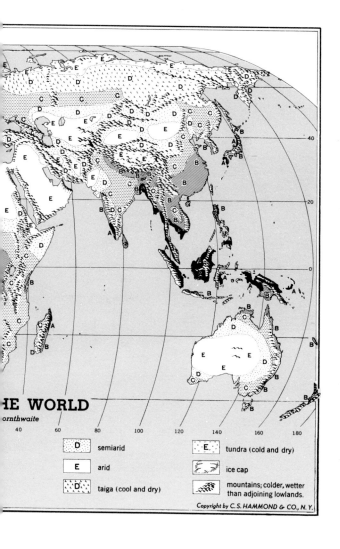

E WORLD

ornthwaite

40   60   80   100   120   140   160   180

D semiarid		**E** tundra (cold and dry)
E arid		ice cap
D taiga (cool and dry)		mountains; colder, wetter than adjoining lowlands.

World–Time Zones

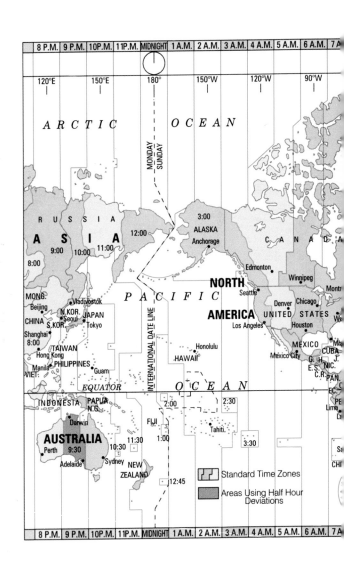

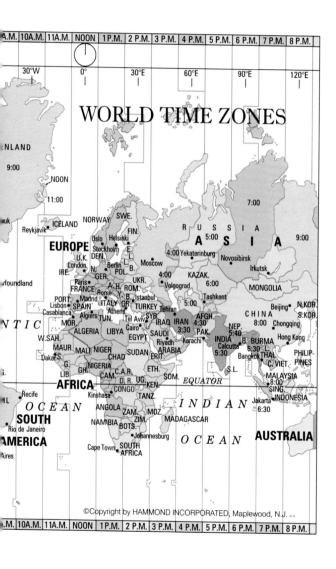

WORLD TIME ZONES

Air Distances Between Major World Cities (in miles)

	Beijing	Cairo	Cape Town	Chicago	Hong Kong	Honolulu	London
Amsterdam	4890	2015	5997	4118	5772	7254	222
Athens	4757	671	4957	5447	5316	8353	1488
Bangkok	2027	4521	6301	8569	1076	6610	5929
Beijing	—	4687	8034	6625	1195	5084	5089
Buenos Aires ...	11,994	7360	4285	5582	11,478	7554	6907
Cairo	4687	—	4510	6116	5057	8818	2158
Cape Town	8034	4510	—	8489	7377	11,534	5988
Chicago	6625	6116	8489	—	7797	4256	3960
Denver	6385	6846	9331	920	7476	3346	4701
Frankfurt	4567	1730	5944	4460	5403	7341	628
Hong Kong	1195	5057	7377	7797	—	5557	5986
Honolulu	5084	8818	11,534	4256	5557	—	7241
Houston	7244	7005	8608	942	8349	3902	4860
Lisbon	6040	2352	5301	4001	6862	7835	989
London	5089	2158	5988	3960	5986	7241	—
Los Angeles	6255	7522	9981	1750	7217	2565	5454
Madrid	5759	2069	5306	4192	6556	7874	786
Melbourne	5632	8700	6428	9667	4605	5501	10,508 1
Mexico City	7772	7677	8516	1688	8789	3791	5558
Montréal	6541	5403	7920	746	7736	4919	3256
Moscow	3627	1770	6277	4984	4443	7049	1556
New Delhi	2350	2752	5769	7486	2339	7413	4178
New York	6867	5598	7801	714	8061	4969	3473
Paris	5138	1973	5782	4145	5992	7452	215
Rio de Janeiro ..	10,778	6153	3773	5288	11,002	8295	5751
Rome	5076	1305	5231	4823	5773	8040	892
San Francisco ..	5934	7436	10,248	1860	6904	2397	5369
Seattle	5432	6809	10,205	1737	6481	2681	4799
Singapore	2754	5143	6007	9376	1608	6728	6747
Stockholm	4197	2084	6422	4288	5115	6873	892
Tokyo	1305	5937	9155	6313	1792	3860	5956
Washington, D.C.	6965	5800	7892	594	8157	4839	3676

	Mexico City	Moscow	New Delhi	New York	Paris	Rio de Janeiro	Rome	San Francisco	Tokyo
6	5735	1337	3958	3654	271	5938	807	5465	5788
7	7021	1387	3120	4938	1305	6030	654	6792	5924
9	9793	4394	1812	8669	5877	9987	5493	7930	2865
2	7772	3627	2350	6867	5138	10,778	5076	5934	1305
9	4580	8369	9823	5279	6857	1231	6925	6455	11,411
0	7677	1770	2752	5598	1973	6153	1305	7436	5937
8	8516	6277	5769	7801	5782	3773	5231	10,248	9155
7	1688	4984	7486	714	4145	5288	4823	1860	6313
5	1438	5501	7730	1631	4900	5866	5887	953	5815
2	6127	961	3550	4028	589	6237	729	5709	5533
5	8789	4443	2339	8061	5992	11,002	5773	6904	1792
1	3791	7049	7413	4969	7452	8295	8040	2397	3860
9	749	5925	8388	1419	5035	5015	5702	1648	6685
8	5396	2433	4844	3377	904	4777	1163	5679	6943
8	5558	1556	4178	3437	215	5751	892	5369	5956
8	1566	6036	7015	2455	5661	6334	6336	349	5476
6	5642	2140	4528	3596	652	5045	849	5806	6704
	8420	8965	6340	10,352	10,442	8218	9940	7850	5070
0	—	6671	9119	2086	5723	4769	6374	1889	7036
0	2315	4397	7012	333	3432	5082	4102	2544	6470
5	6671	—	2703	4680	1550	7162	1477	5884	4663
	9119	2703	—	7319	4103	8747	3684	7691	3638
2	2086	4680	7319	—	3638	4805	4293	2574	6757
2	5723	1550	4103	3638	—	5681	688	5579	6054
8	4769	7162	8747	4805	5681	—	5704	6621	11,535
0	6374	1477	3684	4293	688	5704	—	6259	6140
	1889	5884	7691	2574	5579	6621	6259	—	5148
6	2340	5217	7046	2409	5012	6890	5680	679	4793
7	10,331	5236	2574	9539	6676	9776	6231	8449	3304
3	5965	764	3466	3939	964	6638	1229	5372	5091
0	7036	4663	3638	6757	6054	11,535	6140	5148	—
4	1883	4873	7500	203	3841	4783	4496	2444	6792

World Statistics

The Continents

	Area in: Sq. Miles	Sq. Km.	Percent of World's Land
Asia	17,128,500	44,362,815	29.5
Africa	11,707,000	30,321,130	20.2
North America	9,363,000	24,250,170	16.2
South America	6,875,000	17,806,250	11.8
Antarctica	5,500,000	14,245,000	9.5
Europe	4,057,000	10,507,630	7.0
Australia	2,966,136	7,682,300	5.1

Oceans and Major Seas

	Area in: Sq. Miles	Sq. Km.	Greatest Depth in: Feet	Meters
Pacific Ocean	64,186,000	166,241,700	36,198	11,033
Atlantic Ocean	31,862,000	82,522,600	28,374	8,648
Indian Ocean	28,350,000	73,426,500	25,344	7,725
Arctic Ocean	5,427,000	14,056,000	17,880	5,450
Caribbean Sea	970,000	2,512,300	24,720	7,535
Mediterranean Sea	969,000	2,509,700	16,896	5,150
South China Sea	895,000	2,318,000	15,000	4,600
Bering Sea	875,000	2,266,250	15,800	4,800
Gulf of Mexico	600,000	1,554,000	12,300	3,750
Sea of Okhotsk	590,000	1,528,100	11,070	3,370
East China Sea	482,000	1,248,400	9,500	2,900
Yellow Sea	480,000	1,243,200	350	107
Sea of Japan	389,000	1,007,500	12,280	3,740
Hudson Bay	317,500	822,300	846	258
North Sea	222,000	575,000	2,200	670
Black Sea	185,000	479,150	7,365	2,245
Red Sea	169,000	437,700	7,200	2,195
Baltic Sea	163,000	422,170	1,506	459

Dimensions of the Earth

	Area in Sq. Miles	Sq. Kilometers
Superficial area	196,939,000	510,073,000
Land surface	57,506,000	148,941,000
Water surface	139,433,000	361,132,000

	Miles	Kilometers
Equatorial circumference	24,902	40,075
Polar circumference	24,860	40,007
Equatorial diameter	7,926.4	12,756.4
Polar diameter	7,899.8	12,713.6
Equatorial radius	3,963.2	6,378.2
Polar radius	3,949.9	6,356.8

Maximum distance from Sun	94,600,000 miles	152,000,000 kilometers
Minimum distance from Sun	91,300,000 miles	147,000,000 kilometers

Principal Mountains of the World

	ft./m
Everest, Nepal-China	**29,028/8,848**
Godwin Austen (K2), Pakistan-China	28,250/8,611
Kanchenjunga, Nepal-India	28,208/8,598
Lhotse, Nepal-China	27,923/8,511
Makalu, Nepal-China	27,824/8,481
Dhaulagiri, Nepal	26,810/8,172
Nanga Parbat, Pakistan	26,660/8,126
Annapurna, Nepal	26,504/8,078
Gasherbrum, Pakistan-China	26,740/8,068
Nanda Devi, India	25,645/7,817
Rakaposhi, Pakistan	25,500/7,788
Kamet, India	25,447/7,756
Gurla Mandhada, China	25,355/7,728
Kongur Shan, China	25,325/7,719
Tirich Mir, Pakistan	25,230/7,690
Gongga Shan, China	24,790/7,556
Muztagata, China	24,757/7,546
Ismail Samani Peak, Tajikistan	24,599/7,498
Pobeda Peak, China-Kyrgyzstan	24,406/7,439
Chomo Lhari, Bhutan-China	23,997/7,314
Muztag, China	23,891/7,282
Cerro Aconcagua, Argentina	22,831/6,959
Ojos del Salado, Chile-Argentina	22,572/6,880
Bonete, Chile-Argentina	22,541/6,870
Tupungato, Chile-Argentina	22,310/6,800
Pissis, Argentina	22,241/6,779
Mercedario, Argentina	22,211/6,770
Huascarán, Peru	22,205/6,768
Llullaillaco, Chile-Argentina	22,057/6,723
Nevada Ancohuma, Bolivia	21,489/6,550
Illampu, Bolivia	21,276/6,485
Chimborazo, Ecuador	20,561/6,267
McKinley, Alaska	20,320/6,194
Logan, Canada (Yukon)	19,524/5,951
Cotopaxi, Ecuador	19,347/5,897
Kilimanjaro, Tanzania	19,340/5,895
El Misti, Peru	19,101/5,822
Pico Cristóbal Colón, Colombia	19,029/5,800

	ft./m
Huila, Colombia	18,865/5,750
Citlaltépetl (Orizaba), Mexico	18,855/5,747
El'brus, Russia	18,510/5,642
Damavand, Iran	18,376/5,601
St. Elias, Alaska-Canada (Yukon)	18,008/5,489
Vilcanota, Peru	17,999/5,486
Popocatépetl, Mexico	17,887/5,452
Dykhtau, Russia	17,070/5,203
Kenya, Kenya	17,058/5,199
Ararat, Turkey	16,946/5,165
Vinson Massif, Antarctica	16,864/5,140
Margherita (Ruwenzori), Africa	16,795/5,119
Kazbek, Russia-Georgia	16,512/5,033
Puncak Jaya, Indonesia	16,503/5,030
Tyree, Antarctica	16,289/4,965
Blanc, France	15,771/4,807
Klyuchevskaya Sopka, Russia	15,584/4,750
Dufourspitze (Mte. Rosa), Italy-Switzerland	15,203/4,634
Ras Dashan, Ethiopia	15,157/4,620
Matterhorn, Switzerland	14,691/4,478
Whitney, California, U.S.A.	14,494/4,418
Elbert, Colorado, U.S.A.	14,433/4,399
Rainier, Washington, U.S.A.	14,410/4,392
Shasta, California, U.S.A.	14,162/4,350
Pikes Peak, Colorado, U.S.A.	14,110/4,301
Finsteraarhorn, Switzerland	14,022/4,274
Mauna Kea, Hawaii, U.S.A.	13,796/4,205
Mauna Loa, Hawaii, U.S.A.	13,677/4,169
Jungfrau, Switzerland	13,642/4,158
Cameroon, Cameroon	13,350/4,069
Grossglockner, Austria	12,457/3,797
Fuji, Japan	12,389/3,776
Cook, New Zealand	12,349/3,764
Etna, Italy	11,053/3,369
Kosciusko, Australia	7,310/2,228
Mitchell, North Carolina, U.S.A.	6,684/2,037

Longest Rivers of the World

	Length: mi./kms.		Length: mi./kms.
Nile, Africa	4,145/6,671	Orinoco, S. Amer.	1,600/2,575
Amazon, S. Amer.	3,915/6,300	Zambezi, Africa	1,600/2,575
Chang Jiang (Yangtze), China	3,900/6,276	Paraguay, S. Amer.	1,584/2,549
		Kolyma, Russia	1,562/2,514
Mississippi-Missouri-Red Rock, U.S.A.	3,741/6,019	Ganges, Asia	1,550/2,494
Ob'Irtysh-Black Irtysh, Asia	3,362/5,411	Ural, Russia-Kazak.	1,509/2,428
Yenisey-Angara, Russia	3,100/4,989	Japurá, S. Amer.	1,500/2,414
Huang He (Yellow), China	2,877/4,630	Arkansas, U.S.A.	1,450/2,334
Amur-Shilka-Onon, Asia	2,744/4,416	Colorado, U.S.A.-Mexico	1,450/2,334
Lena, Russia	2,734/4,400	Negro, S. Amer.	1,400/2,253
Congo, Africa	2,718/4,374	Dnieper, Europe	1,368/2,202
Mackenzie-Peace-Finlay, Canada	2,635/4,241	Orange, Africa	1,350/2,173
Mekong, Asia	2,610/4,200	Irrawaddy, Burma	1,325/2,132
Missouri-Red Rock, U.S.A.	2,564/4,125	Brazos, U.S.A.	1,309/2,107
Niger, Africa	2,548/4,101	Ohio-Allegheny, U.S.A.	1,306/2,102
Paraná-La Plata, S. Amer.	2,450/3,943	Kama, Russia	1,262/2,031
Mississippi, U.S.A.	2,348/3,778	Red, U.S.A.	1,222/1,966
Murray-Darling, Australia	2,310/3,718	Don, Russia	1,222/1,967
Volga, Russia	2,194/3,531	Columbia, U.S.A.-Canada	1,214/1,953
Madeira, S. Amer.	2,013/3,240	Saskatchewan, Canada	1,205/1,939
Purus, S. Amer.	1,995/3,211	Peace-Finlay, Canada	1,195/1,923
Yukon, Alaska-Canada	1,979/3,185	Tigris, Asia	1,181/1,901
St. Lawrence, Canada-U.S.A.	1,900/3,058	Darling, Australia	1,160/1,867
		Angara, Russia	1,135/1,827
Rio Grande, Mexico-U.S.A.	1,885/3,034	Sungari, Asia	1,130/1,819
Syrdar'ya-Naryn, Asia	1,859/2,992	Pechora, Russia	1,124/1,809
São Francisco, Brazil	1,811/2,914	Snake, U.S.A.	1,000/1,609
Indus, Asia	1,800/2,897	Churchill, Canada	1,000/1,609
Danube, Europe	1,775/2,857	Pilcomayo, S. Amer.	1,000/1,609
Salween, Asia	1,770/2,849	Magdalena, Colombia	1,000/1,609
Brahmaputra, Asia	1,700/2,736	Uruguay, S. Amer.	994/1,600
Euphrates, Asia	1,700/2,736	Platte-N. Platte, U.S.A.	990/1,593
Tocantins, Brazil	1,677/2,699	Ohio, U.S.A.	981/1,578
Xi (Si), China	1,650/2,655	Pecos, U.S.A.	926/1,490
Amudar'ya, Asia	1,616/2,601	Oka, Russia	918/1,477
Nelson-Saskatchewan, Canada	1,600/2,575	Canadian, U.S.A.	906/1,458
		Colorado, Texas, U.S.A.	894/1,439
		Dniester, Ukraine-Moldova	876/1,410

Largest Islands

	Area in:	
	Sq. Mi.	Sq. Km.
Greenland	840,000	2,175,600
New Guinea	305,000	789,950
Borneo	290,000	751,100
Madagascar	226,400	586,376
Baffin, Canada	195,928	507,454
Sumatra, Indonesia	164,000	424,760
Honshu, Japan	88,000	227,920
Great Britain	84,400	218,896
Victoria, Canada	83,896	217,290
Ellesmere, Canada	75,767	196,236
Celebes, Indonesia	72,986	189,034
South I., New Zealand	58,393	151,238
Java, Indonesia	48,842	126,501
North I., New Zealand	44,187	114,444
Newfoundland, Canada	42,031	108,860
Cuba	40,533	104,981
Luzon, Philippines	40,420	104,688
Iceland	39,768	103,000
Mindanao, Philippines	36,537	94,631
Ireland	31,743	82,214
Sakhalin, Russia	29,500	76,405
Hispaniola, Haiti & Dom. Rep.	29,399	76,143
Hokkaido, Japan	28,983	75,066
Banks, Canada	27,038	70,028
Ceylon, Sri Lanka	25,332	65,610
Tasmania, Australia	24,600	63,710
Devon, Canada	21,331	55,247
Novaya Zemlya (north isl.), Russia	18,600	48,200
Marajó, Brazil	17,991	46,597
Tierra del Fuego, Chile & Argentina	17,900	46,360
Alexander, Antarctica	16,700	43,250

World Statistics

Principal Natural Lakes

	Area in:		Max. Depth in:	
	Sq. Miles	Sq. Km.	Feet	Meters
Caspian Sea, Europe-Asia	143,243	370,999	3,264	995
Lake Superior, U.S.A.-Canada	31,820	82,414	1,329	405
Lake Victoria, Africa	26,724	69,215	270	82
Lake Huron, U.S.A.-Canada	23,010	59,596	748	228
Lake Michigan, U.S.A.	22,400	58,016	923	281
Aral Sea, Kazakh.-Uzbek.	15,830	41,000	213	65
Lake Tanganyika, Africa	12,650	32,764	4,700	1,433
Lake Baykal, Russia	12,162	31,500	5,316	1,620
Great Bear Lake, Canada	12,096	31,328	1,356	413
Lake Nyasa (Malawi), Africa	11,555	29,928	2,320	707
Great Slave Lake, Canada	11,031	28,570	2,015	614
Lake Erie, U.S.A.-Canada	9,940	25,745	210	64
Lake Winnipeg, Canada	9,417	24,390	60	18
Lake Ontario, U.S.A.-Canada	7,540	19,529	775	244
Lake Ladoga, Russia	7,104	18,399	738	225
Lake Balkhash, Kazakhstan	7,027	18,200	87	27
Lake Maracaibo, Venezuela	5,120	13,261	100	31
Lake Chad, Africa	4,000-10,000	10,360-25,900	25	8
Lake Onega, Russia	3,710	9,609	377	115
Lake Eyre, Australia	3,500-0	9,000-0	—	—
Lake Titicaca, Peru-Bolivia	3,200	8,288	1,000	305
Lake Nicaragua, Nicaragua	3,100	8,029	230	70
Lake Athabasca, Canada	3,064	7,936	400	122
Reindeer Lake, Canada	2,568	6,651	—	—
Lake Turkana (Rudolf), Africa	2,463	6,379	240	73
Issyk-Kul', Kyrgyzstan	2,425	6,281	2,303	702
Lake Torrens, Australia	2,230	5,776	—	—
Vänern, Sweden	2,156	5,584	328	100
Nettilling Lake, Canada	2,140	5,543	—	—
Lake Winnipegosis, Canada	2,075	5,374	38	12
Lake Albert, Africa	2,075	5,374	160	49
Kariba Lake, Zambia-Zimbabwe	2,050	5,310	295	90
Lake Nipigon, Canada	1,872	4,848	540	165
Lake Mweru, D.R. Congo-Zambia	1,800	4,662	60	18
Lake Manitoba, Canada	1,799	4,659	12	4
Lake Taymyr, Russia	1,737	4,499	85	26
Lake Khanka, China-Russia	1,700	4,403	33	10
Lake Kioga, Uganda	1,700	4,403	25	8

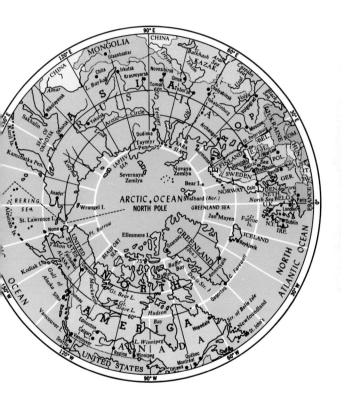

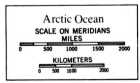

Arctic Ocean

SCALE ON MERIDIANS
MILES

| 0 | 500 | 1000 | 1500 | 2000 |

KILOMETERS

| 0 | 500 | 1000 | 2000 |

© HAMMOND INCORPORATED

World–Political

ARCTIC OCEAN

SEVERNAYA ZEMLYA

C. Chelyuskin

LAPTEV SEA

NEW SIBERIAN ISLANDS

Nordvik

EAST SIBERIAN SEA

Srednekolymsk

Arctic Circle

Lena

Yakutsk

Magadan

RUSSIA

Krasnoyarsk

Irkutsk

SEA OF OKHOTSK

Ulaanbaatar

MONGOLIA

GOBI

Khabarovsk

Amur

Sakhalin Island

Kuril

Lhasa

Beijing

Shenyang

Tianjin

N. KOR.

S. KOR.

Sea of Japan

JAPAN

CHINA

Nanjing

Shanghai

East China Sea

Tokyo

Osaka

Chongqing

Guangzhou

Taipei

Taiwan

Dhaka

BURMA

HONG KONG

Rangoon

South China Sea

PHILIPPINES

Manila

Bangkok

Ho Chi Minh City

MALAYSIA

Celebes

NORTHERN MARIANAS (U.S.)

Guam (U.S.)

Caroline Is.

FED. STATES OF MICRONESIA

SINGAPORE

Borneo

INDONESIA

Jakarta

Java

New Guinea

PAPUA NEW GUINEA

NAURU

SOLOMON IS.

TUVALU

Darwin

CORAL SEA

VANUATU

New Caledonia (Fr.)

INDIAN OCEAN

AUSTRALIA

Townsville

Brisbane

Perth

Adelaide

Melbourne

Sydney

Canberra

TASMAN SEA

Tasmania

Hobart

NEW ZEALAND

Auckland

Wellington

Pt. Barrow

BEAUFORT SEA

Bering Str.

Nome

UNITED STATES

Fairbanks

ALASKA

Anchorage

Juneau

Anadyr

BERING SEA

G. of Alaska

ALEUTIAN IS.

International Date Line

NORTH

PACIFIC

OCEAN

San Francisco

Los Angeles

UNITED

Tropic of Cancer

Midway Is. (U.S.)

HAWAIIAN IS

U.S.

HAWAII

Honolulu

Wake I. (U.S.)

MARSHALL IS.

Equator

Kiritimati

KIRIBATI

SOUTH

Marquesas Is. (Fr.)

SAMOA

Amer. Samoa

FIJI

TONGA

Society Is. (Fr.)

Tahiti

FRENCH POLYNESIA

Tropic of Capricorn

PACIFIC

OCEAN

Easter I. (Chile)

Pr. Patrick I.

QUEEN

McClure Str.

Melville I.

Banks I.

Victoria I.

Amundsen G.

Gt. Bear L.

Gt. Slave

NOR

AME

Edmonton

Vancouver

Seattle

Minn

Denv

Mexi

CI

CE

AM

Edmonton

N

Longitude East of Greenwich

Longitude West of Greenwich

A 120° B 150° C 180° D 150° E 120° F

World–Political

MERCATOR PROJECTION

Capitals of Countries..............

Longitude West of Greenwich   Longitude East of Greenwich

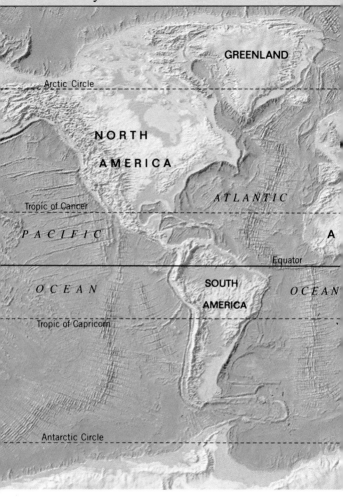

The dramatic map above is a photograph of a sculptured three-dimensional terrain model. In addition to depicting traditional landforms, the model also includes canyons, trenches, rises and ridges of ocean floor topography.

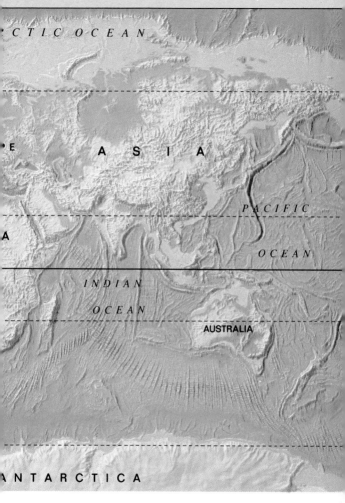

CTIC OCEAN

E

A S I A

PACIFIC

A

OCEAN

INDIAN

OCEAN

AUSTRALIA

NTARCTICA

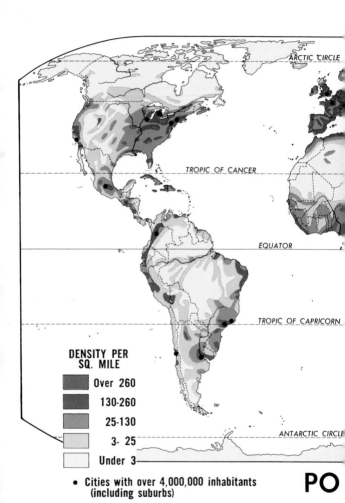

ARCTIC CIRCLE

TROPIC OF CANCER

EQUATOR

TROPIC OF CAPRICORN

**DENSITY PER
SQ. MILE**

Over 260

130-260

25-130

3- 25

Under 3

ANTARCTIC CIRCLE

• Cities with over 4,000,000 inhabitants
(including suburbs)

PO

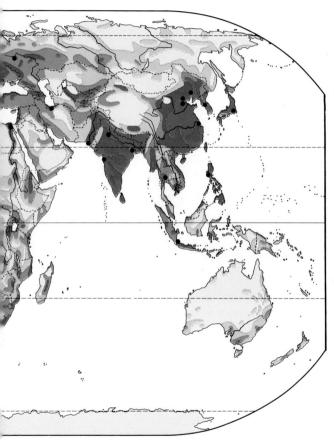

ATION DISTRIBUTION

© Copyright HAMMOND INCORPORATED, Maplewood, N. J.
Printed in U.S.A.

North America

ARCTIC OCEAN

GREENLAND SEA

ICELAND

(Jan Mayen (Nor.))

Reykjavik

Str. of Denmark

GREENLAND

KING FREDERIK VI COAST

KING CHRISTIAN IX LAND

KING CHRISTIAN X LAND

(KALAALLIT NUNAAT)
(Grl.)

PEARY LAND

Thule

Ellesmere I.

QUEEN ELIZABETH IS.

Axel Heiberg I.
SVERDRUP IS.
Prince Patrick I.
Melville I.
M'Clure Str.
Banks I.

Devon I.
Lancaster Sd.
Parry Channel
M'Clintock Channel
Boothia Pen.
G. of Boothia
Victoria I.

Baffin Bay
Davis Strait
Baffin I.
Cumberland Sd.
Foxe Basin
Hudson Str.
Southampton I.
Coats I.
Mansel I.

Davis Strait
Labrador

Newfoundland

Belle Isle Str.
Gulf of St. Lawrence
Cape Breton I.
Sydney
Charlottetown
Halifax
Québec
Ste. Marie
Montréal

C A N A D A

Hudson Bay
BELCHER IS.
James Bay
Moosonee
Timmins
L. Nipigon
Thunder Bay
L. Superior

Chesterfield Inlet
Wager Bay
Repulse Bay

Churchill
Nelson
L. Winnipeg
Winnipeg
Portage
Medicine Hat

Great Slave L.
Reindeer L.
Saskatchewan
Prince Albert
Saskatoon
Edmonton
Calgary
Lethbridge
Spokane

Great Bear L.
Great Radium L.
Yellowknife
Ft. Smith
L. Athabasca
Ft. McMurray
Athabasca

Amundsen Gulf

BEAUFORT SEA

Pt. Barrow

Mackenzie
Ft. Norman
Ft. Wells
Ft. Simpson
Peace
Fraser

Inuvik
Aklavik

Dawson
Whitehorse
Juneau
Ketchikan
Prince Rupert

ALEXANDER ARCH.
Dixon Entrance
QUEEN CHARLOTTE IS.
Vancouver I.
Str. of Juan de Fuca
Victoria
Vancouver
Tacoma
Seattle
Portland

UNITED STATES
ALASKA

Fairbanks
Anchorage
Kodiak I.
Alaska Pen.
Kuskokwim
Yukon

ASIA

Wrangel I.
Anadyr
St. Lawrence I.
Nome
Seward Pen.
Norton Sd.
Bering Str.

Arctic Circle

BERING SEA
Bristol Bay
G. of Alaska

PACIFIC

North Pole

180° 160° 140° 120° 100° 80° 60° 40°
A B C D E F G H I J K

50°
60°
70°
80°

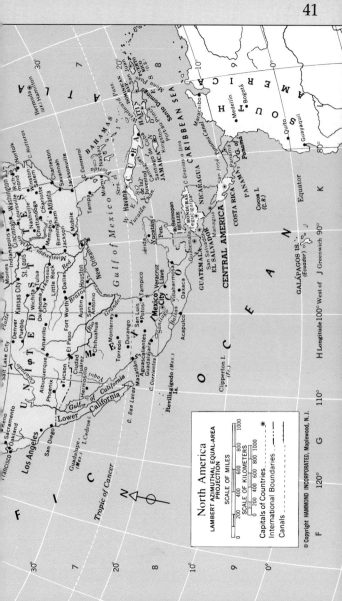

North America

LAMBERT AZIMUTHAL EQUAL-AREA
PROJECTION

SCALE OF MILES

0   200   400   600   800   1000

SCALE OF KILOMETERS

0 200 400 600 800 1000

Capitals of Countries........⊙
International Boundaries.....‒‒·‒‒·‒‒
Canals.........................

© Copyright HAMMOND INCORPORATED, Maplewood, N.J.

Canada

[Map of Canada and northern United States with inset map of southern Ontario / Great Lakes region]

UNITED STATES · ALASKA · YUKON · NORTHWEST TERRITORIES · NUNAVUT · BRITISH COLUMBIA · ALBERTA · SASKATCHEWAN · MANITOBA

PACIFIC OCEAN · BEAUFORT SEA · Banks Island · Victoria I. · Prince of Wales I. · Melville I. · Bathurst

INUVIK REGION · KITIKMEOT REGION · FORT SMITH REGION

Yukon · Porcupine · Circle · Fairbanks · Tanana · Fort Yukon · Arctic Circle · Aklavik · Tuktoyaktuk · Inuvik · Arctic Red River · Paulatuk · Amundsen Gulf · Holman · Read I. · Cambridge Bay · Coppermine · Stewart · Dawson · Mayo · Peel · Norman Wells · Great Bear Lake · Fort Radium · Bathurst Inlet · Garry · Whitehorse · Wrigley · Lac la Martre · Rae · Yellowknife · Dubawnt L. · Fort Reliance · Kasba L. · Nueltin · Watson Lake · Ft. Simpson · Great Slave Lake · Ft. Providence · Ft. Resolution · Teslin · Fort Liard · Trout L. · Hay River · Ft. Smith · Churchill Pk. · Fort Nelson · Vermilion · L. Athabasca · Uranium City · Chipewyan · Wollaston L. · Cree L. · Brochet · Reindeer Lake · Lynn Lake · Amery · Nelso

Sitka · Juneau · Mt. Logan · Mt. St. Elias · Mt. Fairweather · Prince of Wales I. · Ketchikan · Prince Rupert · Stewart · Hecate Str. · Queen Charlotte Is. · Queen Charlotte Sd. · St. John · Dawson Cr. · Peace River · Grande Prairie · Smithers · Burns Lake · Vanderhoof · Prince George · Fort McMurray · Quesnel · Mt. Waddington · Athabasca · Edmonton · Vermilion · Lloydminster · Prince Albert · Flin Flon · Sherridon · The Pas · Courtenay · Nanaimo · Vancouver I. · Str. of Juan de Fuca · Victoria · New Westminster · Kamloops · Kelowna · Jasper · Edson · Wetaskiwin · Camrose · North Battleford · Melfort · Humboldt · Winnipegosis · Berens · Revelstoke · Lake Louise · Banff · Red Deer · Biggar · Saskatoon · Yorkton · Dauphin · Vernon · Trail · Nelson · Cranbrook · Calgary · Drumheller · Medicine Hat · Swift Current · Moose Jaw · Regina · Brandon · Winnipeg · Lethbridge · Cardston · Shaunavon · Weyburn · Estevan · Souris · L. of the Woods · Seattle · Spokane · Portland · Columbia · WASH. · IDA. · MONT. · N. DAK. · S. DAK. · Bismarck · Fargo · MINN. · Minneapolis · Pierre · NEBR. · Niobrara · Missouri · UNITED

[Inset map:]
Lake Huron · Goderich · Walkerton · Orangeville · Newmarket · Cobourg · Listowel · Fergus · Guelph · Cambridge · Oshawa · Toronto · MICH. · Port Huron · Stratford · Kitchener · Lake Ontario · St. Catharines · Woodstock · Brantford · Hamilton · Niagara · Sarnia · London · Simcoe · Welland · Niagara Falls · Wallaceburg · St. Thomas · Welland Canal · Buffalo · Detroit · Chatham · N.Y. · Windsor · Sandwich · L. St. Clair · Long Pt. · Leamington · Lake Erie · Pt. Pelee · Erie

Miles 0 20 40

Longitude

Canada
CONIC PROJECTION
SCALE OF MILES
0 100 200 300 400 500
SCALE OF KILOMETERS
0 100 200 300 400 500

Capitals of Countries _____ ⊕
Provincial & Territorial
Capitals _____ ⊛
Administrative Centers _____ ⊙

© Copyright HAMMOND INCORPORATED, Maplewood, N.J.

GREENLAND
(KALAALLIT NUNAAT) (Den.)

BAFFIN BAY

BAFFIN ISL.

Davis Strait

ATLANTIC OCEAN

HUDSON BAY

James Bay

QUÉBEC

NEWFOUNDLAND

ONTARIO

NEW BRUNS.

NOVA SCOTIA

PRINCE EDWARD IS.

ST. PIERRE & MIQUELON (Fr.)

MAINE

Montréal inset:
Joliette Drummond-ville
St-Jérôme Sorel
Lachine Laval St-Hyacinthe
Verdun Sherbrooke
St-Jean Granby Magog
Valleyfield

United States

United States

POLYCONIC PROJECTION

SCALE OF MILES

0   100   200   300   400

SCALE OF KILOMETERS

0   100   200   300   400

Capitals of Countries _____ ⊛ _____ State Capitals

International Boundaries _____ State Boundaries _ _ _

Copyright by C. S. HAMMOND & Co., N. Y.

Mexico

A 114° B 110° C 106° D

UNITED STATES

Tijuana○ Yuma○ Globe○ Roswell○
Mexicali◉
Ensenada○ Tucson○ Las Cruces○ El Paso
San Nogales○ Bisbee○ Ciudad Juárez
Vicente○ I. Montague Douglas○
S. Felipe Pto. Peñasco○ Heroica Agua Prieta○ Guzmán○ Rio Bravo
Heroica Caborca○ Nogales Cananea○ Ascensión○ Santiago
El Rosario○ 30° Magdalena○ Nva. Casas Mts. Amistad
Ures○ Grandes○ Buenaventura○ Ojinaga○ Piedras
Moctezuma○ Madera○ Manuel Villa
I. Angel Hermosillo◉ Benavides○
de la Guarda Río Sonora Cuauhtémoc○ Chihuahua◉
I. Sebastián Tiburón Mesa Aquiles Serdán○ Saucillo○
Vizcaíno del Seri Sahuaripa○
I. de Ocampo○ Nonoava○ Ciudad Camargo○ Ocampo○
Cedros Guaymas○ Empalme○ Jiménez○
2 Sta. Rosalía○ Río Ciudad Obregón◉ San Francisco Santa
Mulegé○ Navojoa○ del Oro○ Bárbara○ Parral
B. Ballenas Alamos○ San Gómez
Huatabampo○ El Fuerte○ Guadalupe○ Palacio○ San Pe
26° I. del Los y Calvo○ Cd. Lerdo○ Torreón◉
Carmen Mochis○ Guanacevi○
Topolobampo○ Penón Juan
Cabo S. Lázaro Guasave○ Blanco○ Aldama○
I. Sta. I. S. Canatlán○ Gr
Margarita José Navolato○ Vic. Ca
La Paz◉ Culiacán◉ Tayoltita○ Guerrero○
San Antonio○ Eldorado○ Durango◉
Cerralvo○ San Ignacio○ El Salto○ Sombrerete○ Fresnillo○
San José del Cabo○ Mazatlán◉ Jerez○
Cabo S. Lucas Rosario○ Ojocaliente○
22° Acaponeta Colotlán○
R. Aguascalientes◉ ⑨ Lago
Islas Tuxpan○ Ixtlán○ Tlaltenango○
Marías Tepic◉ ⑧ Magdalena○ Le
Pto. Vallarta○ Guadalajara◉
Ameca○ Ira
B. de Banderas JALISCO Ocotlán○ M
Cabo Corrientes Zamora○
Autlán○ Ciudad Guzmán◉ MICH
IS. REVILLAGIGEDO ○ I. S. Benedicto Manzanillo○ ⑩ Colima◉ Ur
(Colima) ○ I. Socorro Tecomán○ Coalcomán○
Infiernillo
18° Res.

PACIFIC OCEAN

Mexico
CONIC PROJECTION

SCALE OF MILES
0   100   200   300
SCALE OF KILOMETERS
0   100   200   300

National Capitals.....☆ State Capitals.....◉

© Copyright HAMMOND INCORPORATED, Maplewood, N.J.

States Indicated by Numbers:

1	Tlaxcala	6	Querétaro
2	Morelos	7	Guanajuato
3	Distrito Federal	8	Aguascalientes
4	México	9	Nayarit
5	Hidalgo	10	Colima

114° B 110° C 106° Longitude D West of

Inset map (upper):

98° F 94° G 90° H 86°

99° 98° 97° 96°

HIDALGO

Chignahuapan

Misantla

Zumpango

Coyotepec

Teziutlán

Teotihuacán

Apan

Altotonga

GULF OF

0 10 20 30

MILES

Azcapotzalco

Texcoco

Calpulálpan

Libres

Nauhcampatépetl

14,045 ft.

(4281 m.)

Jico

Jalapa

Úrsulo Galván

MEXICO CITY

S. Martín

Apizaco

Huamantla

Coatepec

Río Antigua

MEXICO

Coyoacán

Texmelucan

Amecameca

Tlaxcala

Huatusco

de Chicuellar

Veracruz

Xochimilco

D.F.

TLAXCALA

Villa Vicente Guerrero

Tepeaca

Citlaltépetl

18,855 ft. (5747 m.)

Soledad

de Doblado

Cuernavaca

Popocatépetl

17,887 ft. (5452 m.)

Cholula

Puebla

Atzacing Serdán

Orizaba

Córdoba

MORELOS

Cuautla

Atlixco

Tecamachalco

Morelos

Ciudad Mendoza

Jonacatepec

Izúcar de

Matamoros

Cañada

Zongolica

Río Blanco

Jojutla

99° 98° 96°

19°

19°

2

Main map:

Laredo

Corpus Christi

26°

Falcon Res.

GULF

El Azúcar Res.

Brownsville

Reynosa

Matamoros

OF

dereyta Jim.

Montemorelos

Laguna

N

MEXICO

3

Liñares

Madre

Hidalgo

Santander Jiménez

Ciudad Victoria

Tropic of Cancer

Aldama

22°

TOSI

Tula

Cd. Mante

I. Pérez

Cayo Arenas

Cabo Catoche

Cárdenas

Ciudad Madero

Campeche Bank

Cancún

Pánuco

Tampico

Progreso

Tizimín

Jalpan

Tantoyuca

Hunucmá

YUCATÁN

Valladolid

Huejutla

Tuxpan

Mérida

Chichén-Itzá (Ruin)

Cozumel I.

Mineral del Monte

Papantla de Olarte

Bay

Cayo Arcas

Halachó

Ticul

Tekax

4

Juan

Tulancingo

of

Calkiní

Hopelchén

Pachuca

Jalapa

Campeche

Campeche

Felipe Carrillo Puerto

CITY

Teziutlán

Champotón

Sabancuy

I. Bacalar

Tlaxcala

Veracruz

Cd. del

Lag. de

Chetumal

Puebla

Orizaba

Alvarado

San Andrés Tuxtla

Carmen

Términos

CAMPECHE

Xcalak

Iguala

Tehuacán

Coatzacoalcos

Frontera

QUINTANA

Tierra

TABASCO

18°

Tixtla

Huajuápan

Blanca

Tuxtepec

Minatitlán

Villahermosa

Tenosique

Belmopan

Belize City

RERO

OAXACA

Matías

Palenque

Cayo

Dangriga

Tlaxiaco

Mitla (Ruin)

Romero

Tuxtla

S. Cristóbal

Flores

GUATEMALA

Gulf of Honduras

Ometepec

Oaxaca

Gutiérrez

de las Casas

BELIZE

Maldonado

Tehuantepec

Juchitán

Comitán

CHIAPAS

5

Sur

Salina

Cobán

Puerto Ángel

Cruz

Tonalá

Huehuetenango

Zacapa

HONDURAS

Gulf of

Tehuantepec

Huixtla

Quezaltenango

Sta. Rosa

Tapachula

GUATEMALA

98° F 94° G 90° H

Central America

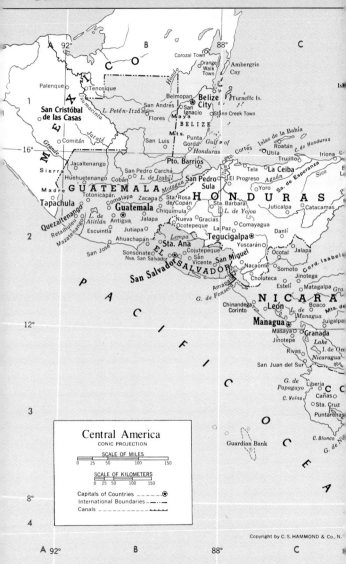

D 80° E 76°

JAMAICA
Kingston

Pedro
Bank

Pedro Cays
(Jam.)

Morant Cays
(Jam.)

1

C A R I B B E A N

Rosalind
Bank

16°

Banco
Gorda

Serranilla
Bank
(Col.)

Bajo Nuevo
(Col.)

*na de
atasca
Caratasca*

Cabo Gracias a Dios

N

Cayos Miskitos

Serrana Bank
(Col.)

2

Pto. Cabezas
(Bragman's Bluff)

Quita Sueño Bank
(Col.)

Prinzapolka

Roncador Cay
(Col.)

*Laguna de
Perlas*

I. de Providencia
(Col.)

S E A

I. de
San Andrés
(Col.)

Corn Is.
(Nic.)

Cayos de
Albuquerque
(Col.)

12°

Monkey Pt.

*San Juan del Norte
(Greytown)*

3

*osé
ago*

Limón

Bahía las Minas   Pta. Manzanillo

G. de San Blas

A

Changuinola

Bocas del Toro

Colón

G. de Urabá

amaca   'Chiriquí

G. de los Mosquitos

*Panama
Canal*

Serranía de San Blas

Pto. Cortés

La Chorrera

Panamá
(Panama
City)

A   M   A

*Arch. de
San Blas*

P A N

La Palma

Golfito

David

Serr. de
Tabasará

Penonomé

Aguadulce

Gulf of

Turbo

Dulce

Santiago

B. de Parita

Arch. de
las Perlas

El Real
de Sta. María

8°

Armuelles   G. de

Chitré

Panama

Pta. Burica   Chiriquí

Pen. de
Azuero

Las Tablas

COLOMBIA

4

I. de Coiba

est of Greenwich   D   80°   E   76°

West Indies

Cuba, Hispaniola & Jamaica

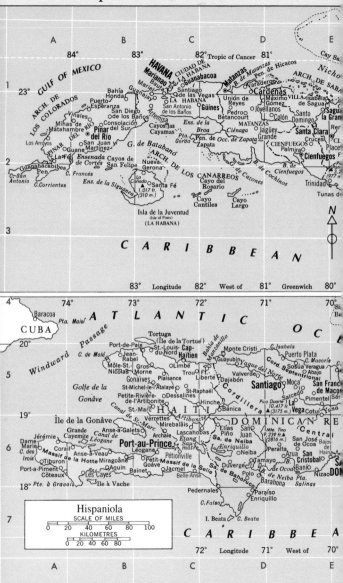

Cuba

SCALE OF MILES
0 20 40 60 80 100

KILOMETRES
0 20 40 60 80 100

LEGEND

Capitals of Countries	☆
Provincial Capitals	◉
International Boundaries	
Provincial Boundaries	

© Copyright HAMMOND INCORPORATED, Maplewood, N. J.

Great Bahama Bank

Cay Lobos

Old Bahama Channel

Cayo Coco

Buena Vista B. Ferro

guajay

s. de Leche Morón

Laguna

Cayo Romano

Cayo Guajaba

Cen. Violeta

Esmeralda

Cayo Sabinal

atibonico DE

Ciego de Avila

AVILA

Senado

Bahía de Nuevitas

Juraco

Cespedes

Nuevitas

Minas

Jumentos Cays

Cay Verde

Mira Por Vos

Cayo Sto. Domingo

Florida

lfo de María

Camagüey

Vertientes

San Pedro

Manati

Sibanicú

Hatuey

Puerto Padre

Chaparra

Guáimaro

Jobabo

Bartle

LAS TUNAS

Victoria de las Tunas

Holguín

HOLGUÍN

C. Lucrecia

Bahía de Nipe

Banes

Santa Cruz del Sur

Francisco

Cauto

San Germán

Velasco Gibara

Jiguani

Preston

Antilla

Gran

Sa. de Cristal

Nicaro

Cayo Mambi

Sagua de Tánamo

Baracoa

Pta Guarico

NES DE LA REINA

Golfo de Guacanayabo

Bayamo

GRANMA

Manzanillo

Campechuela

Niquero

del Toro 1,749 ft. (533 m.)

C. Cruz

Sierra Maestra

Pico Turquino 6,561 ft. (2000 m.)

Palma Soriano

EL Cobre

DE

SANTIAGO

Miranda

Caney

San Luis

Gran Piedra 3,710 ft. (1131 m.)

Jamaica

Cuchillas de Toa

GUANTÁNAMO

Guantánamo

Pta Maisí

Santiago de Cuba

Daiquirí

Bahía de Guantánamo

GUANTANAMO BAY U.S. NAVAL RESERVE

C. Cabrón

C. Samaná

Bahía de Samaná

C. Miches

El Macao

Higüey

La Romana

B. de Yuma

I. Saona

Mona Passage

CARIBBEAN

Montego Bay

Falmouth

Discovery Bay

Runaway Bay

St. Ann's Bay

Otracabessa

Port Maria

Annotto Bay

Buff Bay

Cascade

Lucea

Anchovy

Brown's Town

Dry Harbour

Ocho Rios

Highgate

Hope Bay

St. Margaret's Bay

Green Island

Bethel Town

Montpelier

Clark's Town

Moneague

Christiana

Ewarton

Linstead

Blue Mtn. Peak 7,402 ft. (2256 m.)

Port Antonio

N.E. Pt.

Petersfield

Balaclava

Maggotty

Frankfield

Bog Walk

Spanish Town

Manchioneal

Black River

Lacovia

Santa Cruz

Mandeville

Williamsfield

Porus

Port Royal

Kingston

Bath

Savanna-la-Mar

Cambridge

Luana Pt.

Alligator Pond

May Pen

Old Harbour

Lionel Town

Alley

Great Pedro Bluff

Old Harbour Bay

Portland Ridge Pen.

Portland Pt.

Morant Pt.

Bowden

S. & E. Pt.

Port Morant

Morant Bay

SEA

SEA

Jamaica

SCALE OF MILES
0 10 20 30 40 50

KILOMETRES
0 10 20 30 40 50

Longitude 77° West of Greenwich

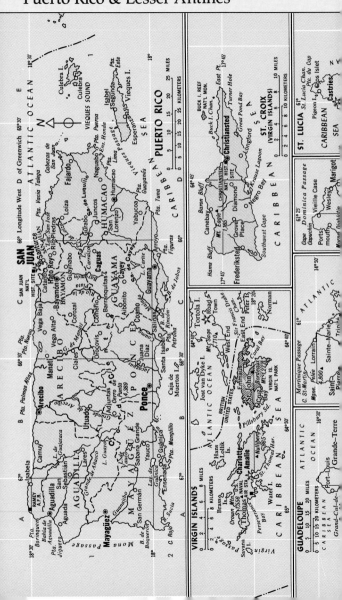

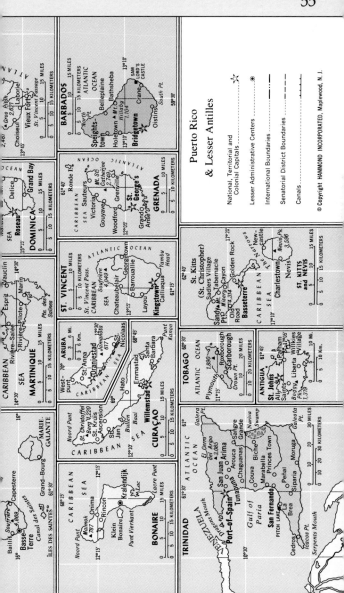

55

BARBADOS

North Pt.
Speightstown
Holetown
ATLANTIC
OCEAN
Belleplaine
Bathsheba
Hillaby 1,104
Crane
SAM
LORD'S
CASTLE
Bridgetown
Oistins
South Pt.
13°10'
59°30'

DOMINICA

SEA
Roseau
Delice
Grand Bay
15°15'

GRENADA

CARIBBEAN
SEA
Victoria
Sauteurs
Ronde I.
Mt. St.
Catherine
2,749
Gouyave
Grenville
St.
George's
Woodford
Grand
Anse
12°05'
61°40'

ST. VINCENT

ATLANTIC
OCEAN
Soufrière
4,049
St. Vincent Pass.
Georgetown
Yambu
Head
CARIBBEAN
SEA
Chateaubelair
Barrouallie
Layou
Kingstown
Calliaqua
13°15'
62°40'

MARTINIQUE

CARIBBEAN
SEA
Rivière-Salée
Marin
Pte. des
Salines
Vauclin
Esprit
14°30'

ARUBA

West
Pt.
St. Anna
Oranjestad
St.
Nicolaas
Santa
Barbara
Punt
Kanon
CARIBBEAN SEA
617
Jamanota
12°30'
70°

CURAÇAO

St. Christoffel
Berg 1,220
St. Kruis
Ascension
Noord Punt
St.
Jan
Bullen
Baai
Hato
Emmastad
Willemstad
Santa
CARIBBEAN SEA
12°10'
69°

BONAIRE

Noord Punt
Malmok
787
Onima
Rincon
Kralendijk
Klein
Bonaire
Lac
Lacre Punt
Punt Vierkant
12°15'
68°15'

Puerto Rico
& Lesser Antilles

National, Territorial and
Colonial Capitals .... ⚝

Lesser Administrative Centers .... ◉

International Boundaries .... —·—·—

Senatorial District Boundaries .... ·········

Canals .... —

© Copyright HAMMOND INCORPORATED, Maplewood, N.J.

ST. KITTS and NEVIS

St. Kitts
(St. Christopher)
Sadlers Village
Sandy
Pt.
Old
Road
Mt. Misery
3,714
Cayon
Tabernacle
Golden
Rock
Basseterre
Narrows
New-
Castle
Nevis Pk.
3,596
Charlestown
Nevis
CARIBBEAN SEA
17°20'
17°10'
62°40'

TOBAGO

ATLANTIC
OCEAN
Plymouth
Roxborough
Scarborough
Crown Pt.
1,890
11°15'
60°30'

ANTIGUA

St. John's
All-
Saints
Bolans
Liberta
Parham
Willikies
Village
Boggy Pk.
1,319
61°45'

TRINIDAD

ATLANTIC
OCEAN
Galera
Pt.
El Cerro
del Aripo
3,085
San Juan
Tunapuna
Arima
Arouca
Sangre
Grande
Chaguanas
Couva
Biche
Nariva
Swamp
Princes Town
Marabella
Dragons Mouth
Gulf of
Paria
Peñal
Galeota
Pt.
San Fernando
La
Brea
Moruga
Siparia
PITCH LAKE
Cedros
Point
Icacos Pt.
Serpents Mouth
VENEZUELA
10°30'
61°30'
61°

South America—Northern Part

South America–Southern Part

D Campo URUBUPUNGA
Grande DAM
Trés Lagoas

la Vista
Dourados

Y Maringá Londrina

Sete Quedas Falls
ITAIPU Res.
DAM Iguaçu
Falls

BRAZIL

Passo Fundo• Lages•
Cruz Alta•
guaiana Santa Maria•
Alegrete•
Cachoeira do Sul•

Santana do Livramento•
Bagé•

Melo•
Emb. del
Rio Negro

NGUAY
Canelones•

Montevideo
ata

San Antonio

Plata

Belo Horizonte• •Itabira Colatina•

50° Represa Ribeirão •Pico da Vitória•
de Furnas Prêto Bondeiro 9,482 ft. (2890 m.)
Poços de Caldas• •Juiz de Fora Barbacena• Cachoeiro de Itapemirim•
Marília• Bauru• Campinas• Paraíba •Campos
Piracicaba• Nova Iguaçu C. de São Tomé
Sorocaba• Volta Redonda•
São Paulo• Rio de Janeiro
•Santos Niterói•
I. de São Sebastião C. Frio

Ponta Grossa• Tropic of Capricorn
Curitiba•

Paranaguá•

Blumenau• •Joinvile
Itajaí•
I. de Santa Catarina
Florianópolis•

Tubarão•

Caxias do Sul• Canoas•

Porto Alegre
Lagoa dos Patos

Pelotas•

Rio Grande•
Lagoa Mirim

Pta. del Este

A T L A N T I C

O C E A N

N

South America
Southern Part

AZIMUTHAL EQUAL-AREA PROJECTION

MILES

| 0 | 100 | 200 | 400 | 600 |

KILOMETERS

| 0 | 100 200 | 400 | 600 |

Capitals of Countries .... ⊛

Other Capitals .... ⊛

International Boundaries .... ▬ ▬ ▬

Canals ....

® Copyright HAMMOND INCORPORATED, Maplewood, N. J.

West of 50° Greenwich E   40°   F   30°   G   20°

Africa—Northern Part

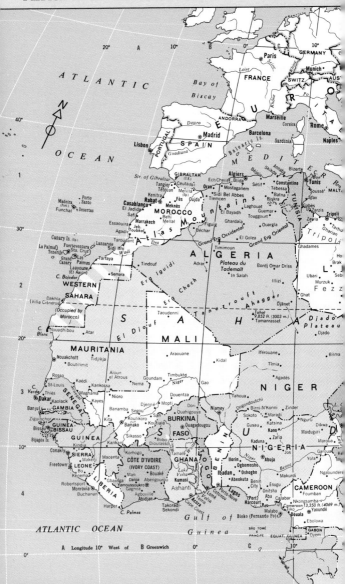

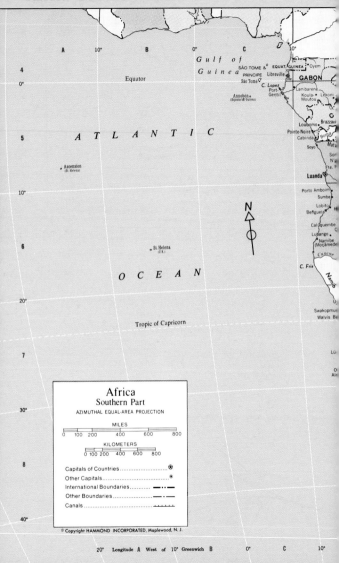

Gulf of Guinea

Equator

4
0°

A   10°   B   0°   C   10°

SÃO TOMÉ & PRÍNCIPE   EQUAT. GUINEA   •Oyem

São Tomé   Libreville   GABON

Annobón•
(Equatorial Guinea)   C. Lopez   Lambaréné   •Lékoni
Port-   Koula-
Gentil   Moutou

Louboma   •Brazzavi
Pointe-Noire   Pointe-Noire
Cabinda   Bom
Soyo   Mata

Sor
N'z
Fte. F

5   A T L A N T I C   Luanda

Porto Amboim
Sumbe
Lobito
Benguela

Caluquembe
10°   Lubango   C
Namibe
(Moçâmede)

6   •Ascension
(St. Helena)   Cunene

•St. Helena   C. Fria
(U.K.)   Namib

O C E A N

20°   Tropic of Capricorn   Swakopmul
Walvis Ba

7   Lü

O
Al

N

Africa
Southern Part
AZIMUTHAL EQUAL-AREA PROJECTION

MILES
0   100 200   400   600   800

KILOMETERS
0 100 200   400   600   800

Capitals of Countries ....⊛
Other Capitals ....⊛
International Boundaries........... ▬▬▬
Other Boundaries .... ▬ ▪ ▬
Canals .... ▬ ▪ ▬

8

40°

20°   Longitude A West of 10° Greenwich B   0°   C   10°

SUDAN

Belet
Weyne · El Dere
Baydhabo · Giohar
Bur Acaba · G · Mogadishu (Muqdisho)
Bardera · Afgoi
Uanle · Marka
Uen · Brava
Jamma
Chisimayu

Yangambi
·Stanley (Boyama) Falls·
Kisangani
(Zaïre)
L. Albert
Bunia
Margherita
16,795 ft.
Butembo
L. Edward
Goma
Port Kindu
Lodja
Saukuru
Lusambo
Kongolo
Kalemie
Kamina
Manono
Kananga
·Mbuji-Mayi
Katanga
Kolwezi Panda·
Kambove
Likasi
Kipushi
Chililabombwe
Chingola
Mufulira·
Ndola
Kitwe·
Luanshya·
Kolwezi

UGANDA
Elgon
4,178 ft.
Kioga
Mbale
Kampala
5199 m.
L. Kivu
Entebbe
Bukavu
Bujumbura
RWANDA
Kigali
Musoma
BURUNDI
Jigoma-Ujiji
Mwanza
Shinyanga
Singida
Tabora
Mpanda
Lake
Tanganyika
Mbala
Kasama
L. Mweru
Kasanga
Mbeya

KENYA
Lake
Turkana
Marsabit
Moyale
Wajir
Kitale
Eldoret
Kisumu
L.
Victoria
Nakuru
Nairobi
Kilimanjaro
19,340 ft.
Arusha
Moshi
5895 m.
Voi
Kenya
17,058 ft.
5199 m.

SOMALIA
Belet
Baydhabo
Bur Acaba
Bardera

Garissa
Malindi
Lamu
Mombasa
Tanga
Zanzibar
Zanzibar
Dar es Salaam
Mafia

TANZANIA
Dodoma
Morogoro
L. Rukwa
Iringa
Rufiji
Songea
Lindi
Rovuma
Mtwara-Mikindani
C. Delgado
Njazidja
Moroni
Mwali
Mayotte
(Fr.)

Aldabra Is.
(Seychelles)
Astove (Seychelles)
Cosmoledo Is.

COMOROS
Nzwani
C. Bobaomby
Antsiranana
Hell-Ville
Moromokotro
9,436 ft.
(2876 m.)
Ambanja

ZAMBIA
Mongu
Lusaka
Mazabuka
Kabwe

MALAWI
Chipata
Lilongwe
Lake
Nyasa
Mzimba
Lichinga
Pemba
Nacala
Nampula
Angoche

Mocambique

MOZAMBIQUE
Blantyre
Mulanje
7,936 ft.
Tete
9,843 ft. (3000 m.)
Namuli
2419 m.
Quelimane
Chinde

Mahajanga
Marovoay
Antananarivo
Tsiafajovona
8,671 ft.
2643 m.
Morondava
Mangok
Toliara
Ambatondrazaka
Ambatolampy
Antsirabe
Ambositra
Fianarantsoa
Manakara
Farafangana
Toamasina
Moramanga
Mananjary

MADAGASCAR
Ambatondrazaka
Toamasina
Antalaha

Juan de Nova
(Reunion)

Bassas da India
(Reunion)

Europa
(Reunion)

Mozambique Channel

ZIMBABWE
Harare
(Salisbury)
Kadoma
Kwekwe
Gweru
Chimoio
Beira
Hwange
Bulawayo
Zvishavane
Nyanda

Makgadikgadi
Salt Pan
Tonota
Serowe
Mahalapye

BOTSWANA
Mongu
Kalahari
Molepolole
Gaborone
Kanye
Mochudi

Desert
Upington
Kimberley
Bloemfontein

C. Vohimena
Faradofay

Limpopo
Chinde

Xai-Xai
Inhambane
Inharrime
Maputo

Pietersburg
Mbabatho
Pretoria
Germiston
Johannesburg
Mbabane
SWAZILAND
Vereeniging
Welkom
Maseru
LESOTHO
Bethlehem
Ladysmith
Pietermaritzburg
Durban
Port
Shepstone
Bloemfontein
Queenstown
Umtata
Cradock
King William's Town
East London
Uitenhage
Grahamstown
Mossel Bay
Port Elizabeth

REP. OF THE CONGO

Luvua
Kabambare

Kamina

Lake
Malombe

Victoria Falls
(Mosi-Oa-Tunya)
Livingstone
Caprivi Strip

Vaal

Kroonstad

INDIAN

OCEAN

4
0°

5

10°

6

20°

7

30°

8

40°

A   30°   B   20°   C   10°   D   0°   E   10°

70°

Arctic Circle

Lofoten Is.

Reykjavik ICELAND Akureyri

3

Faroe Is. (Den.)

Shetland Is.

N Trondh

Bergen

O

Stavanger

Oslo

ATLANTIC OCEAN

BRITISH

HEBRIDES

Orkney Is.

GREAT BRITAIN

SCOTLAND

NORTH

Göteborg

Skagerrak

Kattegat

Hälsir

Mair

ISLES

Glasgow
Edinburgh

UNITED

DENMARK

Copenhagen

BA

50°

NO. IRELAND

Belfast

SEA

Köln

KINGDOM

Berlin

Pozr

IRELAND

IRISH

Manchester

Amsterdam

Hamburg

Dublin

SEA

Liverpool

The Hague

Bremen

Leipzig

Dresden

Cork

St. George's Channel

ENGLAND

Birmingham

Antwerp

Essen

Cologne Bonn

Frankfurt

CZECH

Bristol

London

BEL.

Brussels

LUX.

Prague

Land's End

English Channel

Nürnberg

Viet

Brest

Le Havre

Rouen

Paris

Nancy

Munich

AUSTRIA

Rennes

Seine

FRANCE

Strasbourg

SWITZ.

LIECH.

Graz

Bay of Biscay

Nantes

Tours

Dijon

Geneva

Bern

Ljubljana

SLOVEN

Rijk

Limoges

St-

Lyon

Milan

Venice

ADRIATIC

40°

C. Finisterre

Gijon

Bordeaux

Étienne

Rhône

Turin

Genoa

Vigo

Bilbao

Pyrenees

Toulouse

Nice

Florence

SAN

Oporto

Valladolid

Saragossa

ANDORRA

Marseille

MONACO

MARINO

Lisbon

PORTUGAL

SPAIN

Madrid

Barcelona

Corsica

Ajaccio

VATICAN

Rome

CITY

ITALY

Tagus

Valencia

BALEARIC IS.

Sardinia

Naples

C. St. Vincent

Cordoba

Murcia

Minorca

TYRRHENIAN

Cadiz

Seville

Majorca

SEA

Str. of Gibraltar

Málaga

GIBRALTAR (U.K.)

MEDITERRA

Cagliari

Palermo

Tangier

Rabat

Algiers

Tunis

Sicily

Catan

AFRICA

MALTA

5

Europe

LAMBERT AZIMUTHAL EQUAL-AREA PROJECTION

SCALE OF MILES

0 100 200 300 400 500 600

SCALE OF KILOMETRES

0 100 200 300 400 500 600

Capitals of Countries ..... ⊚   International Boundaries ___

Internal Boundaries ....

Copyright by C.S. HAMMOND & CO., N.Y.

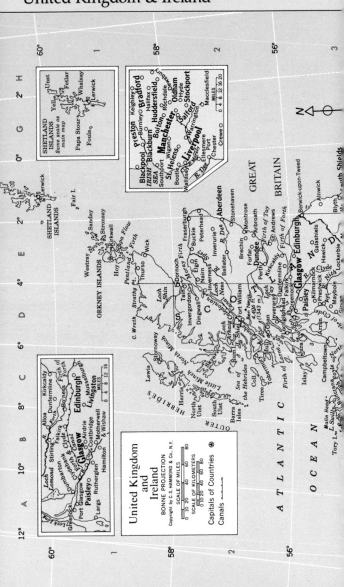

SHETLAND ISLANDS
Same scale as main map

Unst
Yell
Fetlar
Whalsay
Lerwick
Papa Stour
Foula

Blackpool
Preston
Keighley
Burnley
Bradford
Halifax
Blackburn
Huddersfield
Bolton
Oldham
IRISH SEA
Southport
Wigan
Rochdale
St. Helens
Manchester
Stockport
Bootle
Salford
Macclesfield
Liverpool
Warrington
Wallasey
Widnes
Ellesmere
Chester
Crewe

MILES
0 4 6 8 12 16 20

SHETLAND ISLANDS
Fair I.
Lerwick

ORKNEY ISLANDS
Westray
Sanday
Stronsay
Kirkwall
Hoy
Scapa Flow
Pentland Firth
C. Wrath
Strathy Pt.
Thurso
Wick

Lewis
Stornoway
Harris
North Uist
South Uist
Barra
Isles
OUTER HEBRIDES
Sea of the Hebrides
Coll
Tiree
Mull
Jura
Islay
Campbeltown
Malin Head
Tory I.
Little Minch
North Minch
Loch Shin
Loch Ness
Loch Linnhe
Dornoch Firth
Tain
Invergordon
Dingwall
Inverness
Nairn
Elgin
Moray Firth
Ballater
Fraserburgh
Buckie
Peterhead
Inverurie
Aberdeen
Brechin
Stonehaven
Forfar
Montrose
Perth
Arbroath
Dundee
Firth of Tay
St. Andrews
Kirkcaldy
Dunfermline
Firth of Forth
Falkirk
Edinburgh
Berwick-upon-Tweed
Galashiels
Hawick
Alnwick
Blyth
South Shields

Ben Nevis
4,406 m.
(1343 m.)
Fort William
Loch Lomond
Loch Fyne
Firth of Lorne
Oban
Inveraray
Tarbert
Campbeltown
Dumbarton
Paisley
Glasgow
Kilmarnock
Ayr
Maybole
Girvan
Firth of Clyde
Lockerbie
Dumfries

GREAT BRITAIN

N
ATLANTIC OCEAN

SHETLAND ISLANDS
Alloa
Kirkcaldy
Stirling
Dunfermline
R. Forth
Firth of Forth
Boness
Falkirk
Edinburgh
Musselburgh
Livingston
Airdrie
Coatbridge
Motherwell & Wishaw
Glasgow
Rutherglen
Hamilton
Paisley
Port Glasgow
Greenock
Dumbarton
Clydebank
Clyde & Forth Canal
R. Clyde
Largs
Loch Lomond

MILES
0 4 8 12 16

United Kingdom and Ireland
BONNE PROJECTION
Copyright by C.S. HAMMOND & Co., N.Y.

SCALE OF MILES
0 10 20 40 60 80

SCALE OF KILOMETERS
0 10 20 40 60 80

Capitals of Countries
Canals

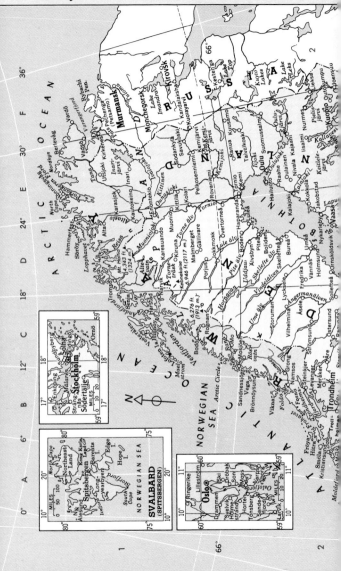

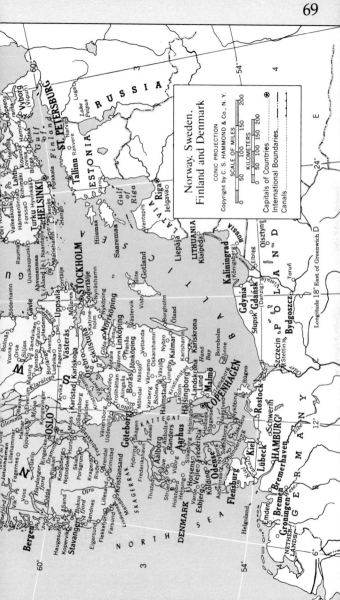

Norway, Sweden,
Finland and Denmark

CONIC PROJECTION

Copyright by C. S. HAMMOND & Co., N. Y.

SCALE OF MILES

50   100   150   200

KILOMETERS

50 100 150 200

Capitals of Countries ⊛
International Boundaries.
Canals

Germany

Germany
CONIC PROJECTION

SCALE OF MILES
SCALE OF KILOMETERS

Capitals of Countries
State & District Capitals
Canals

© Copyright HAMMOND INCORPORATED, Maplewood, N.J.

BALTIC SEA

NORTH SEA

DENMARK

POLAND

NETHERLANDS

WEST FRISIAN ISLANDS

NORTH FRISIAN ISLANDS

SCHLESWIG-HOLSTEIN

MECKLENBURG

WESTERN POMERANIA

BRANDENBURG

SAXONY-ANHALT

LOWER SAXONY

NORTH RHINE

HAMBURG
BERLIN
Bremen
Lübeck
Kiel
Flensburg
Rostock
Wismar
Schwerin
Stralsund
Szczecin (Stettin)
Magdeburg
Hannover
Brunswick
Hildesheim
Osnabrück
Bielefeld
Münster
Oldenburg
Wilhelmshaven
Bremerhaven
Cuxhaven
Frankfurt
Cottbus
Potsdam

Rügen
Fehmarn
Helgoland
Sylt
Föhr

Elbe
Weser
Ems
Oder
Rhine

CZECH REPUBLIC

Prague

Plzeň

B o h e m i a n   F o r e s t

B a v a r i a n   F o r e s t

Linz

Wels

(Moldau)

Vltava

Písek

Tábor

Beroun

Benešov

Ústí n. L.

Sebnitz

Pirna

Freital

Freiberg

Mittweida

Chemnitz

Zwickau

Glauchau

Altenburg

Gera

Jena

Weimar

Erfurt

Gotha

Arnstadt

Eisenach

T H U R I N G I A

Meiningen

Suhl

Coburg

Kronach

Bamberg

Bayreuth

Weiden

Amberg

Regensburg

Straubing

Deggendorf

Passau

Landshut

Pfarrkirchen

Braunau

Salzburg

Berchtesgaden

Königssee

Watzmann

Bad Reichenhall

Traunstein

Rosenheim

Wasserburg

Mühldorf

Erding

MUNICH
(München)

Freising

Ingolstadt

Neuburg

Augsburg

Dachau

Aichach

B A V A R I A

Donauwörth

Nördlingen

Nuremberg
(Nürnberg)

Fürth

Erlangen

Schwabach

Ansbach

Würzburg

Schweinfurt

Aschaffenburg

Frankfurt

Darmstadt

Mainz

Wiesbaden

H E S S E

Marburg

Fulda

Gießen

Limburg

Koblenz

R H I N E L A N D -
P A L A T I N A T E

Trier

Luxembourg

LUXEMBOURG

Saarbrücken

Kaiserslautern

Ludwigshafen

Mannheim

Heidelberg

Heilbronn

Stuttgart

Karlsruhe

Pforzheim

Baden-Baden

BADEN-
WÜRTTEMBERG

Reutlingen

Tübingen

Ulm

Freiburg

Konstanz

Constance

Bregenz

S W I T Z E R L A N D

Basel

Zürich

St. Gallen

F R A N C E

Strasbourg

Metz

Saarbourg

B E L G .

Danube

Rhine

Inn

Lech

Isar

Of Greenwich
Longitude East   12°

48°

50°

14°

Netherlands, Belgium & Luxembourg

CONIC PROJECTION

SCALE OF MILES

0   10   20   30   40   50

KILOMETRES

0   10   20   30   40   50

Capitals of Countries .... ☆

Provincial Capitals .... ◉

International Boundaries ....

Provincial Boundaries ....

Canals ....

IJSSELMEER

MARKER WAARD

NORTH EAST POLDER

FLEVOLAND

WEST FRISIAN ISLANDS

WADDEN SEE

AMSTERDAM

ROTTERDAM

The Hague ('s Gravenhage)

Hook van Holland (Hoek van Holland)

Scheveningen

Leiden

Haarlem

Utrecht

Groningen

Leeuwarden

Arnhem

Nijmegen

Emden

Norden

Borkum

Enschede

Emmen

Assen

Meppel

Zwolle

Deventer

Apeldoorn

Amersfoort

Hilversum

Gouda

Delft

Dordrecht

Alkmaar

Den Helder

Texel

Vlieland

Terschelling

Ameland

Schiermonnikoog

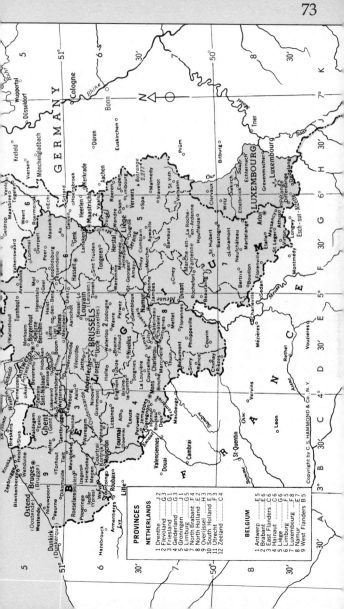

73

France

NORTH SEA

ENGLISH CHANNEL

UNITED KINGDOM

NETHERLANDS

GERMANY

BELGIUM

LUX.

Paris and Environs

Amsterdam · Rotterdam · The Hague · Haarlem · Utrecht · Leiden · Eindhoven · Arnhem · Maastricht · Enschede · Zwolle · Groningen · Leeuwarden · Emmen · Apeldoorn · Breda · Tilburg · Den Helder · Alkmaar · Texel

Brussels · Antwerp · Ghent · Bruges · Ostend · Flushing · Mechelen · Louvain · Namur · Liège · Verviers · Charleroi · Mons · Tournai · Courtrai · Roeselare

Cologne · Düsseldorf · Essen · Dortmund · Bonn · Münster · Osnabrück · Wiesbaden · Mainz · Saarbrücken · Strasbourg · Freiburg · Basel · Colmar · Mulhouse · Belfort · Trier · Luxembourg

London · Norwich · Cambridge · Peterborough · Colchester · Luton · Ipswich · Croydon · Brighton · Hastings · Dover · Canterbury · Ramsgate · Southampton · Portsmouth · Bournemouth · Exeter · Plymouth · Brest

Calais · Boulogne · Dunkirk · Lille · Roubaix · Tourcoing · Valenciennes · Cambrai · Arras · Douai · Lens · Amiens · Abbeville · Dieppe · Le Havre · Rouen · Beauvais · Compiègne · Soissons · Reims · Épernay · Châlons · Verdun · Metz · Nancy · Épinal · Troyes · Auxerre · Dijon · Besançon · Paris · Versailles · Orléans · Blois · Tours · Le Mans · Laval · Rennes · Nantes · St-Nazaire · Lorient · Quimper · Vannes · St-Brieuc · St-Malo · Cherbourg · Caen · Bayeux · Alençon · Angers

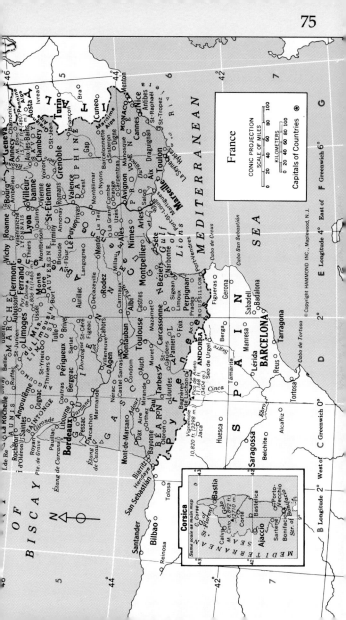

Spain & Portugal

Spain and Portugal

CONIC PROJECTION

SCALE OF MILES

0   25   50   75   100   125   150

SCALE OF KILOMETERS

0   25   50   75   100   125 150

Capitals ----- ⊛ International Boundaries -----

Italy

CONIC PROJECTION

SCALE OF MILES

0 20 40 60 80 100 120

SCALE OF KILOMETERS

0 20 40 60 80 100 120

Capitals of Countries ⊗

Regional Capitals ◉

YUGOSLAVIA

BOSNIA & HERZEGOVINA

Sarajevo ⊗

Mostar

CROATIA

SLOVENIA

Ljubljana ◉

Klagenfurt

Graz

Bruck

AUSTRIA

Niedere Tauern

Hohe Tauern

Innsbruck

Kufstein

Landeck

GERMANY

LIECHTENSTEIN

Bregenz

Lake Constance

SWITZERLAND

St. Gallen

Zürich

Winterthur

Schaffhausen

Basel

Bern

Geneva

Lausanne

Lake Geneva

La Chaux-de-Fonds

Neuchâtel

Solothurn

Lucerne

Glarus

Chur

Davos

St. Moritz

Lugano

Locarno

Lepontine Alps

Great St. Bernard Pass

Mont Blanc 15,771 ft. (4807 m)

M. Blanc 15,203 ft. (4634m)

Frejus Pass

Cottian Alps

FRANCE

Nice

MONACO

Ventimiglia

San Remo

Imperia

LIGURIA

Savona

Genoa

Gulf of Genoa

La Spezia

Carrara

Massa

Viareggio

LIGURIAN SEA

Leghorn (Livorno)

Pisa

Lucca

Pistoia

Florence

Empoli

Volterra

Siena

Grosseto

Elba

Piombino

Portoferraio

CORSICA

Bastia

Calvi

Corte

PIEDMONT

Turin

Cuneo

Mondovì

Saluzzo

Pinerolo

Alba

Asti

Alessandria

Vercelli

Novara

Biella

Aosta

VALLE D'AOSTA

LOMBARDY

Milan

Pavia

Cremona

Brescia

Bergamo

Como

Lecco

Monza

Varese

Sondrio

Piacenza

Parma

Reggio nell'Emilia

Modena

Bologna

EMILIA-ROMAGNA

Ferrara

Ravenna

Forlì

Cesena

Rimini

Imola

Faenza

Comacchio

Venice

VENETO

Verona

Vicenza

Padua

Treviso

Rovigo

Mantua

Belluno

TRENTINO

Trento

Bolzano

Bressanone

Merano

Brunico

Rovereto

Bassano

FRIULI-VENEZIA GIULIA

Udine

Gorizia

Trieste

Monfalcone

Pordenone

Carnic Alps

Julian Alps

Dolomites

Pula (Pola)

Rijeka (Fiume)

Karlovac

Zadar (Zara)

Šibenik

Split

Dubrovnik

Cetinje

ADRIATIC SEA

MARCHE

Ancona

Pesaro

Senigallia

Macerata

Fermo

Ascoli Piceno

San Benedetto

Civitanova

Fabriano

Urbino

TUSCANY

Arezzo

UMBRIA

Perugia

Foligno

Spoleto

Terni

Orvieto

Gubbio

ABRUZZI

L'Aquila

Pescara

Chieti

Teramo

Vasto

Lanciano

LAZIO

Rieti

Viterbo

Civitavecchia

Bolsena

Orbetello

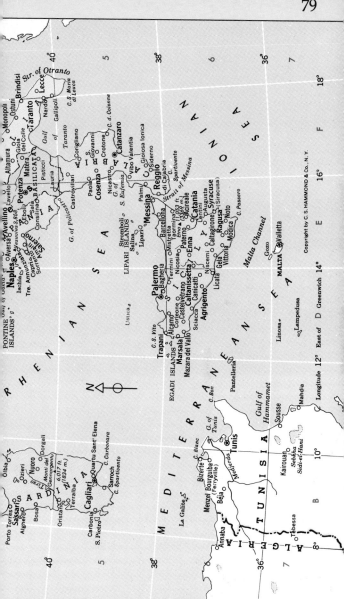

Str. of Otranto

Brindisi
Lecce
C. S. Maria
di Leuca
Monopoli
Altamura
Nardo
Gallipoli
Taranto
Gulf of
Taranto
Gioia
del Colle
Giovanni
Matera BASILICATA
Pisticci
Corigliano
Crotone
C. d. Colonne
Catanzaro
Potenza
Lavello
Avellino
Eboli
Lauria
Consiglana
Castrovillari
Paolo
Cosenza
Nicastro
S. Eufemia
Vibo Valentia
Siderno
Gioiosa Ionica
C. Spartivento
Strait of Messina
Palmi
Reggio
Messina
Stromboli
LIPARI ISLANDS
Salina
Lipari
Barcellona
Mistretta
Patti
Milazzo
Enna
Etna
10,958 ft.
Paterno
Acireale
Catania
Lentini
Augusta
Syracuse
Noto
C. Passero
Palermo
Bagheria
Termini
Corleone
Castelvetrano
Sciacca
Agrigento
Canicatti
Castrogiovanni
Niscemi
Gela
Vittoria
Licata
Ragusa
Siracusa
Modica
Comiso
Alcamo
C. S. Vito
Trapani
Marsala
Mazara del Vallo
EGADI ISLANDS
Ustica
Pantelleria

I O N I A N   S E A
T Y R R H E N I A N   S E A
M E D I T E R R A N E A N   S E A

Malta Channel
Gozo
MALTA
Valletta

Copyright by C. S. HAMMOND & CO. N. Y.

Linosa
Lampedusa

SARDINIA
Sassari
Porto Torres
Alghero
Bosa
Oristano
Nuoro
Monti del
Gennargentu
6,017 ft.
(1834 m.)
Olbia
Ozieri
Orosei
Dorgali
Terralba
Iglesias
Carbonia
S. Pietro
Cagliari
Quartu Sant'Elena
Carbonara
C. Spartivento

Olbia

G. of
Tunis
C. Blanc
C. Bon
Bizerte
Tunis
Gulf of
Hammamet
Sousse
Mahdia
Kairouan
Sebkha
Sidi-el-Hani
Menzel Bourguiba
(Ferryville)
Béja
Medjerda
La Galite
Annaba
Tébessa
ALGERIA
TUNISIA

Longitude 12°   East of   D Greenwich 14°   E   16°   F   18°
10°   B   36°
8°   7   A   36°
5   38°   40°
40°   5   6   38°   36°   7

A 6° B 7° 8°

Luxeuil-les-Bains

Thann
Müllheim
Schwar
Mulhouse
Belfort
Altkirch
Lörrach
BASELSTADT
Basel
Riehen
Säck
Héricourt
Allschwil
Dornach
Rheinfelden
Frick
Montbéliard
Boncourt
Audin-
court
Alle
Liestal
Sissach
Oberdorf
BASELLAND
Porrentruy
Courgenay
Delémont
Läufen
Trimbach
Olte
Zof
JURA
Aare
Besançon
Doubs
Baume-les-Dames
Saignelégier
Moutier
Courroux
Balsthal
Niederbipp
Langenthal
Ognon
Moron 4,396
Tramelan
Birs
Grenchen
Oensingen
SOLOTHURN
Herzogen-
buchsee
Huttwil
Ornans
La Chaux-de-Fonds
5,272 ft.
(1607 m.)
St-
Imier
Lengnau
Biel
Solothurn
Büren
Kirchberg
Emme
1

Le Locle
Chasseral
Cernier
Neuveville
Nidau
Lyss
Münchenbuchsee
Burgdorf
Samp
Napf
4,619 ft
1408 m
Lützelflüh

47°
Salins-les-
Bains
Doubs
Brévine
Peseux
La
Blaise
Ins
Bolligen
Langnau
Pontarlier
Fleurier
Gouvet
Boudry
Neuchâtel
Morat
Köniz
Bern
Münsingen
Champagnole
Lac de
St-Point
Chasseral
5,272 ft.
(1607 m.)
Ste-
Croix
Estavayer
le Lac
Grandson
Avenches
Düdin
gen
Belp
Schwarzen-
burg
Steffisburg
Brienzer Rothorn
Unterseen
Baulmes
Orbe
Yverdon
FRIB.
Payerne
Tafers
Sense
Thunersee
Thun
Brienzer
see
Interlaken

Le Lieu
Vallorbe
Chavornay
Treyvaux
La Roché
Romont
Bulle
Boltigen
Zweisimmen
Grindelwald
Lauterbrunnen
Mürren
Le Sentier
Lac
de Joux
La Sarraz
Echallens
Moudon
Siviriez
Gruyères
Broc
Vanil Noir
7,838 ft.
(2389 m.)
Saanen
Lenk
Adelboden
Kander
Oberl
2
Morez
Mt. Tendre 5,512 ft.
(1608 m.)
Cossonay
Renens
Châtel-St-
Denis
Zweisimmen
Gsteig
Wildhorn
10,656 ft.
(3248 m.)
Aletschhorn
13,763 ft.
(4195 m.)
Bière
Aubonne
Morges
Pully
Lausanne
Vevey
Montreux d'Oex
Saanen
Château-
d'Oex
LÖTSCHBERG
TUNNEL
Bietschhorn
12,907 ft. (3934 m.)
Naters
Brig
La Dôle
5,502 ft.
(1677 m.)
Rolle
St-Prex
Chexbres
Lake Geneva
Villeneuve
Bernese
Leysin
Leuk
Visp
Simplon
Pass
Gex
Céligny
Nyon
Thonon-
les-Bains
Cornettes de Bise
7,999 ft.
(2438 m.)
Aigle
Diablerets
10,570 ft.(3222 m.)
Ayent
Savièse
Oberl
St.
Niklaus
Simplon
Versoix
Évian-
les-Bains
Monthey
Bex
Conthey
Sion
Chalais
GENEVA
Geneva
Annemasse
Carouge
Drance
St-
Maurice
Chamoson
Fully
Nendaz
Hérémence
Sierre
Ayer
VALAIS
Dom 14,91
(4545
La Roche
Arve
Cluses
Mt. Bouet
10,200 ft.
(3109 m.)
Dents du Midi
10,686 ft.
(3257 m.)
Martigny
Saxon
Le Châble
Évolène
Weisshorn
14,780 ft.
(4505 m.)
Zermatt
Rimpfischhorn
(4199
46°
FRANCE
Annecy
Sallanches
Argentière
Mt. Dolent
12,533 ft.
(3820 m.)
Bourg-
St-Pierre
Grand
Combin
14,154 ft.
(4314 m.)
Dent
d'Hérens
13,684 ft.
(4171 m.)
Matterhorn
14,691 ft.
4478 m.)
Monte
Rosa
Dufourspi
15,203
4634
La Roche
Chamonix
MT. BLANC
TUNNEL
Hospice
GT. ST. BERNARD
ROAD TUNNEL
Dent Blanche
Châtillon
Favergas
St-Gervais-les-Bains
Mont Blanc
15,771 ft.
(4807 m.)
Great
St. Bernard Pass
Courmayeur
Aosta
Dora Baltea
ITA
Albertville
Little St. Bernard
Pass
Bourg-
St-Maurice
Graian
Alps
Verres

6° 7° C Longitude 8°

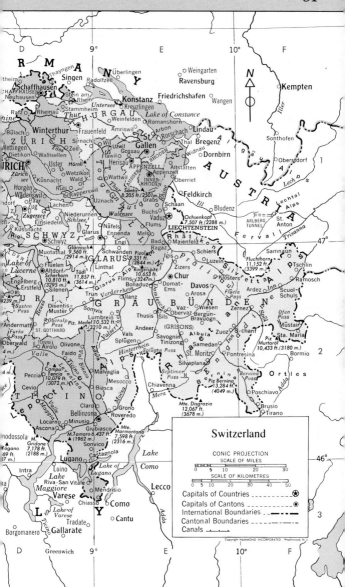

Switzerland

CONIC PROJECTION

A 12° B 14° C 16°

Gera
Chemnitz
Rumburk Warnsdorf
Jelena Góra
Zwickau
Trnova
Podmokly
Děčín
Liberec
Plauen
Teplice
Ústí nad Labem
Česká Lípa
Jablonec
Turnov
Sněžka b. 264
P
Coburg
Krušné Hory (Erzgebirge)
Most
Litoměřice
Jizera
Jičín
Trutnov
Aš
Jáchymov
Chomutov
Bílina
Mělník
Mladá Boleslav
Dvůr Králové
Náchod
Hradec Králové
Bayreuth
Krásno
Sokolov
Karlovy Vary
Ohře
Žatec
Louny
Kladno
Nymburk
Nový Bydžov
Rychn
Fürth
Cheb
Bochov
Rakovník
PRAGUE (Praha)
Český Brod
Kolín
Labe
Pardubice
50°
Nuremberg
Mariánské Lázně
Mže
Beroun
Radnice
Kutná
Čáslav
Chrudim
Vysoké
Tachov
Plzeň
Příbram
Benešov
Sedlčany
Chotěboř
Litomyšl
Svitavy
Regen
Dobřany
Rožmitál
Nepomuk
Tábor
Pacov
Humpolec
Havlíčkův Brod
Velké Meziříčí
Sňatka
Regensburg
Klatovy
Blatná
Písek
Vltava
Kamenice
Jihlava
Telč
Třebíč
Jihlava
Straubing
Sušice
Strakonice
Netolice
Týn
České Budějovice
Jindřichův Hradec
Mor. Budějovice
Znojmo
GERMANY
Landshut
Passau
Aigen
Vimperk
Český Krumlov
Gmünd
Retz
Freistadt
Greiner Wald
Zwettl
Horn
Eggenburg
Mistelbach
Danube (Donau)
Isar
Schärding
Urfahr
Greim
Spitz
Hollabrunn
Stockerau
MUNICH
Inn
Raab
Ried
Linz
Krems
Tulln
Mödling
Wels
Steyr
Ybbs
St. Pölten
Braunau
Amstetten
Berndorf
Wiener Neustadt
Salzburg
Mond see
Garsten
Scheibbs
Neunkirchen
Eiser
stadt
Chiemsee
Gmunden
Weyer
Mariazell
Semmering Pass
Gloggnitz
Bavarian Alps
Hallein
Ebensee
Eisenerz
Mürzzuschlag
Deu
Bad Ischl
Selzthal
Bruck an der Mur
Kapfenberg
Pinkafeld
Kufstein
Bischofshofen
Stainach
Mürz
Hartberg
Solbad Hall
Wörgl
Zell am See
Kaprun
Niedere Tauern
Leoben
Fürstenfeld
Kö
Innsbruck
Kitzbühel
A U S T R I A
Murau
Knittelfeld
Judenburg
Voitsberg
Gleisdorf
Graz
Raab
Szentgott
Steinach
Hohe Tauern
Großglockner 12,461
Bad Gastein
St. Michael
Neumarkt
Deutsch Landsberg
Zalaeg
Brenner Pass
Brunico
Ober Vellach
Gmünd
Althofen
Wolfsberg
Leibnitz
Radkersbur
Bressanone
Lienz
Spittal
St. Veit
Klagenfurt
Maribor
I T A L Y
Carnic Alps
Drau
Villach
Karawanken
Drava
Varaždin
Tarvisio
SLOVENIA
Celje
Koprivn

L. of Constance (Bodensee)   Same scale as main map
Bregenz
GERMANY
Reutte
46°
Rhein
Dornbirn
Feldkirch
LIECHT.
Bludenz
Lech
Imst
Inn
Landeck
Pfunds
Wildspitze 12,381
47
Gorizia
Novo Mesto
Sava
Ljubljana
Rhätikon
S W I T Z E R L A N D
10
I T A L Y
ADRIATIC SEA
Trieste
Zagreb
Bjelo

A 12° B 14° C Longitude 16° East of

Austria, Czech Republic,
Slovakia & Hungary

Conic Projection

SCALE OF MILES

0   20   40   60   80   100

SCALE OF KILOMETRES

0   20   40   60   80   100

Capitals of Countries   ⊛
International Boundaries   - - - - -
Canals   +++++

UKRAINE

MOLDOVA

ROMANIA

HUNGARY

CROATIA

SLOVENIA

BOSNIA

HERZEGOVINA

MONTENEGRO

SERBIA

KOSOVO

BULGARIA

POLAND

SLOVAKIA

CZECH REP.

AUSTRIA

GERMANY

VOJVODINA

BLACK SEA

ADRIATIC SEA

Bucharest • Sofia • Belgrade (Beograd) • Zagreb • Ljubljana • Sarajevo • Chișinău • Iași • Constanța • Varna • Bürgas • Galați • Brăila • Ploiești • Pitești • Craiova • Timișoara • Cluj-Napoca • Oradea • Arad • Subotica • Novi Sad • Szeged • Budapest • Bratislava • Vienna • Graz • Klagenfurt • Maribor • Rijeka • Split • Dubrovnik • Mostar • Tuzla • Banja Luka • Niš • Kragujevac • Priština • Pleven • Ruse • Pernik • Plovdiv • Vidin • Turnu Severin • Focșani • Bacău • Piatra Neamț • Suceava • Botoșani • Satu Mare • Debrecen • Nyíregyháza • Miskolc • Kecskemét • Kraków • Katowice • Ostrava • Olomouc • Brno • Prague • Plzeň • Linz • Salzburg • L'viv • Ivano-Frankivsk • Chernivtsi • Uzhhorod • Košice • Berdychiv • Vinnytsya

Danube • Dniester • Prut • Tisza • Siret • Drava • Sava • Morava • Vardar

44° • 48° • 20° • 24° • 28° • 16°

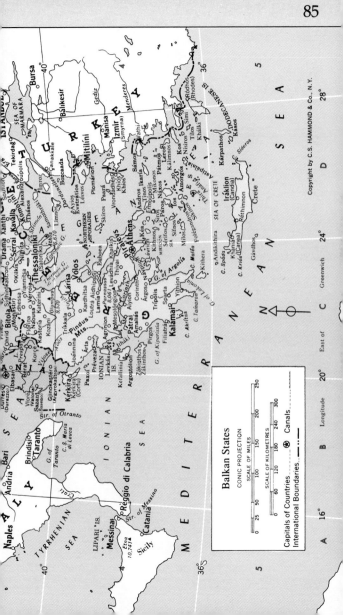

Balkan States

CONIC PROJECTION

SCALE OF MILES

0   25   50   100   150   200   250

SCALE OF KILOMETRES

0   60   120   180   240   300

Capitals of Countries .... ⊛   Canals .... ····
International Boundaries .... ▬▬▬

Copyright by C.S. HAMMOND & Co., N.Y.

Poland

DENMARK

BALTIC SEA

Pomeranian Bay

Rügen

Stralsund

Greifswald

Uznam (Usedom)

Rostock

Güstrow

Neubrandenburg

Neustrelitz

Müritzsee

Eberswalde

Berlin

Brandenburg

Potsdam

Luckenwalde

Wittenberg

Dessau

G E R M A N Y

Leipzig

Lauchhammer

Cottbus

Forst

Meissen

Dresden

Chemnitz

Zwickau

Ústí nad Labem

Świnoujście

Oder-Haff

Police

Szczecin

Gry. inn.

Chojna

Myślibórz

Górzyca

Dębno

Kostrzyn

Słubice

Rzepin

Świebodzin

Sulechów

Krosno

Odrz.

Guben

Lubsko

Żary

Żagań

Przemków

Bolesławiec

Zgorzelec

Görlitz

Zittau

Liberec

Bogatynia

Cieplice Śl.

Zdrój

Jelenia Góra

Kamienna

Góra

Kowary

Wolin

Kamień Pomorski

Gryfice

Nowogard

Goleniów

Stargard Szcz.

Pyrzyce

Barlinek

Strzelce

Kraj.

Witnica

Gorzów Wlkp.

Międzychód

Skwierzyna

Międzyrzecz

Nowy

Tomyśl

Zbąszyń

Wolsztyn

Zielona Góra

Nowa Sól

Wschowa

Głogów

Sława

Szprotawa

Kożuchów

Polkowice

Lubin

Chojnów

Legnica

Złotoryja

Jawor

Strzegom

Świdnica

Świebodzice

Dzierżoniów

Bielawa

Nowa

Ruda

Kłodzko

Bystrzyca

Kłodzka

Międzylesie

Kudowa

Zdrój

Głuchołazy

Ustka

Słupsk

Darłowo

Sławno

Koszalin

Białogard

Połczyn-Zdrój

Świdwin

Łobez

Drawsko

Pomorskie

Złocieniec

Szczecinek

Wałcz

Złotów

Piła

Trzcianka

Czarnków

Czarnkowo

Wronki

Szamotuły

Pniewy

Buk

Luboń

Mosina

Śrem

Kościan

Leszno

Góra

Rawicz

Milicz

Wołów

Brzeg Dolny

Oleśnica

Wrocław

Oława

Brzeg

Strzelin

Ziębice

Ząbkowice Śl.

Nysa

Prudnik

Głubczyce

Racibórz

Wodzisław

Śl.

Ostrava

Cieszyn

Łeba

Puck

Wejherowo

Reda

Rumia

Lębork

Kartuzy

Sopot

Władysławowo

Kościerzyna

Bytów

Miastko

Człuchów

Chojnice

Tuchola

Sępólno

Kraj.

Koronowo

Więcbork

Nakło n.

Szubin

Kcynia

Chodzież

Rogoźno

Wągrowiec

Oborniki

Poznań

Swarzędz

Środa

Wlkp.

Września

Gniezno

Witkowo

Mogilno

Janikowo

Słupca

Konin

Turek

Koło

Jarocin

Kożmin

Pleszew

Gostyń

Krotoszyn

Ostrów Wlkp.

Kalisz

Ostrzeszów

Kępno

Namysłów

Kluczbork

Olesno

Opole

Krapkowice

Kędzierzyn

Bydgoszcz

Żnin

Gniewkowo

Mogilno

Strzelno

Trzemeszno

Świecie

Łabiszyn

Starogard Gd.

Tczew

Łeba

Słupia

Brda

Noteć

Warta

Warta

Prosna

Barycz

Nysa Łużycka

Nysa Kłodzka

Oder

Oder

Odra

Odra

Bóbr

Kwisa

Sprewa (Spree)

Havel

Havel

Spree

Elbe

Mulda

Neisse

Łaba (Elbe)

Morava

C Z E C H   R E P.

Šumperk

Olomouc

Přerov

Brno

Pferov

Odra

Sudety

Krzyż

Dobiegniew

Drezdenko

Rogoźno

Wyrzysk

Inset map

MI.

KM.

Tarnowskie

Góry

Piekary

Śl.

Wojkowice

Ząbkowice

Będzin

Czeladź

Dąbrowa Górnicza

Sławków

Bukowno

Bytom

Siemianowice Śl.

Chorzów

Sosnowiec

Zabrze

Ruda Śląska

Świętochłowice

Gliwice

Katowice

Mysłowice

Knurów

Kłodnica

Brynica

Przemsza

Czarna Przemsza

Jaworzno

Jeleń

Trzebinia-

Siersza

Chrzanów

Knurów

Orzesze

Mikołów

Łaziska

Górne

Tychy

Leszczyny

Poland

CONIC PROJECTION

SCALE OF MILES

0 10 20 40 60 80

SCALE OF KILOMETERS

0 10 20 40 60 80

Capitals of Countries .... ★

Other Capitals .... ◉

International Boundaries .... — ·· —

Internal Boundaries .... — · —

Canals ....

Poland is divided into 49 provinces (bearing the same name as their capitals) and the autonomous cities of Warsaw, Łódź and Kraków.

RUSSIA

LITHUANIA

BELARUS

UKRAINE

SLOVAKIA

Kaliningrad
Baltiysk
Braniewo
Frisches Haff
Elbląg
Pasłęk
Orneta
Morąg
 Iława
Lubawa
Nowy Miasto
Lubawskie
Brodnica
Rypin
Żuromin
Sierpc
Płock
Sochaczew
Gostynin
Łowicz
Głowno
Zgierz
Łódź
Pabianice
Andrespol
Piotrków
Trybunalski
Radomsko
Włoszczowa
Koniecpol
Myszków
Wolbrom
Olkusz
Kraków
Wieliczka
Wadowice
Myślenice
Andrychów
Rabka
Nowy
Targ
Zakopane
High
Rysy
8,199 ft.
(2499 m.)

Pregolya
Lyna
Bartoszyce
Lidzbark Warm.
Dobre Miasto
Biskupiec
Barczewo
Olsztyn
Ostróda
Olsztynek
Działdowo
Nidzica
Chorzele
Mława
Przasnysz
Ciechanów
Pułtusk
Nasielsk
Nowy Dwór Maz.
Legionowo
Pruszków
Błonie
Żyrardów
Grodzisk Maz.
Skierniewice
Rawa Maz.
Grójec
Warka
Tomaszów Maz.
Opoczno
Końskie
Szydłowiec
Iłża
Suchedniów
Skarżysko-Kam.
Starachowice
Ostrowiec Swkrz.
Opatów
Kielce
Jędrzejów
Staszów
Pińczów
Miechów
Kazimierza Wlk.
Busko-Zdrój
Nowa Nisko
Dęba
Mielec
Dąbrowa Tarnowska
Bochnia
Tarnów
Limanowa
Nowy Sącz
Stary
Sącz
Gorlice
Krynica
Bardejov

Chernyakhovsk
Gołdap
Węgorzewo
Gižycko
Reszel
Mrągowo
Orzysz
Ełk
Szczytno
Pisz
Kolno
Łomża
Ostrołęka
Ostrów Maz.
Zambrów
Łapy
Wyszków
Wołomin
Warsaw
Otwock
Piaseczno
Garwolin
Kozienice
Radom
Zwoleń
Pionki
Puławy
Poniatowa
Bełżyce
Kraśnik Fabryczny
Kraśnik
Janów
Lub.
Sandomierz
Tarnobrzeg
Stalowa Wola
Nowa
Leżajsk
Rudnik
Łańcut
Przeworsk
Rzeszów
Jarosław
Dębica
Strzyżów
Brzozów
Jasło
Krosno
Sanok
Ustrzyki
Dolne
DUKLA
PASS

Kapsukas
Suwałki
Olecko
Sejny
Augustów
Jez. Mamry
Jez. Śniardwy
Grajewo
Biebrza
Sokółka
Mońki
Czarna Biał.
Wasilków
Białystok
Narew
Wysokie Maz.
Bielsk Podlaski
Hajnówka
Bug
Sokołów Podlaski
Łosice
Siemiatycze
Terespol
Brest
Biała Podlaska
Łuków
Międzyrzec Podl.
Radzyń Podl.
Parczew
Włodawa
Lubartów
Lublin
Świdnik
Chełm
Krasnystaw
Zamość
Hrubieszów
Szczebrzeszyn
Biłgoraj
Tomaszów Lubelski
Lubaczów

Kobrin
Yasel'da
Pripyat'
Kovel'
Volodymyr-
Volyns'kyy
Novovolyns'k
Luts'k
Chervonohrad
Brody
L'viv
Przemyśl
Horodok
Sambir
Drohobych
Boryslav
Stryy
Zolochiv
Berezhany
Stryy
Kalush
Dnister

Gerlachovka
8,707 ft.
(2654 m.)

Warmia
Lynia
Mazury
Jez. Zegrzyńskie
Vistula
Wkra
Pilica
Wieprz
Bug

N

20° 22° 24° 26°

54° 52° 50°

2 3 4

longitude 20° East of Greenwich 22° 24° F

Eastern Europe

Eastern Europe

CONIC PROJECTION

MILES
0 50 100 200 300

KILOMETRES
0 100 200 300

National Capitals ⊛
International boundaries
Canals

© Copyright HAMMOND INCORPORATED, Maplewood, N.J.

ARCTIC OCEAN

KARA SEA

Gulf of Ob'

Yamal Pen.

Novaya Zemlya I.

Mezhdusharskiy I.

North Cape

NORWAY

Varangerfjord

Kirkenes

Inari

L. Inari

L. Inandra

Pechenga

Polyarnyy

Rybachiy Pen.

Iokan'ga

Murmansk

Monchegorsk

Kola Pen.

Oktovsk

Kandalaksha Pen.

WHITE SEA

Kem'

Kaleviala

Vygozero

Belomorsk

Povenets

Ust'-Usa

Vorkuta

Arctic Circle

Ust'-Tsilma

Pechora

Nar'yan-Mar

Kozhva

Usa

Ural Mts.

North Ural Mts.

Syktyvkar

Koslan

Ukhta

Vym'

Leshukonskoye Ridge

Timan

Mezen'

G. of Mezen

Kanin Pen.

Kolguyev I.

Pinega

Northern Dvina

Archangel (Arkhange'sk)

Onega

Onega B.

Onega

Plesetsk

Nyandoma

Vel'sk

Kargopol'

Kotlas

Velikiy Ustyug

Totma

Sokol

Vologda

SWEDEN

Stockholm

Sundsvall

Umeå

Gulf of Bothnia

Vaasa

Tampere

Turku

Helsinki

FINLAND

L. Oulu

Kemi

L. Päijänne

L. Ladoga

Vyborg

ST. PETERSBURG

Novgorod

L. Ilmen

Staraya Russa

Pskov

Velikiye Luki

ESTONIA

Tallinn

Narva

Tartu

L. Peipus

BALTIC SEA

Gulf of Finland

Riga

Gulf of Riga

LATVIA

Daugavpils

LITHUANIA

Klaipėda

Šiauliai

Liepāja

Ventspils

Kyshtym

Yekaterinburg (Sverdlovsk)

Zlatoust

Ufa

Perm (Molotov)

Izhevsk

Kirov

Yoshkar-Ola

Kostroma

Ivanovo

Yaroslavl'

Rybinsk

Rybinsk Res.

Cherepovets

Russia and Neighboring Countries

© Copyright HAMMOND INCORPORATED, Maplewood, N.J.

Russia and Neighboring Countries

CONIC PROJECTION

SCALE OF MILES
200   400   600   800

SCALE OF KILOMETERS
200   400   600   800

Capitals of Countries .... ⊛
International Boundaries .... ▬▬▬

Longitude 120° East of Greenwich

PHILIPPINES
Luzon
Manila
Mindoro
Panay
Negros
Mindanao
Davao
SULU SEA
Kota Kinabalu
SABAH
Kuching
SARAWAK
BRUNEI
Borneo
Banjarmasin
Madagascar
Celebes
CELEBES SEA
Manado
SULA
MOLUCCAS
Timor
FLORES SEA
JAVA SEA
Surabaja
BANDA SEA
SUNDA IS.
Christmas I. (Austr.)

SOUTH CHINA SEA
Hainan
Hanoi
G. of Tonkin
VIETNAM
LAOS
Vientiane
THAILAND
BANGKOK
Da Nang
Ho Chi Minh City (Saigon)
Phnom Penh
G. of Thailand
MALAYA
MALAYSIA
Kuala Lumpur
Str. of Malacca
SINGAPORE
George Town
Medan
Padang
Palembang
Jakarta
Bandung
Semarang
SUMATRA
JAVA
INDONESIA

BURMA
Mandalay
BANGLADESH
DACCA
Sittwe
Moulmein
RANGOON
Andaman Is. (India)
Nicobar Is. (India)

INDIA
Nagpur
Calcutta
Chandernagore
Indore
Ahmadabad
Bombay
Poona
Panjim
Hyderabad
Bangalore
Madras
Pondicherry
Karikal
Cannanore (Laccadive) Is. (India)
Mahe
Madura
SRI LANKA (CEYLON)
Kandy
Colombo
Vanam
Daman
Diu

ARABIAN SEA
Kuria Muria Is.
BAY OF BENGAL

MALDIVES
Male
Diego Garcia
BRIT. IND. OC. TERR.
Cocos Is. (Austr.)

SEYCHELLES

INDIAN OCEAN

Equator
Tropic of Capricorn

AUSTRALIA
Broome
Perth

AFRICA
YEMEN
Aden
G. of Aden
Djibouti
Socotra (Yemen)
Mukalla

Madagascar

N

20°
40°

60° E   Longitude 80°   East of   G   Greenwich   100°   H   120°   J

© Copyright HAMMOND INCORPORATED, Maplewood, N.J.

Asia
LAMBERT AZIMUTHAL
EQUAL-AREA PROJECTION
SCALE OF MILES
0   300   600   900   1200
SCALE OF KILOMETERS
0   300   600   900   1200
Capitals of Countries..............●
International Boundaries...........
Canals...................................

A 25° 30° C 35° D 40° E 45°

Edirne
Thessaloníki Istanbul
Sea of Marmara Bosporus
Adapazari Sakarya Zonguldak Sinop BLACK SEA P'ot'i GEORGIA
Bursa Eskişehir Ankara Samsun Trabzon Bat'umi Tbilisi RUSSIA Derber
Balikesir AEGEAN Afyon Çorum Kizilirmak Sivas Kars ARM. Ganca AZER. Nul
İzmir Khíos SEA Konya Kayseri L. Tuz Erzurum Ararat Yerevan Sevan Aras Khvoy Ardab
Athens Denizli Taurus Mts. Malatya Diyarbakir 16,946 ft. (5165 m.) L. Van. Urmia Tabriz
Iráklion (Candia) Antalya Mersin Adana Maraş Urfa Urmia Aras
Crete Rhodes G. of Antalya Antakya El Haseke Mosul Erbil Kirkuk Ham
CYPRUS Aleppo SYRIA Tigris Bakhtara
MEDITERRANEAN Nicosia Hama Latakia Tadmur El Hamad Baghdad
SEA Tripoli Homs Mesopotamia IRAQ Kut
LEBANON Beirut Damascus (Dimashq) Syrian Desert Karbala An Najaf Hilla
LIBYA Sidi Barrani Alexandria Port Said Haifa Tel Aviv-Jaffa Jerusalem Sea of Galilee Amman An Nasiriya Basra
Suez Canal ISRAEL Gaza JORDAN Wadi Sirhan KUWAIT
Siwa Oasis Qattara Depression Cairo Giza Suez Elat Al 'Aqaba Jauf Sakaka
El Faiyûm Sinai Pen. Gulf of Aqaba Nefud
El Minya Nile Arabian Desert Taima Jebel Shammar Hail SAUDI
EGYPT Asyût Qena El Karnak Khaibar Buraida Wadi Rima Shaqra
Dakhla Oasis Sohag El Karnak Wejh Umm Lajj Medina ARAB Riya
Khârga Oasis ASWAN HIGH DAM Aswân Yenbo Al Hil
Lake Nasser Rabigh Sufeina Laila
Lake Nubia Nubian Desert Jidda Mecca
3rd Cataract Dongola Jebel Oda 7,412 ft. (2259 m.) Taif Al Lidam
4th Cataract Abu Hamed Port Sudan Qunfidha
SUDAN 5th Cataract Merowe Suakin Abha Aba as Su'ud (Najran)
6th Cataract Atbara Farasan Is. Sa'ada Bahr es (Al Ah
Omdurman Khartoum North Kassala Massawa Dahlak Arch. Shib
Khartoum Agordat Asmara Kamaran Y San'a
Wad Medani Gedaref Ras Dashan 15,157 ft. (4620 m.) Hodeida Dhamar
En Nahud El Obeid Wad Medani Adwa Ta'izz Madinat
White Nile Blue Nile ETHIOPIA Gondar Mocha Ash Sha'b Aden
Kosti Kassala L. Tana DJIBOUTI Perim Lahej G. of Mandeb

© Copyright HAMMOND INC., Maplewood, N.J.

B 30° 35° D 40° F

Near and Middle East

CONIC PROJECTION

SCALE OF MILES

0   100   200   300   400

KILOMETERS

0   100   200   300   400

Capitals of Countries .... ⊛
International Boundaries ___
Other Boundaries ....

Turkey, Syria, Lebanon & Cyprus

BULGARIA
GREECE
BLACK SEA

Svilengrad Edirne Kırklareli İstranca Mts. Demirköy İğneada C.
Lüleburgaz Demirköy
Ergene Çorlu Bosporus (Karadeniz Boğazı) Cide İnebolu
Uzunköprü Tekirdağ Şile Karadeniz Boğazı Küre Mountains Kastamo
Enez Keşan Silivri Kandıra Akçakoca Ereğli Safranbolu Taşköprü
Zonguldak Hisarönü Araç
İstanbul Kaynarca Karabük Soğanlı Devrez İskilip
Gallipoli Sea of Marmara İzmit (Kocaeli) Adapazarı Bolu Gerede Çerkeş Çankırı Tosya
Çanakkale Biga Gönen Karacabey Yenişehir Gölpazarı Mudurnu Beypazarı Altındağ Kızılırmak
Bandırma Gemlik L. İznik İnönü Sakarya Ankara Kırıkkale
İLİUM (TROY) Bayramiç Mustafa Kemalpaşa Bilecik Polatlı Kaman Delicermak
Ayvacık Edremit Dursunbey Tavşanlı İnegöl Eskişehir Sivrihisar Haymana Kırşehir
C. Baba Ayvalık Bigadiç Kütahya Türkmen Dağı 5,138 Emiroğlu Tepesi 7,352 Cihanbeyli Şereflikochisar Nevşehir
Lésvos Bergama Kırkağaç Simav Gediz Afyon Bolvadin Lake Tuz Yeşilh
G. of Çandarlı Dikili Akhisar Demirci Uşak Sandıklı L. Akşehir Aksaray Hasan Dağı 10,673 Niğde
Khíos Çeşme Menemen Manisa Salihli Alaşehir Borlu Sultan Akşehir Sille Konya Karapınar
İzmir (Smyrna) Turgutlu Buldan Civril Eğridir Kadınhanı Ereğli
Sámos Kuşadası EPHESUS Tire Nazilli Çal Dinar L. Beyşehir Cumra Karaman Tarsu
İkaria Söke Aydın Menderes L. Acı Isparta Beyşehir Kara Dağ 7,451 Mersin (İçel)
Pátmos L. Bafa Denizli Tavas Burdur Eğridir Seydişehir Hadım C. İnceku
G. of Mandalya Bodrum Muğla Tefenni Bucak Akseki Mut Taurus Mts. Silifke
Kós G. of Kerme Marmaris Daçmen L. Söğüt Antalya (Adalia) Serik Ermenak Göksu Anamur
Astipalaía Datça Elmalı Korkuteli Alanya
Tílos Rodhos (Rhodes) Fethiye Finike Gulf of Antalya
Rhodes Kaş C. Gelidonya
Kárpathos Kastellórizon

Crete MEDITERRANEAN SEA

C. Kormakiti Kyrenia Yialousa
C. Arnauti Morphou Nicosia Famagu
Paphos SOVEREIGN BASE AREA (U.K.) CYPRUS C. Greco
SOVEREIGN BASE Larnaca
AREA (U.K.) Limassol
C. Gate
Tel Aviv-Jaffa

Inset 1 (Gallipoli)

26° 30'
Gulf of Saros
Bolayır
Gallipoli (Gelibolu)
C. Büyük Kemikli Galata Dardanelles Boğazı
Büyük-anafarta Lâpseki
Eceabat Çanakkale
Dardanelles Kilitbahir
İntepe Koca
Kumkale
MILES
0 5 10 15 20
26° 30'

Inset 2 (İstanbul)

29°
BLACK SEA
Kilyos
Sarıyer
Beykoz
Yeniköy
Beyoğlu (Pera) Beşiktaş
Eyüp Üsküdar
İSTANBUL Kadıköy
Sea of Marmara
Kartal
MILES
0 5 10
Adalar
29°

Turkey, Syria,
Lebanon & Cyprus
CONIC PROJECTION

MILES
0 25 50 75 100 125 150

KILOMETRES
0 25 50 75 100 125 150

Capitals of Countries ⊛
International Boundaries ---·---
Ruins ∴

Israel & Jordan

Kiswe

En Nabatiye

Litani

Merj 'Uyun

Qana

'Aazziye

Tibnin

Bent Jubail

En Naqura

Rosh Haniqra

Sur (Tyre)

Es Sanamein

Nava

Sheikh Miskin

Tibneh

De'ra

Nessib

Jabir

Er Ramtha

El Mafraq

Ba'ama

El Madwar

El Kitta

El Husn

Irbid

Hawara

Kitirn

Et Taiyiba

Tibra

Suf

Jerash

Kufrinja

Kuraiyima

Anjara

'Ajlun

'Ajlun

Jebel 'Ajlun

Mt. (1247 m.)

I R B I D

Jobbin H. (1247 m.)

Hasbani

Hermon

9,232 ft. (2814 m.)

Metula

Kefar Gil'adi

Qiryat Shemona

Dan

Banyias

Kefar Blum

Mishmar Hayarden

Dafna

Malkiyya

Hula

Yesud Hama'ala

Jish

Rafid

El Quneitra

GOLAN HEIGHTS (Occupied by Israel)

S Y R I A

W A D I

Wadi er Ruqqad

Wadi esh Shallala

Er Rafid

Samar

Harima

Et Taiyiba

Waqqas

Deir Abu Sa'id

Kefar Ruppin

Tirat Zvi

El Yarmuk

Geshir

Alumot

Bizra Zababida

Ez Zababida

El Husn

D R U Z E

Meron 3,963 ft. (1208 m.)

Zefat (Safad)

Rosh Pinna

Hazor

Qatane

NORTHERN

Arrabe

Sakhnin

GALILEE

Kefar Hananya

Maghar

Migdal

Tiberias

Sea of Galilee (Lake Kinneret)

Ginnosar

Kinneret

'En Gev

Fiq

Ma'ad

Ein Harod

Jalbun

Beisan

Bet She'an

Geshir

Kfar Yasif

Kafr Kanna

Zippori

Nazareth

Nazerat

Iksal

Mizra

Afula

Ha Emeq Qishon

Megiddo

Zububa

Jenin

Qabatiya

Siris

'Anza

Siris

Tubas

Tammun

Mt. (1084 m.)

Tirat Karmel

Cape Carmel

Daliyat al-Karmel

'Atlit

Dor

Habonim

Newe Yam

Bat Shelomo

Zikhron Ya'aqov

Binyamina

Pardes Hanna

Hadera

Givat Ada

Mikhmoret

Kefar Vitkin

Netanya

Avihayil

Even Yehuda

Kefar

Qadima

Shefayim

Eyashiv

Qalansuwe

Tel Abba

Qiryat Haim

Qiryat Ata (Akko)

Acre

Bay of Haifa

Haifa

Qir. Motzkin

Qir. Yam

Qir. Bialik

Nesher

1,791 ft. (546 m.)

Shefar'am

Turi'an

M E D I T E R R A N E A N   S E A

Tulkarm

Shuweika

Silat Dhahr

Ya'bad

'Attil

'Ajja

Jaba'

Burqa

Anabta

CENTRAL

WEST

Ba'un

Falama

SCALE OF MILES

SCALE OF KILOMETERS

Israel & Jordan

CYLINDRICAL PROJECTION

© Copyright HAMMOND INCORPORATED, Maplewood, N.J.

Copyright by C.S. HAMMOND & Co., N.Y.

Capitals of Countries

Internal Capitals

International Boundaries

Internal Boundaries

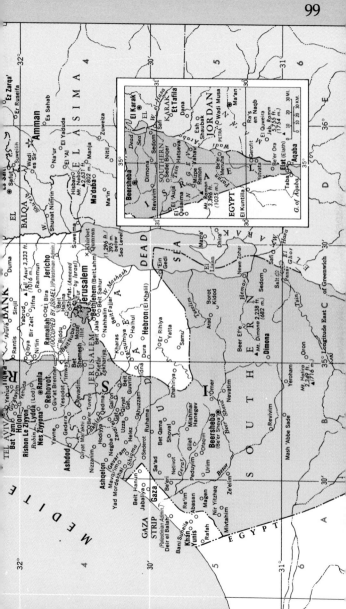

Iran & Iraq

38° | A | 40° | B | 42° | C | D | 44° | E | 46° | F | 48° | G | 50°

TURKEY

Malatya · Elâzığ · Murat · Bingöl Daği · Karaköse · Iğdır · Ararat 16,916 · ARAS · Xankändi · Kura · 50°

Adiyaman · Suphan Daği 13,697 · Malazgirt · Doğubayazit · Makü · Naxçivan · AZER. · Salyan

Lice · Bitlis · Lake Van · 12,809 · AZERBAIJAN

Siverek · Diyarbakir · Dicle · Siirt · Başkale · Khvoy · Lânkäran

Viransehir · Mardin · Çölemerik · Salmas · Marand · Sufian · Astara · Ardabil · Bandar-e Anzali

Urfa · Cizre · Amadiya · Urmia · Lake Urmia · TABRIZ · Mianeh · Särab · Rasht

Tel Kotchek · El Haseke · Al Qosh · Mahabad · Saqqez · Saeendey · Safid Rud · Qezel Owzan · Zanjan

SYRIA · J. 'Abdul 'Aziz · Khabur · Nineveh · Haji Ibrahim 12,000 · Qarah Su

El Rashid · **Mosul** · Erbil (Arbela) · Great Zab · 11,000 · Dezh Shahpur · Bijar · Abhar

Deir ez Zor · Al Qaiyara · Little Zab · Kirkuk · Sulaimaniya · Shirvan · Sanandaj (Sinneh) · Qorveh · **Hamadan**

Es Sukhne · Euphrates · Qal'a Sharqat · Tauq · Diyala · Maidan · Kangavar

Abu Kemal · **Tikrit** · Kifri · Khanaqin · **Bakhtaran** · Malayer · Arak

'Ana · Al Qa'im · Samarra · Naft Kaneh · Eslamabad · Borujerd

El Hamad · Hit · Naft-i-Shah · Ilam · Golpayegan · Delija

(Syrian Desert) · Ramadi · Habbaniya · Ba'quba · **BAGHDAD** · Zagros · 10,500 · Khorramabad · 14,088

Rutba · Habbaniya · Ctesiphon · Karkheh · Dezful · Dez

Jeb. 'Aneiza 3,100 · W. 'Ubaiyidh · Al 'Aziziya · Babylon · Kut · Shushtar

Karbala · Hilla · Masjed Soleyman · Ahvaz · Haft Gel

An Najaf · Diwaniya · Amara · Al 'Azair · Ramhormoz · Bandar-e Ma'sh

Rumaitha · Hor al Hammar · Bandar-e Khomeyni · Agha

SAUDI · W. 'Arar · Samawa · An Nasiriya · Ma'qil · **Basra** · Khorramshahr · Gach Sa

Sakaka · Az Zubair · Abadan · Karun · Bubiyan I. · Bandar-e

Jauf · **ARABIA** · Shatt-al-'Arab · Fao · **KUWAIT** · Kharg

W. al Batin · **Al Kuwait** · Burgan · PERSIAN

Jubba · Ras Tanajib · Bushe

Abu Hadriya

Dammam · Dhahran · Ta

Abqaiq · BAH

Hofuf

Iran and Iraq
CONIC PROJECTION

MILES
0 · 25 · 50 · 100 · 150 · 200

KILOMETRES
0 · 25 · 50 · 100 · 150 · 200

⊛ Capitals of Countries
– ·· – International Boundaries
Ruins
Elevations in Feet

Copyright by C.S. HAMMOND & Co., N.Y.

TURKMENISTAN

Kara kum
(Desert)

Gyzylarbat
Kara-Kala
Gasan-Kuli
Bandar-Torkeman
Gorgan
Gonbad-e Kavus
Bojnurd
Shirvan
Darreh Gaz
Quchan
Ashgabat
Artyk
Kaakhka
Tejen
Dushak
Mary
Ravnina
Bayramaly
Kavakli
Amu-Dar'ya
Repetek
Burdalyk
Chärjew
UZB.
Farab
Pristan'

Sari
Babol
Damavand
18,376
Firuzkuh
Semnan
Gorgan
(Asterabad)
Jajarm
Sabzevar
Neyshabur
Meshed
Sarakhs
Torbat-e
Heydariyeh
Torbat-e
Jam
Gushgy
Takhta-Bazar
Bala
Murghab
Kushk
Tirpul
Paropamisus
Herat
11,795
Obeh

HRAN
M
t
s
Emamshahr
Damghan
Torud
Qal'eh Now
Turan
Kashmar
Bejestan
Khvat
Qayen
Namaksar
Farsi
Kuh-i-Wala
12,680
Daulatabad

Dasht-e Kavir
Khvor
Ferdows
Siah Kuh
Yazdan
Sabzawar
Anardarra

Ardestan
Anarak
Na'in
Kuhpayeh
Meybod
Tabas
Birjand
Khusf Rud
Tabas
Duruho
Juwain
Khash

AFGHANISTAN
Farah Rud

Yazd
Taft
Shir
13,369
Bafq
Nay Band
Nehbandan
Daryacheh-ye
Sistan
Zabol
SEISTAN
Dasht-i-
Margo
Helmand

Abadeh
Abarqu
Anar
Madvar
11,811
Ravar
Shahdad
Kerman
Dasht-e Lut
Namakzar-e
Shahdaa
Chahar Burjak
Rudbar
Gaud-i-Zirreh

Deh Bid
Rafsanjan
Mahan
Laieh Zar
14,340
Robat Qila
Zahedan
Chagai Hills
PAKISTAN

Zargan
Persepolis
I. Tashk
Bakhtegan
Neyriz
Sa'idabad
Baft
Bam
Mirjaveh
Nok Kundi

raz
Kor
Mand
Estahbanat
Fasa
Safidar
10,459
Darab
Jahrom
Tarom
Rigan
Bazman
11,447
Taftan
13,201
Khash
Slana
Ladgasht
Talab
Saravan

Hamun-e Jaz
Murian
Gasht
Sarbaz

Lar
Mehran
Bandar
Abbas
Minab
Bampur
Iranshahr
(Fahrej)
Bampur
BALUCHISTAN
Nahang
Tump
PAKISTAN
MAKRAN

Nay Band
Sheykh
Sho'eyb
Bandar-e
Lingeh
Qeys
Hormuz
Qeshm
Ruus al Jibal
(To Oman)
Musandam
Strait
of Hormuz
Larak
Nikshahr
Qasr-e
Qand
Dashtiari
Gavater
Gwadar

GULF
UNITED ARAB
EMIRATES
Dibah
Jask
Ras-e
Meydani
Bir Bala
Chah Bahar

G. of
Oman

LARISTAN

TURKMEN. UZBEK. TAJIKISTAN

Pamir

Kashmir

Khorugh

Kulob

Balkh

Andkhvoy

Sheberghan

Mazar-i-Sharif

Feyzabad

Shache (Yarkant)

Pishan

Guma

Takla Ma

Ka

Yecheng

Qandahar

Marar-i-Sharif

Meymaneh

Bamian

Zibak

Hindu Kush

Baltit

Gilgit

Hotan

Yutian

K U N

Muztag 23,891 ft. (7282 m.)

Qayen Shindand

Gushgy

Farsi

Chitral

K2 (Godwin Austen) 28,250 ft. (8611 m.)

Kashi

Zhaxigang

Birjand

Dowlat Yar

Charikar

Chilas

Kargil

AFGHANISTAN

Herat

KABUL

Jalalabad

Khyber Pass

Peshawar

Leh

Rutog

Farah

Ghazni

Kohat

Islamabad

Rawalpindi

Srinagar

Chushul

T I

Lashe-Joveyn

Zabul

Sakhar

Qalat

Bannu

Ismail Khan

Jammu

Dharamsala

Gar

Coqê

Qandahar

Khash

Quetta

Sibi

Ft. Sandeman

Sialkot

Amritsar

Jullundur

Simla

Zaranj

Kalat

Chaman

Loralai

Sulaiman Ra.

Lahore

Ludhiana

Chandigarh

Dehra Dun

Almora

Jumla

Gangdi

Iranshar

Kundi

Khuzdar

Nushki

Dera Ghazi Khan

Montgomery

Faisalabad

Ferozepore

Patiala

Ambala

Saharanpur

Meerut

Moradabad

Shahjahanpur

Nainital

Kathm

Panjgur

Siahan

Bela

Jacobabad

Shikarpur

Sukkur

Bahawalpur

Sutlej

Bikaner

Churu

DELHI

Aligarh

Bareilly

Sallyana

P

Tump

Turbat

Khairpur

Larkana

Nawabshah

Jaisalmer

Jodhpur

Great Indian Desert

NEW DELHI

Mathura

Agra

Faizabad

Gorakhpur

Gwalior

Lucknow

Kanpur

Varanasi

Gaya

Gwadar

PAKISTAN

Karachi

Hyderabad

Nagar Parkar

Sirohi

Ajmer

Beawar

Jaipur

Tonk

Kota

Datia

Jhansi

Allahabad

Chapra

Patna

Ganges

Jamuna

Mirpur

Sonmiani

Mandvi

Bhuj

Rann of Kutch

Viramgam

Abu Road

Udaipur

Neemuch

Sironj

Sagar

Rewa

Daltonganj

Ranchi

Jamshed

Tropic of Cancer

Jamnagar

Rajkot

Baroda

Ahmadabad

Ratlam

Ujjain

Indore

Vindhya

Narmada

Jubbulpore

Chirmiri

Chindwara

Seoni

Bilaspur

Porbandar

Junagadh

Bhavnagar

Surat

Dhulia

Khandwa

Balaghat

Raipur

Samb

Veraval

Diu

Daman

Navsari

Jalgaon

Akola

Amravati

Nagpur

Bhandara

Bolangir

Sonpur

Kalyan

Nasik

Ahmadnagar

Warangal

Yeotmal

Chanda

Russelkonda

Jagdalpur

Jeypore

ARABIAN

BOMBAY

Murud

Poona

Bidh

Nizamabad

Godavari

Kanker

Chica

SEA

Mahabaleshwar

Barsi

Secunderabad

Warangal

Vizianaga

Ratnagiri

Sholapur

Gulbarga

Hyderabad

Eluru

Rajahmundry

Visakhap

Kolhapur

Bijapur

Raichur

Vijayawada

Kakinada

Yanam

Malvan

Belgaum

Guntur

Machilipatnam

Panjim

Hubli

Kurnool

Karwar

Davangere

Bellary

Anantapur

Chirala

Kavali

Kumta

Shimoga

Tumkur

Cuddapah

Nellore

Udipi

Mangalore

Bangalore

Kolar Gold Fields

Chetlat

CANNANORE (LACCADIVE) ISLANDS (India)

Mahe

Kozhikode

Mysore

Vellore

Kanchipuram

Madras

Pondicherry

Cuddalore

Karikal

Kavaratti

Coimbatore

Trichur

Thanjavur

Nagapattinam

Kalpeni

Tiruchirappalli

Minicoy

Eight Degree Channel

Alleppey

Trivandrum

Madurai

Jaffna

Tirunelveli

Tuticorin

SRI LANKA (CEYLON)

Trincomalee

MALDIVES

Nagercoil

C. Comorin

Mannar

Gulf of Mannar

Anuradhapura

Batticaloa

Negombo

Kandy

Badulla

Colombo

Moratuwa

Galle

N

ARABIAN SEA

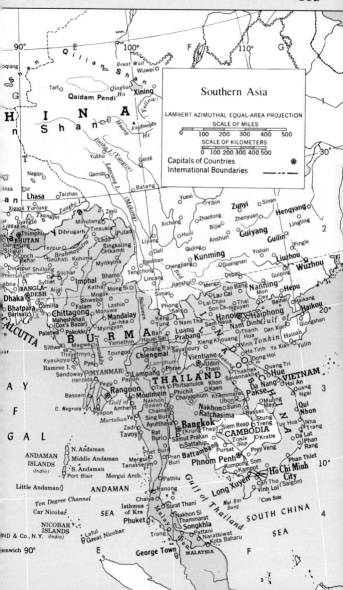

China & Mongolia

KAZAKHSTAN

Lake Balkhash

Semey

Kyzyl

Cheremkhov

Irkutsk

Hövsgöl Nuur

Balqash

Taldyqorghan

Tacheng

Ölgiy

Hovd

Ulaangom

Mörön

Ulaanb

Almaty

Yining

Karamay

Junggar Pendi

Uliastay

Tsetserleg

KARAKORUM Dz

Issyk-Kül

Pobeda Pk.
24,406 ft.
(7439 m.)

KYRGYZSTAN

Ürümqi

Qitai

Turpan

M O N G O L

Altay

Arvayheer

O

Tian Shan

XINJIANG
UYGUR

Hami

Dalandzadgad

G

Kashi

Aksu

Kuqa

Korla

Bay

Bachu

Tarim He

Lop Nur

GANSU

Shache (Yarkant)

ZIZHIQU

Ruoqiang

Anxi

Pishano

Hotan

Qiemo

Minfeng

Yutian

Mangnai

Qaidam Pendi

Yumen

Jiuquan

Zhangye

Alxa Zuoqi

Wuwei

Karakoram

28,250 ft.
(8611 m.)
Leh

Kun Lun Shan

Ulu Muztag
25,340 ft.
(7723 m.)

Golmud

Qinghai Hu

Xining

Yongdeng

Lanzhou

NINGXIA
HUIZU
ZIZHIQU

Jingyuan

Pir

Gé'gyai

A r Jin Shan

QINGHAI

Bayan Har Shan

Linxia

GANSU

Tianshui

Baoji

Tibet

Qing Zang Gaoyuan

(Yangtze)

Gar

XIZANG ZIZHIQU

Gangdisê Shan

Amdo

Yushu

Wudu

Wen Xian

Pingwu

Nagqu

Nu J. (Salween)

Qamdo

Garzê

SICHUAN

Nanchong

Wan

Mt. Everest
29,028 ft.
(8848 m.)

Nyainqêntanglha Shan

Lhasa

Yarlung Zangbo J.

Xigazê

Gyangzê

Brahmaputra

Batang

Chengdu

Hechuan

Cho

Neijiang

Zigong

Lucknow

N E P A L

Kathmandu

BHUTAN

I N D I A

Putao

Yibin

GUIZH

Guiyang

Myitkyina

Xiaguan

Mekong

Zigong

Anshun

GUANG

Liu

Kathmandu

H I M A L A Y A

Tengchong

Lincang

YUNNAN

Kunming

Gejiu

Mengzi

Z

Lao Cai

B U R M A

Chiang Mai

Vientiane

Hanoi

Haip

Gulf of Tonkin

M Y A N M A R

L A O S

THAILAND

VIET

China and Mongolia

CONIC PROJECTION

MILES

0   100 200 300 400 500

KILOMETERS

0   100 200 300 400 500

Capitals of Countries _____ ⊛

Provincial Capitals _____ ◉

International Boundaries _____

Provincial Boundaries _____

Japan & Korea

A 124° B 128° C 132° D 136°

1
44° Changchun

Mudanjiang

Lake Khanka

Spassk-Dal'niy Tetyukhe

Plas

Jilin

Suifenhe RUSSIA

Liaoyuan

Ussuriysk

Ol'ga

Kaiyuah

Songhua Hu

Tunhwa

Hunchun

Artem Margaritovo

Fushun

Hailong

Tumen
Yanji

Vladivostok
Peter the Great Bay

Suchan

2

CHINA

Tonghua

Changbaek-sanmaek

Tumen

Hoeryong

Rashino

Musan Najin

Ch'ŏngjin
Nanam
Chuŭronjang

SEA OF

Ch'osan

Manp'o

Changbai

Aoji-dong

Kapsan

Paekam

Kilchu

P'ungsan

Kanggye
Changjin Res.

Puksubaek
8,274 ft
(2522 m.)

Kimch'aek
Tanch'ŏn

Sinŭiju

Hŭich'ŏn

Hongwŏn

Pukch'ŏng

40°

Dandong

Sŏnch'ŏn

Anju

Hamhŭng

Hŭngnam

KOREA

NORTH

West Korea Bay

Namp'o

P'yŏngyang

Yŏnghŭng

East Korea Bay

JAPAN

Anak

Sariwŏn

Wŏnsan

Haeju

Kaesŏng

Ch'ŏrwŏn

Changjŏn

3

YELLOW SEA

Inch'ŏn

Seoul

P'anmunjŏm

Yangyang

Ch'unch'ŏn

Kangnŭng

Ullŭng (Dagelet)

Wŏnju

Samch'ŏk

Tok-to (Takeshima)
(Claimed by S. Kor. & Jap.)

Ch'ŏngju

SOUTH

Toebaek
5,121 ft
(1561 m.)

Oki Is.

Wajima
Noto Pen.

Pt

Sŏsan

KOREA

Dozen

Dogo

Matsu

Takaoka

Noto

Kanazawa

Komatsu

36°

Taejŏn

Chiri
6,283 ft
(1915 m.)

Andong

Kimch'ŏn

Sangju

P'ohang

Izumo

Tottori

Wakasa Bay

Takayama

Fukui

Takefu

Tsuruga

Kunsan

Chŏnju

Ŏlji

Taegu

Ulsan

Hamada

Miyoshi

Yonago
Fukuchiyama

Biwa

Ōgaki
Gifu

Kwangju

Namwŏn

Miryang

Masan

Izumo

Okayama

Kyoto

Yokkaichi

Tsu

Mokp'o

Chinju

Chinhae

Pusan

Masuda

Hiroshima

Tsuyama

Himeji

Osaka

Izumisano

Sunch'ŏn

Kŏje

Tsu Is.

Kōji

Yamaguchi

Tokuyama

Fukuyama

Kure

Harima

Awaji

Wakayama

Owase

Cheju Strait

Korea Strait

Shimonoseki

Iki

Ube

Suo Sea

Takamatsu

Tokushima

Kōbe

Shingu

Tanabe

4

Cheju

Kitakyushu

Iyo

C. Shiono

Cheju (Quelpart)

Fukuoka

Karatsu

Nakatsu

Matsuyama

Uwajima

Kōchi

Muroto

Saga

Beppu

Ōita

Susaki

SHIKOKU

Goto Is.

Sasebo

Ōmuta

Kumamoto

Sukumo

Pt. Ashizuri

Nagasaki

Amakusa Is.

Nobeoka

Hitoyoshi

EAST

Kobayashi

Miyazaki

KYUSHU

PACIFIC

32°

CHINA

Kagoshima

Miyakonojo
Nichinan

Mi
K
Akas

SEA

Kanoya

OCEAN

135°

5

B 128° C 132° D 136° Lon

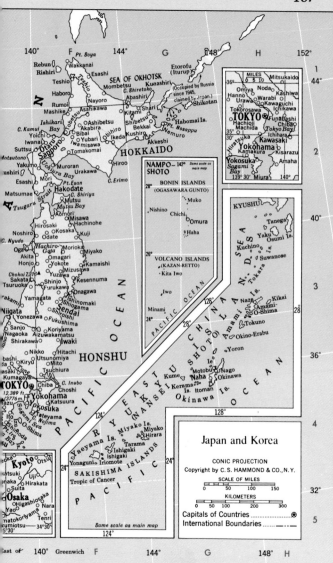

Japan and Korea

CONIC PROJECTION

Copyright by C.S. HAMMOND & CO., N.Y.

SCALE OF MILES

0   50   100   150

KILOMETERS

0   50   100   200   300

Capitals of Countries .... ⊛

International Boundaries .... —·—·—

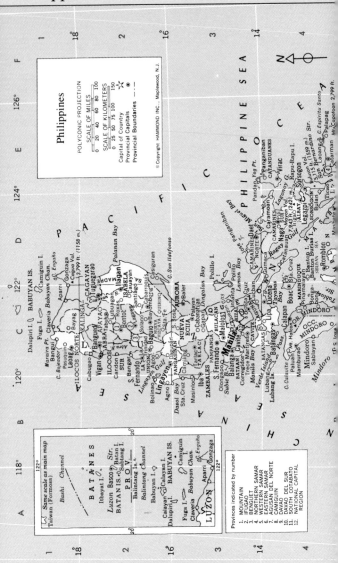

Philippines

POLYCONIC PROJECTION

SCALE OF MILES
0 20 40 60 80 100

SCALE OF KILOMETERS
0 25 50 75 100 150

Capital of Country .... ✪
Provincial Capitals .... ●
Provincial Boundaries ---- ⦿

© Copyright HAMMOND INC.., Maplewood, N.J.

Provinces indicated by number
1. MOUNTAIN
2. IFUGAO
3. BENGUET
4. NORTHERN SAMAR
5. WESTERN SAMAR
6. EASTERN SAMAR
7. AGUSAN DEL NORTE
8. CAMIGUIN
9. DAVAO
10. DAVAO DEL SUR
11. SOUTH COTABATO
12. NATIONAL CAPITAL REGION

PACIFIC

PHILIPPINE SEA

SOUTH CHINA SEA

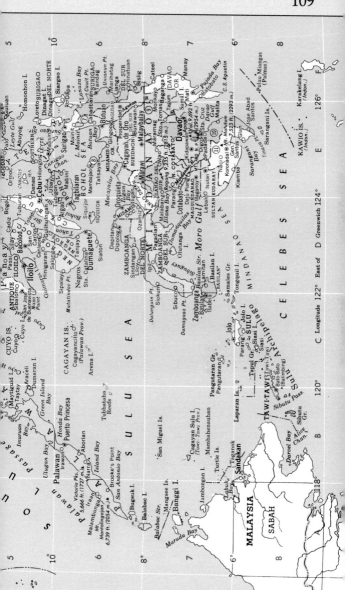

Burma, Thailand, Indochina & Malaya

Burma, Thailand,
Indochina & Malaya

CONIC PROJECTION

SCALE OF MILES
0   50   100   200   300

SCALE OF KILOMETERS
0   50 100   200   300

Capitals of Countries..........⊛
Capitals of States..............◉
International Boundaries......— ·· — ··

CHINA

Zhaotong

Kunming

Zhongdian   Lijiang   Huize   Guangnam

Panzhihua   Xiguan   Baoshan

Simao

INDIA

Dibrugarh   Sadiya   Ledo   Sumprabum   Ft. Hertz   Putao

Tezpur   Nowgong   Jorhat

Shillong   Kohima   Imphal

BANGLADESH   Agartala   Sylhet

Chittagong

BHUTAN   Bumthang

BAY OF BENGAL

Mandalay   Myitkyina   Mogaung   Tengchong   Bhamo   Lashio

BURMA (MYANMAR)

Rangoon

Pegu   Yoma

Bassein   Moulmein   Mudon

Akyan   Sittwe

THAILAND

Chiang Mai   Lampang   Chiang Rai

Plain of Jars

LAOS   Vientiane

Luang Prabang

VIETNAM   Hanoi   Haiphong

Da Nang   Hue   Quang Tri

HAINAN   Haikou   Zhanjiang

Beihai   Nanning   Guiping

Phu Bia 9,252

Gulf of Tonkin

SOUTH CHINA SEA

Southeast Asia

Southeast Asia

LAMBERT AZIMUTHAL EQUAL-AREA PROJECTION

SCALE OF MILES

0   100   200   400   600

SCALE OF KILOMETERS

0   100 200   400   600

Capitals of Countries .... ⊛
Administrative Center .... ⊚
International Boundaries _____
Territorial Boundaries _____

JAVA

0 25 50 75 MI.
0 25 50 75 KM.

Jakarta, Serang, Bogor, Bandung, Indramayu, Cirebon, Tegal, Pekalongan, Semarang, Kudus, Rembang, Karimunjawa Is., Bawean, Madura, Pamekasan, Madura Str., Surabaya, Probolinggo, Pasuruan, Malang, Mt. Semeru 12,060 ft. (3676 m.), Banyuwangi, Blitar, Kediri, Madiun, Solo, Surakarta, Yogyakarta, Magelang, Mt. Slamet, Cilacap, Ciamis, Sukabumi

JAVA SEA
INDIAN OCEAN

PHILIPPINES

Taiwan (Formosa), Batan Is., Babuyan Is., Laoag, Vigan, Tuguegarao, Baguio, Luzon, Cabanatuan, Tarlac, ...ayen, Manila, Batangas, ...aga, Catanduanes I., Legazpi, Mindoro, ...lamian ...oup, Masbate, Catbalogan, Samar, Panay, Iloilo, Cebu, Tacloban, Leyte, Bacolod, Bohol, Negros, Puerto ...rincesa, SULU SEA, Cagayan de Oro, Oroquieta, Mindanao, Davao, Zamboanga, Basilan, Moro Gulf, Sarangani, ...u, Sulu Arch., ...dakan

PACIFIC OCEAN

Sonsorol Is., Koror ⊛ **PALAU**, Merir, Tobi

N

CELEBES SEA, C. Malangka, Manado, Gorontalo, Gulf of Tomini, Poso, ...alopo, Mt. Rantekombola 11,335 ft. (3455 m.), Kendari, Gulf of Bone, Bonthain, Baubau, Tukangbesi, Butung, Buru, Ambon, BANDA SEA, Banda Is., Penyu Is., Kawio Is., Talaud Is., Sangihe Is., Morotai, Jailolo, Ternate, Bacan, Weda, Halmahera, Asia Is., Waigeo, Raja, Ampat Gr., Salawati, Sorong, Misool, Obi Is., Sula Is., Banggai Arch., MOLUCCA SEA, CERAM SEA, Doberai Pen., Fakfak, Ceram, Mapia Is., Manokwari, Biak, Schouten Islands, C. Perkam, Mamberamo, Cenderawasih Bay, Kaimana, Maoke Mts., Puncak Jaya 16,503 ft. (5030 m.), IRIAN JAYA, Jayapura (Hollandia), Kai (Ewab), Aru Is., Digul, Kolepom, C. Vals, Merauke, PAPUA NEW GUINEA

...ELEBES, ...ORES SEA, Ruteng, Flores, Ende, Waingapu, Savu Sea, Sawu, Roti, Kupang, Timor, Lomblen, Alor, Dili, Wetar, Damar Is., Babar Is., Saumlaki, Tanimbar Is., TIMOR SEA, ARAFURA SEA, Melville I., **AUSTRALIA**, Wessel Is.

Australia & New Zealand

120°   B   130°   C

I N D O N E S I A

1 Java   Dili
Bar Sumbawa Sumba Timor   ARAFURA
S U N D A   Kupang   I S. TIMOR SEA
10°   Bathurst I. Melville I.
                        Van Diemen Gulf Darwin
                        C. Talbot Joseph ARNHEM LAND Pine Creek
                              Bonaparte Katherine
                              Gulf Daly Roper
                                          Birdum
Collier B.   Wyndham Ord
2 C. Leveque   Victoria • Newcastle Wate
                  Derby Fitzroy   • L. Woods
Broome   Goldfield NORTHER
            St. George   Murchison Ra.
            Range   • Barrow Creek
            Port Hedland   Goldfield
20° Barrow I. Roebourne   L. Mackay T E R R I T O R Y
North West C. Marble Bar   Alice Springs
            Fortescue Great Sandy Desert Macdonnell Ranges
            W E S T E R N L. Disappointment
Ashburton   Gibson Desert   • L. Amadeus Simp
                                    Dese
                  L. Carnegie   Musgrave Ranges
3 Sha Carnarvon Meekathara Wiluna   Oodnadatta
Dirk B. L. Austin Goldfield   Stuarts L.
Hartog I. A U S T R A L I A   Coober Pedy Eyre S O U T
Steep Pt. Northampton Leonora L. Great   A U S T R A L I
            Geraldton Murchison Carey Victoria Desert Mar
            L. Goldfield
            Moore L. Barlee Goldfield
30°   Kalgoorlie Boulder   L. Whya
            Northam Merredin Norseman Fowler's Bay Gairdner Port P
        Perth Narrogin   Streaky Bay
    Fremantle Collie Esperance Great Port Lincoln
        Bunbury Northcliffe C. Arid Australian Bight Spence
C. Naturaliste   Albany   Kangaroo
40°
5   110° A   120° B   130° C Long

Australia and New Zealand
BONNE PROJECTION
SCALE OF MILES
0   200   400   600   800

SCALE OF KILOMETERS
0   200   400   600   800

National Capitals _ _ _ ⊛   State and Territorial Capitals _ _ _ ⊛

PAPUA NEW GUINEA

Port Moresby

SOLOMON
ISLANDS

Honiara
Guadalcanal

C. York

The

C. Flattery

CAPE
YORK
PEN.

Coen

Cooktown

Cairns

C O R A L

S E A

Mitchell

rmanton

Forsayth

Townsville

NEW
CALEDONIA
(Fr.)

Charters Towers

ughenden

Noumea

Great

Q U E E N S L A N D

Barrier

Reef

Tropic of Capricorn

Aramac

Longreach

Barcaldine

Blackall

Clermont

Emerald

Mackay

C. Manifold

Rockhampton

Dividing

Charleville

Roma

Maryborough

Bundaberg

Great Sandy I.

Gympie

St. George

Toowoomba

Ipswich

Range

C. Byron

Brisbane

Bulloo L.

Moree

Lismore

Grafton

Darling

Bourke

Armidale

roken Hill

Cobar

Tamworth

N E W

S O U T H

Dubbo

Mildura

Orange

Lithgow

Blue Mts.

Newcastle

W A L E S

Wagga Wagga

Cootamundra

Sydney

Wollongong

Canberra
AUSTRALIAN
CAP. TERR.

ham

Bendigo

Albury

V I C T O R I A

C. Howe

maine

larat

Bairnsdale

elong

Melbourne

Wonthaggi

Wilson's Promontory

g I.

Bass Str.

Furneaux
Group

Devonport

Launceston

enstown

T A S M A N I A

Hobart

T A S M A N

S E A

North Cape

Whangarei

Auckland

Bay of
Plenty

North
Island

Hamilton

New Plymouth

Gisborne

Wanganui

Tasman

Napier
Hastings

Palmerston
North

Nelson

Wellington

Cook Str.

Greymouth

Southern

Alps

Christchurch

South
Island

Timaru

Oamaru

Dunedin

Invercargill

Stewart I.

New Zealand
Same scale as main map.

P A C I F I C

O C E A N

Copyright by C.S. HAMMOND & CO., N.Y.

Pacific Ocean

Copyright by C.S. HAMMOND & Co., N.Y.

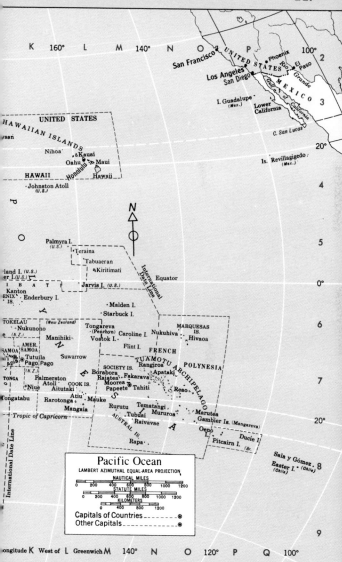

K   160°   L   140°   M   N   O   P   100°

UNITED STATES

San Francisco
Los Angeles   Phoenix   El Paso
San Diego   MEXICO
I. Guadalupe (Mex.)   Lower California

C. San Lucas   20°

Is. Revillagigedo (Mex.)

UNITED STATES
HAWAIIAN ISLANDS

Nihoa   Kauai
Oahu   Maui
HAWAII   Honolulu   Hawaii   4

Johnston Atoll (U.S.)

N

Palmyra I. (U.S.)   5
Teraina
Tabuaeran
Kiritimati

land I. (U.S.)
er I. (U.S.)   Jarvis I. (U.S.)   Equator   0°
Kanton
ENIX   Enderbury I.   International Date Line
IS.

Malden I.
Starbuck I.   6

TOKELAU   (New Zealand)
Nukunono   Tongareva (Penrhyn)   MARQUESAS IS.
Manihiki   Caroline I.   Nukuhiva
SAMOA   AMER.   Vostok I.   Hivaoa
SAMOA   Suwarrow   Flint I.   FRENCH
Apia   Tutuila   POLYNESIA
Pago Pago   SOCIETY IS.   Rangiroa   TUAMOTU ARCHIPELAGO
TONGA   Bora bora   Apataki   7
Palmerston   Raiatea   Fakarava
Atoll   Moorea   Papeete   Tahiti   Reao
Niue   Aitutaki   COOK IS.
Tongatabu   Rarotonga   Atiu   Mauke
Mangaia   Rurutu   Tematangi
Tubuai   Mururoa
Tropic of Capricorn   Raivavae   Marutea
AUSTRAL IS.   Gambier Is. (Mangareva)   20°
Oeno I.   Ducie I. (Br.)
Rapa   Pitcairn I. (Br.)

Sala y Gómez
Easter I. (Chile)   8

Pacific Ocean
LAMBERT AZIMUTHAL EQUAL-AREA PROJECTION
NAUTICAL MILES
0   200   400   600   800   1000   1200
STATUTE MILES
0   200   400   600   800   1000   1200
KILOMETERS
0   400   800   1200
Capitals of Countries _____ ⊛
Other Capitals _____ ◉

9

ongitude K West of L Greenwich M 140° N   O   120°   P   Q   100°

International Date Line

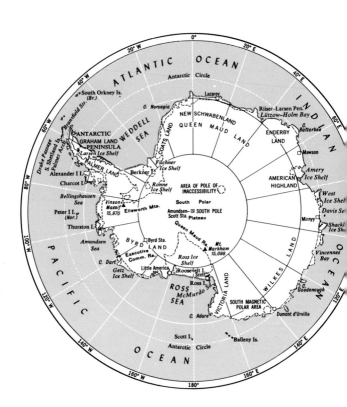

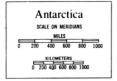

Antarctica

SCALE ON MERIDIANS

MILES

0   200   400   600   800   1000

KILOMETERS

0 200 400 600 800 1000

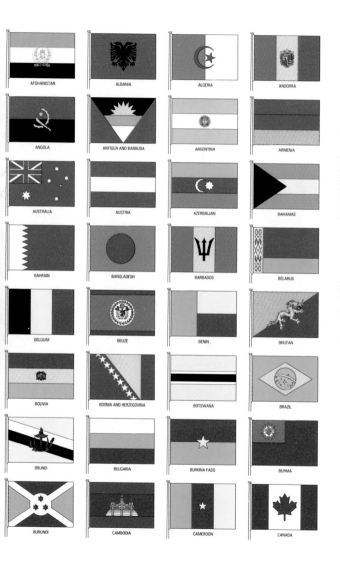

AFGHANISTAN

ALBANIA

ALGERIA

ANDORRA

ANGOLA

ANTIGUA AND BARBUDA

ARGENTINA

ARMENIA

AUSTRALIA

AUSTRIA

AZERBAIJAN

BAHAMAS

BAHRAIN

BANGLADESH

BARBADOS

BELARUS

BELGIUM

BELIZE

BENIN

BHUTAN

BOLIVIA

BOSNIA AND HERZEGOVINA

BOTSWANA

BRAZIL

BRUNEI

BULGARIA

BURKINA FASO

BURMA

BURUNDI

CAMBODIA

CAMEROON

CANADA

Flags of the World

CAPE VERDE

CENTRAL AFRICAN REPUBLIC

CHAD

CHILE

CHINA

COLOMBIA

COMOROS

CONGO, DEM. REP. OF THE

CONGO, REP. OF THE

COSTA RICA

CÔTE D'IVOIRE

CROATIA

CUBA

CYPRUS

CZECH REPUBLIC

DENMARK

DJIBOUTI

DOMINICA

DOMINICAN REPUBLIC

ECUADOR

EGYPT

EL SALVADOR

EQUATORIAL GUINEA

ERITREA

ESTONIA

ETHIOPIA

FIJI

FINLAND

FRANCE

GABON

GAMBIA, THE

GEORGIA

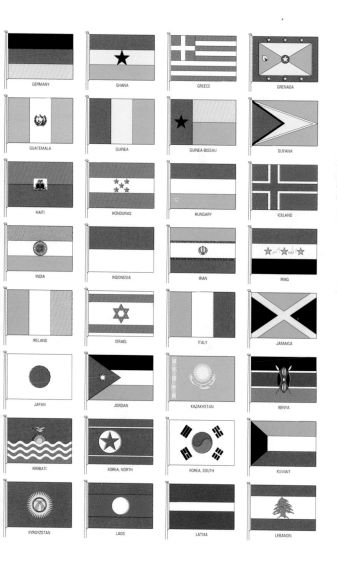

GERMANY

GHANA

GREECE

GRENADA

GUATEMALA

GUINEA

GUINEA-BISSAU

GUYANA

HAITI

HONDURAS

HUNGARY

ICELAND

INDIA

INDONESIA

IRAN

IRAQ

IRELAND

ISRAEL

ITALY

JAMAICA

JAPAN

JORDAN

KAZAKHSTAN

KENYA

KIRIBATI

KOREA, NORTH

KOREA, SOUTH

KUWAIT

KYRGYZSTAN

LAOS

LATVIA

LEBANON

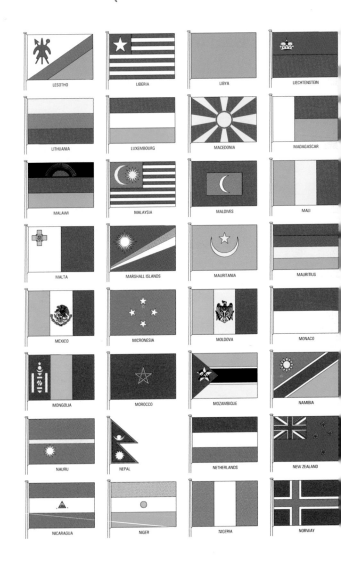

LESOTHO

LIBERIA

LIBYA

LIECHTENSTEIN

LITHUANIA

LUXEMBOURG

MACEDONIA

MADAGASCAR

MALAWI

MALAYSIA

MALDIVES

MALI

MALTA

MARSHALL ISLANDS

MAURITANIA

MAURITIUS

MEXICO

MICRONESIA

MOLDOVA

MONACO

MONGOLIA

MOROCCO

MOZAMBIQUE

NAMIBIA

NAURU

NEPAL

NETHERLANDS

NEW ZEALAND

NICARAGUA

NIGER

NIGERIA

NORWAY

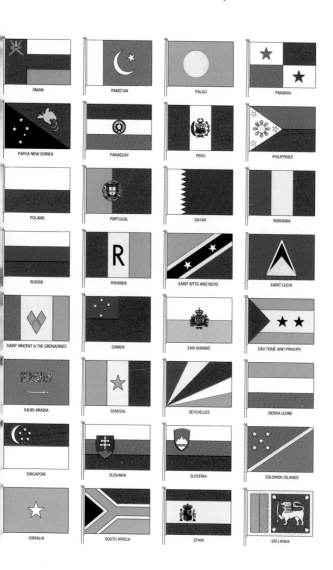

OMAN	PAKISTAN	PALAU	PANAMA
PAPUA NEW GUINEA	PARAGUAY	PERU	PHILIPPINES
POLAND	PORTUGAL	QATAR	ROMANIA
RUSSIA	RWANDA	SAINT KITTS AND NEVIS	SAINT LUCIA
SAINT VINCENT & THE GRENADINES	SAMOA	SAN MARINO	SÃO TOMÉ AND PRÍNCIPE
SAUDI ARABIA	SENEGAL	SEYCHELLES	SIERRA LEONE
SINGAPORE	SLOVAKIA	SLOVENIA	SOLOMON ISLANDS
SOMALIA	SOUTH AFRICA	SPAIN	SRI LANKA

Flags of the World

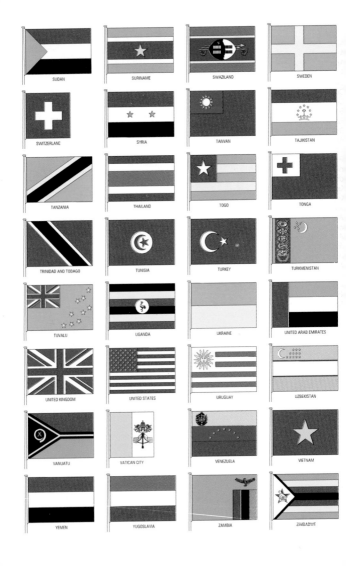

SUDAN

SURINAME

SWAZILAND

SWEDEN

SWITZERLAND

SYRIA

TAIWAN

TAJIKISTAN

TANZANIA

THAILAND

TOGO

TONGA

TRINIDAD AND TOBAGO

TUNISIA

TURKEY

TURKMENISTAN

TUVALU

UGANDA

UKRAINE

UNITED ARAB EMIRATES

UNITED KINGDOM

UNITED STATES

URUGUAY

UZBEKISTAN

VANUATU

VATICAN CITY

VENEZUELA

VIETNAM

YEMEN

YUGOSLAVIA

ZAMBIA

ZIMBABWE

UNITED STATES 126
Alabama 128
Alaska 129
Arizona 130
Arkansas 131
California 132
Colorado 134
Connecticut 136
Delaware 139
Florida 140
Georgia 142
Hawaii 129
Idaho 143
Illinois 144
Indiana 145
Iowa 146
Kansas 147
Kentucky 148
Louisiana 150
Maine 151
Maryland 139
Massachusetts 136
Michigan 152
Minnesota 153
Mississippi 154
Montana 156
Nebraska 157
Nevada 132

New Hampshire 158
New Jersey 159
New Mexico 135
New York 160
North Carolina 162
North Dakota 164
Ohio 166
Oklahoma 168
Oregon 169
Pennsylvania 170
Rhode Island 137
South Carolina 162
South Dakota 165
Tennessee 148
Texas 172
Utah 174
Vermont 158
Virginia 139
Washington 175
West Virginia 138
Wisconsin 176
Wyoming 177
CANADA 126
Alberta 191
British Columbia 190
Manitoba 189
New Brunswick 182
Newfoundland 183
Nova Scotia 183

Ontario 186
Prince Edward
    Island 183
Québec 184
Saskatchewan 188
METROPOLITAN
    AREAS
Atlanta 142
Baltimore 139
Boston 137
Buffalo 160
Calgary 191
Charlotte 163
Chicago 178
Cincinnati 167
Cleveland 167
Dallas 172
Denver 178
Detroit 178
Edmonton 191
Fort Worth 172
Greensboro 163
Houston 173
Kansas City 155
Los Angeles 179
Louisville 149
Memphis 148
Miami 141
Milwaukee 176

Minneapolis 153
Montréal 184
Nashville 148
New Orleans 150
New York 180
Norfolk 138
Orlando 140
Ottawa 186
Philadelphia 171
Phoenix 130
Pittsburgh 170
Portland, Ore. 180
Rochester 160
Salt Lake City 174
St. Louis 155
St. Paul 153
St. Petersburg 140
San Diego 180
San Francisco 133
Seattle 175
Tampa 140
Toronto 187
Vancouver 190
Washington, D.C. 139
Winston-Salem 163
MEXICO 181
MILEAGE TABLE 192

SYMBOLS

▬▬▬	Limited Access Highways	———	Major Highways
▬▬▬	Toll Roads	———	Other Important Roads
═══	National Parkways	- - - - -	Ferries
▬▬▬	Selected Scenic Routes	┤ 32 ├	Mileage Between Points
🛡90	U.S. Interstate Route Numbers	▢▪	Points of Interest
150	Federal Route Numbers	♠	State Parks, Recreation Areas
15	State and Other Route Numbers	✈	Major Airports
⬟	Trans-Canada Highway	◉	National Capitals
◀191	Adjoining Map Pages	✹	State and Provincial Capitals

United States, Canada

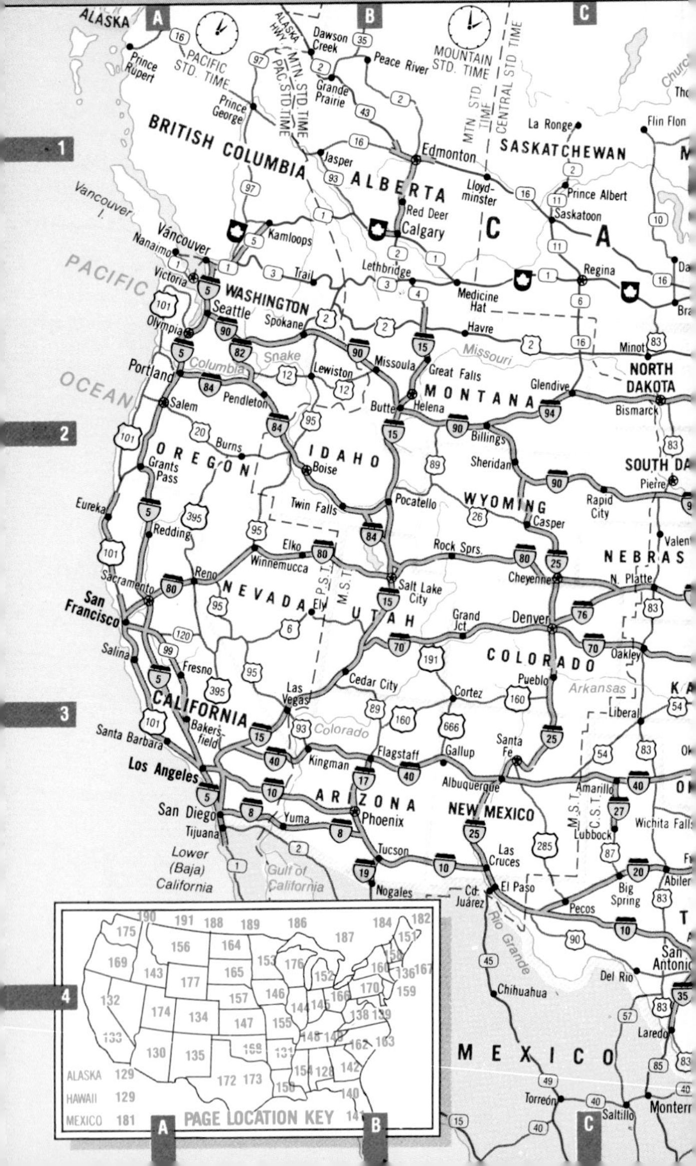

© HAMMOND INCORPORATED

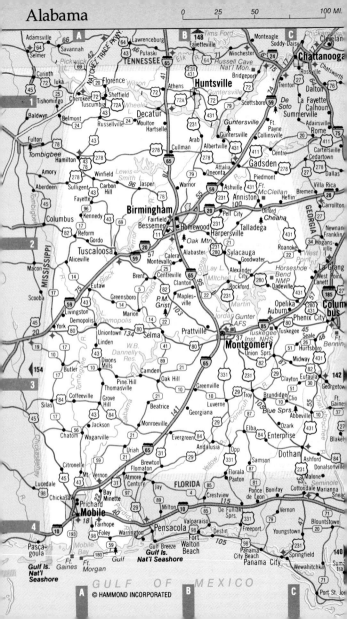

Alabama

0   25   50   100 MI.

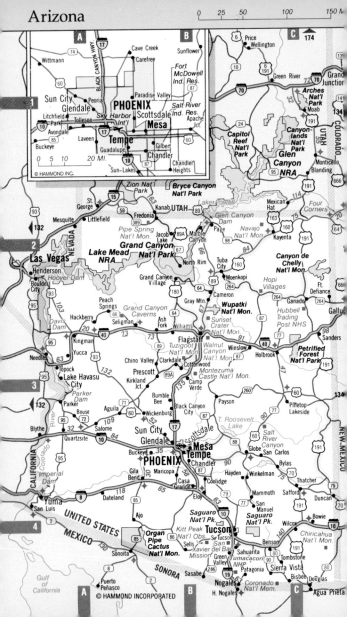

A
B
C

4

UTAH

NEVADA

Wendover

174

6
50

Baker

Medora
319

Rogerson

Jackpot

Montello

Wells

80

93
A

Currie

McGill

Ely

Preston
Lund

Great Basin
Nat'l Park
487

Pioche

Cathedral
Gorge
Caliente

93

64

61

233

69

28

318

Grasmere

Owyhee

225

Elko

Ruby Mtn.
Scenic Area

93

78

Eureka

50

79

Copper Pit

Currant

6

Lunar Crater

375

143
51

IDAHO

NEVADA

Carlin

Dinner
Station

Tuscarora

226

Battle
Mtn.

Geysers

305

Austin

70

50

RANGE

TOIYABE

376

Berlin-
Ichthyosaur

Belmont
Courthouse

Warm
Springs

6

Round Mtn.

Tonopah

95

Goldfield

IDAHO
OREGON

S. FK. Owyhee R.

McDermitt

Orovada

73

Golconda

71

Mill City

Middlegate

Gabbs

Luning

66

360

NEV.
CALIF.

95

ORE.   NEV.

395

Denio

140

Winnemucca

Humboldt
Sink

50

Fallon

Schurz

Walker
Lake

Hawthorne

359

120

Mono

169

BLACK

ROCK

DESERT

Rye Patch
Res.

Lovelock

SMOKE
CREEK
DESERT

Empire

447

Pyramid
Lake

19

Carson
Sink

Large
Earthquake
Faults

95

Nixon

447

Silver
Springs

35

Yerington

Wellington

208

176

Lee
Vining

120

Yosemite
Nat'l Park

Fernley

80

Va. City

Carson City

Minden

88

89

108

Bridgeport

395

NEVADA

CALIFORNIA

395

Honey
Lake

445

Sparks

Reno

30

Lake Tahoe

50

Markleeville

Angels
Camp

Sonora

Oakdale

Yosemite
Nat'l Park

2

Goose
Lake

Lakeview

Alturas

Canby

139

299

Ild

Susanville

Westwood

Quincy

36

89

Sierraville

13

Truckee

Squaw
Valley

49

Placer-
ville

20

Jackson

Lodi

Stockton

Manteca

Tracy
72

Klamath
Falls

140

Lassen
Volcanic
Park

Almanor

Chester

32

L. Oro-
ville

Grass
Valley

Citrus
Hts.

Carmichael

Sacramento

5

Lava
Beds
Nat'l
Mon.

387

Mt. Shasta

Burney

Shasta Dam

44

Chico

99

Gridley

Marysville

Yuba
City

70

113

Woodland

Davis

4

Concord

Pittsburg

37

Medford

66

Ashland

OREGON

Yreka

96

Weed

5

Whiskeytown-
Shasta-Trinity
NRA

Clair
Engle
L.

Shasta
L.

Redding

Anderson

Red Bluff

36

Colusa

Williams

192

5

505

Calistoga

St. Helena

Napa

Vacaville

Fairfield

Vallejo

34

29

Napa

Pt. Reyes
Seashore

San Rafael

Novato

SAN FRANCISCO

Oakland

1

199

CALIFORNIA

Crescent
City

88

299

Willow Creek

Weaverville

Trinity L.

Trinity
R.

COAST

RANGE

Corning

Orland

Upper Lake

20

Clear L.

Healdsburg

Santa
Rosa

Rohnert
Park

Petaluma

Brookings

Pt. St.
George

Redwood
Nat'l
Park

Arcata

Eureka

Fortuna

101

Mendocino
C.

Humboldt
Redwoods

Leggett

Ft. Bragg

Mendocino

282

20

Willits

Ukiah

Cloverdale

Eel

Mud

Mad R.

Mattole R.

Eel R.

Sacramento R.

Feather R.

101

Colorado, New Mexico

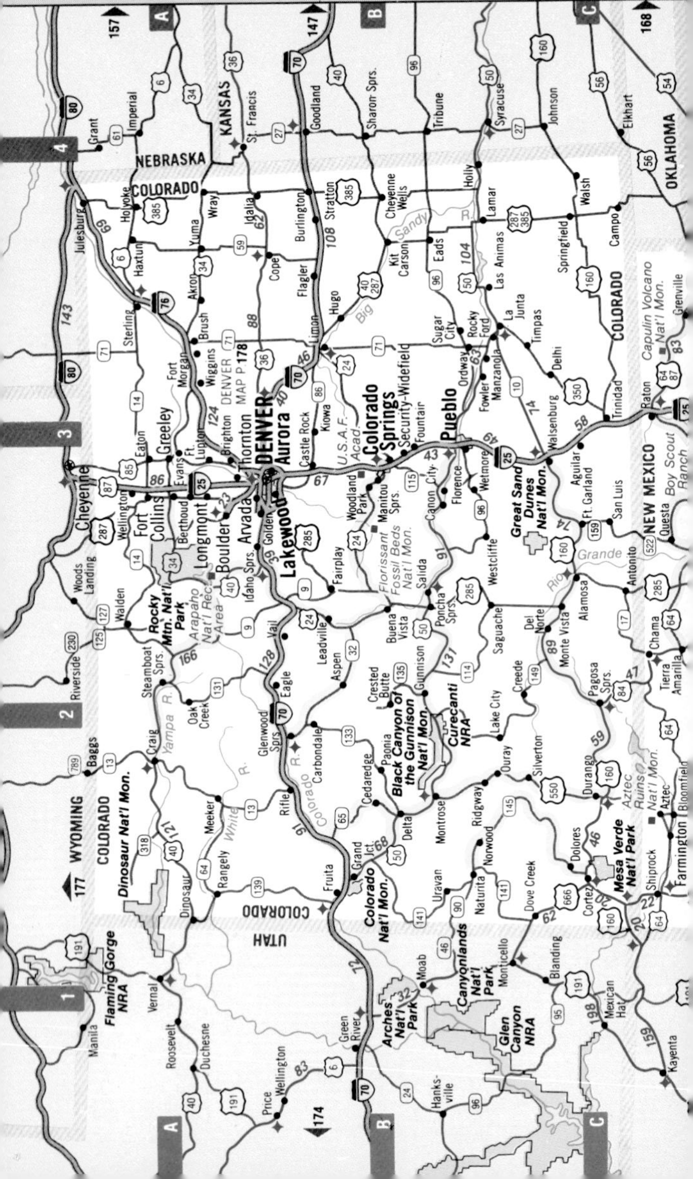

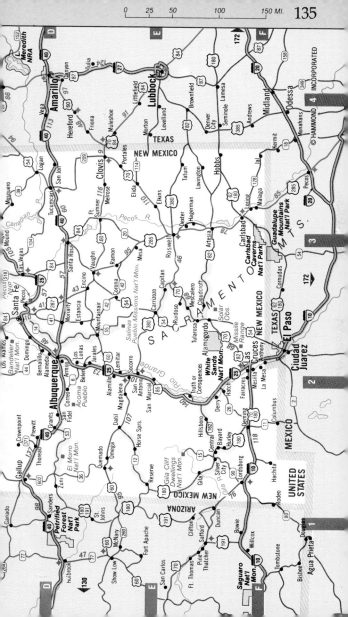

Connecticut, Massachusetts, Rhode I.

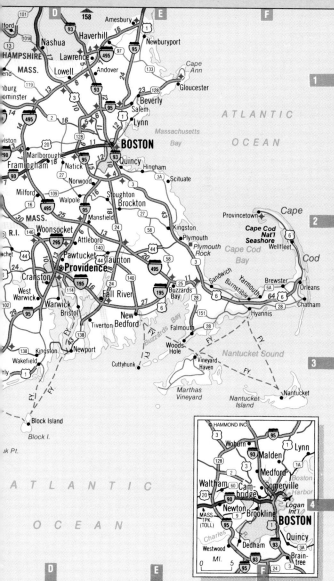

0 5 10 20 30 40 MI.

D
158
E
F

101

HAMPSHIRE

MASS.

93 Haverhill
Amesbury
16
Nashua
13
101A
95
Newburyport
1
Lawrence
495
97
Lowell
Andover
24
133
Cape Ann
8
93
23
128
Gloucester
3
10
Beverly
495
6
5
11
Salem
Lynn
16
12
Massachusetts Bay

ATLANTIC

OCEAN

128
BOSTON
20
Marlborough
95
12
Quincy
Hingham
18
Natick
15
93
14
90
Framingham
27
Norwood
3
3A
Scituate
90
Milford
109
16
Walpole
Stoughton
Brockton
43
Provincetown
Cape
Mansfield
27
Cape Cod Nat'l Seashore
6
495
25
140
58
Kingston
2
Woonsocket
24
Plymouth
Wellfleet
Cod
146
R.I.
295
Attleboro
Plymouth Rock
Cape Cod Bay
Brewster
6A
44
Pawtucket
44
Taunton
20
44
58
Sandwich
Barnstable
Yarmouth
6
Orleans
24
Providence
140
495
6A
6
Cranston
195
11
Buzzards
Chatham
114
25
Bay
64
West
24
6
Warwick
Fall River
27
151
6
102
16
195
28
Hyannis
95
Bristol
Buzzards
Falmouth
28
New
138
Bay
Nantucket Sound
Tiverton
Bedford
FY
Woods
Kingston
Newport
Hole
Vineyard
Nantucket
FY
Haven
1
Wakefield
Cuttyhunk
FY
erly
FY
Marthas
Nantucket
Vineyard
Island
FY
FY

ATLANTIC

Block Island

Block I.

k Pt.

OCEAN

© HAMMOND INC.
3
95
Woburn
1
Lynn
128
93
Malden
1A
3
Medford
Boston
Waltham
60
Somerville
Harbor
Cambridge
90
20
Logan Int'l.
Newton
9
Brookline
BOSTON
MASS. TPK (TOLL)
95
1
Quincy
Charles
Westwood
Dedham
93
3A
MI.
Brain-tree
0
5
95
F
24
3

Delaware, Maryland, Virginia, West Virginia

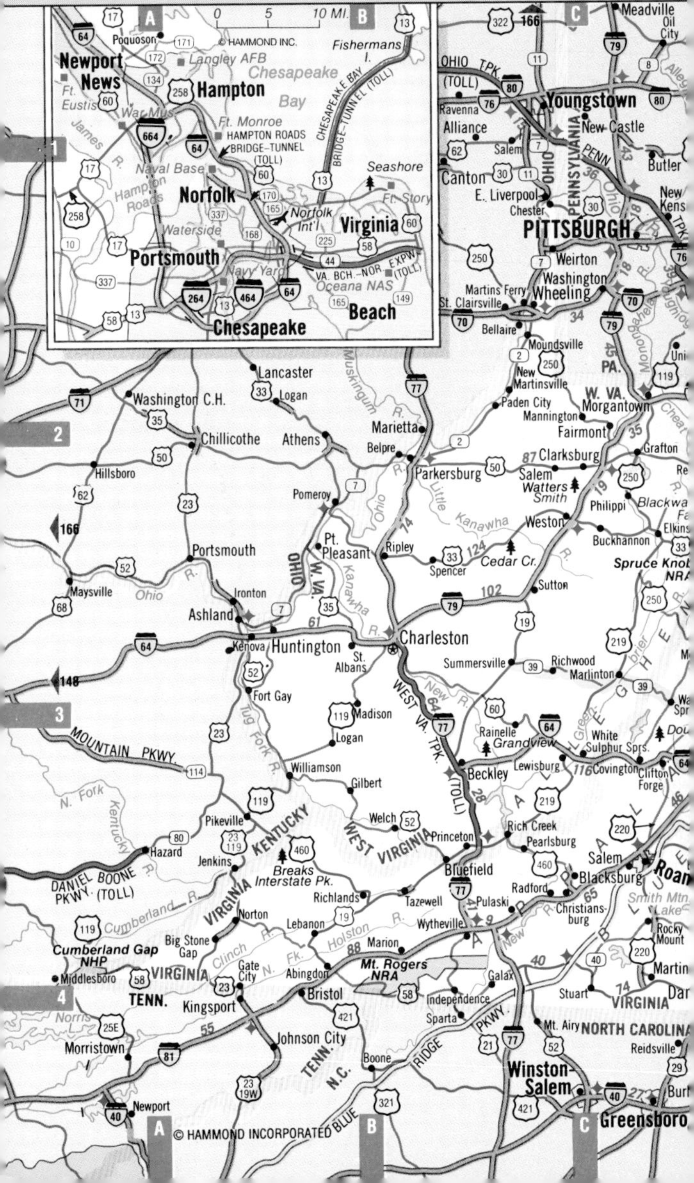

© HAMMOND INCORPORATED

100 MI.

25 50

0 5 MI.

© HAMMOND INC.

0 5 MI.

© HAMMOND INC.

D **E** **F**

CAPITAL

95

BELTWAY

Bethesda

Silver Spring

Takoma Pk.

Greenbelt

495

Canal NHP

355

Chevy Chase

College Pk.

29

WASHINGTON

Hyattsville

White House

50

595

McLean

123

1

Arlington

Capitol

D.C.

214

MD

Church

66

50

295

Hillcrest-Hts.

395

Annandale

395

236

1

Andrews AFB

5

Alexandria

BELTWAY

95

1

Towson

83

695

Pikesville

Parkville

695

NORTH

PKWY

95

140

Pimlico Race Tr.

83

45

147

Overlea

BALTIMORE

Mem. Sta.

40

150

70

40

895

695

Catonsville

Essex

Arbutus

Fort McHenry Nat'l Mon.

895

HARBOR TUNNL (TOLL)

Dundalk

Elkridge

895

KEY BR. (TOLL)

Sparrows Pt.

95

BALTO WASH PKWY

895

695

Patapsco R.

B.-W. Int'l.

97

1

SYLVANIA

230

70

170

81

Gettysburg

83

Wilmington

159

Cumberland

Hancock

97

MARYLAND

DEL. TPK. (TOLL)

95

N.J.TPK. (TOLL)

A.C. EXPWY. (TOLL)

Keyser

522

Hagerstown

Westminster

Reisterstown

Bel Air

66

Elkton

Odessa

NEW JERSEY

Martinsburg

15

Frederick

Towson

Havre de Grace

Aberdeen

G. ST. PKWY. (TOLL)

43

50

Harpers Ferry

Harpers Ferry

45

BALTIMORE

Smyrna

DELAWARE

Charles Town

270

Gaithersburg

Laurel

Ft. Meade

300

Dover

WEST VIRGINIA

Winchester

Leesburg

Rockville

95

Milford

13

Cape Henlopen

a Rocks

Berryville

7

301

404

FY.

Lewes

Strasburg

56

Marshall

Arlington

WASHINGTON

Annapolis

Rehoboth Beach

Woodstock

Front Royal

66

19

Alexandria

65

Seaford

Georgetown

DEL.

New Market

211

Warrenton

Ft. Belvoir

13

Laurel

1

Luray

Culpeper

Quantico

Waldorf

La Plata

Cambridge

Berlin

MD.

Salisbury

Ocean City

SKYLINE DRIVE

Shenandoah Nat'l Park

Orange

Gordonsville

3

301

Lexington Park

G. Wash. Birthpl. Nat'l Mon.

Pocomoke City

Snow Hill

MD.

3

Charlottesville

64

33

Warsaw

Crisfield

Chincoteague

VA.

Assateague Island Nat'l Seashore

64

66

Ashland

295

Tappahannock

360

Sprouses

15

Richmond NBP

17

Kilmarnock

Exmore

13

Lynchburg

Richmond

RICH.- PETERSBG. TPK. (TOLL)

23

Colonial NHP

Appomattox C.H. NHP

360

17

Williamsburg

Yorktown

Cape Charles

ATLANTIC

Appomattox

Petersburg

51

Hopewell

10

Langley AFB

Hampton

Farmville

51

Wakefield

460

Smithfield

Newport News

CHESAPEAKE BAY BR.-TUN. (TOLL)

South Hill

95

40

Blackstone

McKenney

58

Norfolk

Naval Base

Virginia Beach

Ft. Story

44

Keysville

15

Portsmouth

Suffolk

21

Boggs Island Lake

116

Emporia

Franklin

Chesapeake

OCEAN

4

85

Oxford

Roanoke Rapids

13

Ahoskie

Elizabeth City

17

168

Durham

162

64

95

Rocky Mount

Edenton

158

Kitty Hawk

Windsor

Albemarle Sd.

D **E** **F**

Florida

0 25 50 100 MI.

Dickinson
Stuart
West Palm Beach
Riviera Beach
Jupiter
Palm Beach
Lake Worth
Boynton Beach
Delray Beach
Boca Raton
Pompano Beach
Fort Lauderdale
Hollywood
Dania
Miami Beach
Miami
Coral Gables
Biscayne Nat'l Park

Okeechobee
Canal Point
Pahokee
Belle Glade
South Bay
Clewiston
Moore Haven
La Belle
Immokalee
Hialeah
Florida City
Homestead
Key Largo
John Pennekamp Coral Reef
Key Largo
Islamorada
Long Key
Craig
Dolphin Research Center
Marathon
Sugarloaf Key
Key West

FLORIDA'S TPK (TOLL)
EVERGLADES PARKWAY 80 (TOLL)
TAMIAMI TRAIL
Everglades Nat'l Park
Cape Sable
East Cape
Flamingo
Everglades City
Ten Thousand Islands
Cape Romano
Marco Island
Collier-Seminole
Naples
Bonita Springs
Fort Myers
Cape Coral
Punta Gorda
Port Charlotte
Venice
Sarasota
Ringling Museums & Circus Hall of Fame
Circus Winter Hdqrts.
Highlands Hammock
Arcadia
Solana
Sanibel I.
Everglades Wonder Gardens
African Safari at Caribbean Gardens
Palmdale Gatorama
Big Cypress Swamp
Okaloacoochee Slough

MEXICO
GULF OF MEXICO
Straits of Florida
Florida Keys
Marquesas Keys
Biscayne Bay
Florida Bay

THE EVERGLADES

ALABAMA
Seminole
Chattahoochee
Bristol
Hosford
Marianna
Florida Caverns
Blountstown
Torreya
Apalachicola R.
Dead L.
Port St. Joe
Apalachicola
Cape St. George
Cape San Blas
St. Joseph Peninsula
Graceville
Chipley
Bonifay
Panama City
Tyndall AFB
De Funiak Springs
Freeport
Florala
Crestview
Valparaiso Niceville
Eglin AFB
Fort Walton Beach
Gulfarium
Santa Rosa I.
Gulf Is. Nat'l Seashore
Pensacola
Pensacola NAS
West Pensacola
Atmore
Perdido R.
Choctawhatchee R.
Yellow R.
Dead L.

© HAMMOND INCORPORATED

Plantation
Ft. Laud.
Dania
Hallandale
Hollywood
Pembroke Pines
Miramar
North Miami
Miami Beach
Davie
Opa-Locka
Hialeah
Miami Int'l
Miami
Coral Gables
Key Biscayne
Virginia Key
Cape Florida
West Monroe
Carol City

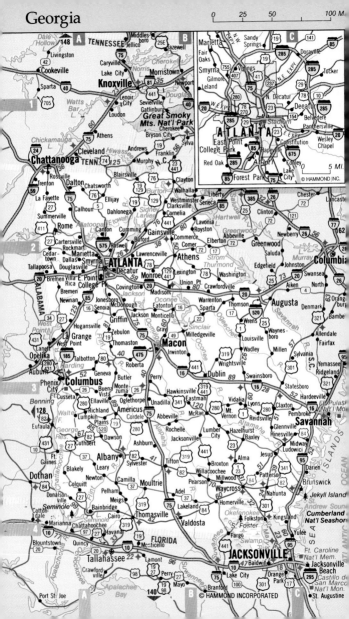

Georgia

Idaho 143

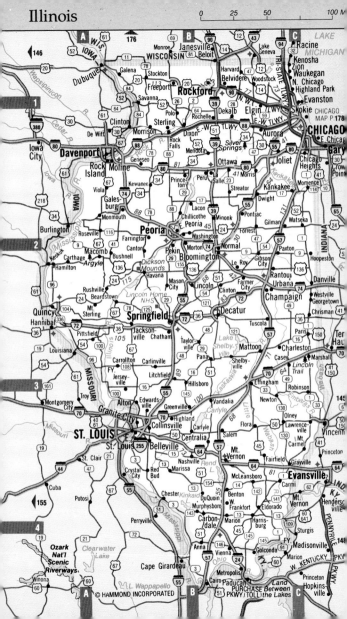

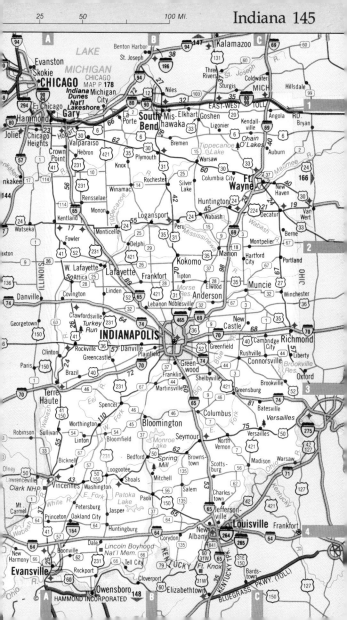

Iowa

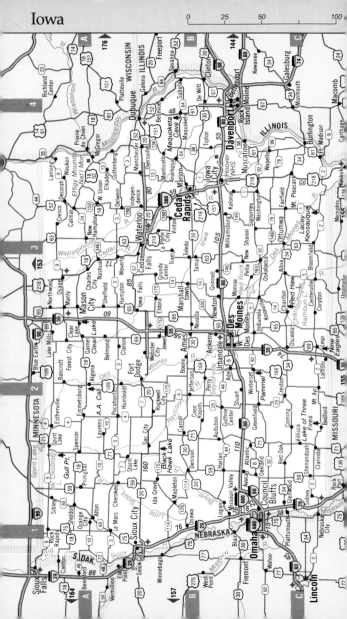

0   25   50   100

Kentucky, Tennessee

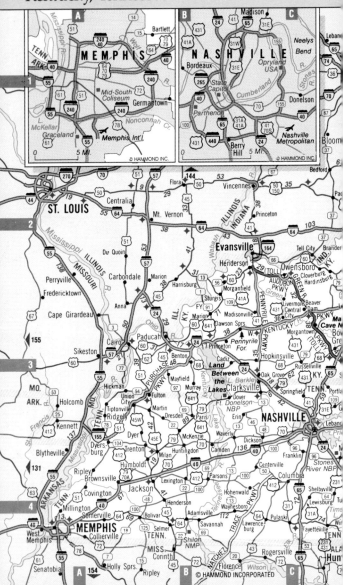

MEMPHIS

14 · Bartlett · 51 · 15 · 240 · 40 · 79 · 64 · TENN. · ARK. · 40 · 70 · 79 · 55 · 61 · 51 · 240 · Mid-South Coliseum · 72 · 240 · Germantown · 51 · 240 · 78 · Nonconnah Cr. · McKellar · Graceland · 61 · 55 · Memphis Int'l · 0 · 5 MI. · © HAMMOND INC.

NASHVILLE

Madison · 24 · 41A · 65 · 31E · 431 · 41A · 31W · 155 · Neelys Bend · Bordeaux · 31E · Opryland USA · 265 · State Capitol · Cumberland R. · Stones R. · Donelson · 40 · 70 · 155 · 40 · Parthenon · 31A · 41A · 100 · 65 · 41 · 70S · Nashville Metropolitan · 431 · 440 · Berry Hill · 24 · 0 · 5 MI. · © HAMMOND INC.

270 · 70 · 51 · 57 · Flora · 144 · 50 · 53 · 67 · Bedford · 50 · 150 · 35 · Vincennes · 44 · 19 · 50 · Centralia · 9 · 29 · 45 · ILLINOIS · INDIANA · 38 · Princeton · Pac · 55 · ST. LOUIS · 55 · Mt. Vernon · 33 · 64 · 43 · 64 · 103 · 37 · MISSOURI · ILLINOIS · 51 · 38 · 53 · Wabash R. · Evansville · 41 · Tell City · Brander · Du Quoin · 57 · 31 · 164 · 66 · KY. · Perryville · Carbondale · Marion · 13 · 56 · 60 · 22 · Henderson · 29 (TOLL) · Owensboro · 231 · Cloverdg · Hardinsburg · 79 · Fredericktown · Harrisburg · Morganfield · 41A · AUDU · BON · Livermore · Beaver · 67 · Anna · 1 · Sturgis · FY · 91 · 109 · PENNYRILE PKWY · Central · Dam · Cave M · 155 · Cape Girardeau · 3 · 45 · Marion · 60 · 641 · Dawson Sprs. · 41 · 36 · Morgantown · Bo · Gre · Cairo · Paducah · Ohio R. · 24 · 62 · W · Pennyrile For. · KENTUCKY PKWY · PKWY · 60 · Sikeston · 57 · 21 · Benton · 68 · Cadiz · 431 · Hopkinsville · 68 · Russellville · 57 · 55 · PURCHASE PKWY · Mayfield · 45 · Princeton · 24 · Land Between the Lakes · Oak Grove · 62 · KY. · MO. · 53 · Hickman · 94 · Murray · 97 · L. Barkley · Clarksville · Springfield · TENN. · ARK. · Holcomb · Union City · Fulton · 641 · 79 · Ft. Donelson NBP · 13 · 41 · 109 · Kennett · 25 · Tiptonville · Martin · Dresden · 69 · Paris · 79 · Erin · 46 · NASHVILLE · 31E · Lebano · 412 · 137 · Ridgely · 45W · 22 · McKenzie · 13 · Waverly · 70 · Blytheville · Dyer · 45E · Milan · Huntingdon · Camden · 136 · Dickson · 100 · 24 · 131 · Dyersburg · 104 · 412 · 40 · 40 · Centerville · Franklin · 96 · Stones River NBP · Ripley · Humboldt · 19 · 412 · Parsons · 50 · Columbia · Lebani · Brownsville · 70A · Lexington · 22 · 100 · Hohenwald · NATCHEZ TRACE PKWY · 412 · 65 · Shelbyville · 64 · Lewisburg · 31 · 63 · Jackson · 41 · 18 · Henderson · Waynesboro · 64 · 31A · Millington · 113 · Somerville · 64 · 69 · Bolivar · Adamsville · 112 · Pulaski · Fayetteville · 231 · Hun · West Memphis · MEMPHIS · Collierville · 18 · 125 · Selmer · 64 · Savannah · Lawrenceburg · 43 · 55 · 7 · 22 · Shiloh NMP · MISS. · 72 · Rogersville · 65 · Senatobia · A · 154 · Holly Sprs. · Ripley · 45 · B · Corinth · Florence · Wilson L. · © HAMMOND INCORPORATED · C

0 25 50 100 MI.

Inset map (Louisville area):

Sellersburg
311
65 62 42
Prospect
150
265 Clarks-ville
71
64 Jeffersonville
New Albany
42 St. Mathews
265
Louisville
111 60 31W
Douglas Hills
65 155
64
Shively
264
Jeffersontown
Pleasure Ridge Park
Standiford Field
Okolona Fern Cr.
Valley Sta. 841
265 31E
Hillview 31E 150
0 5 10 MI.
© HAMMOND INC.

Main map:

69
27 INDIANA OHIO
75 166
E
D
F

Anderson
Richmond
Troy
Springfield
70 27 100
70
IANAPOLIS
Dayton
675
27
Kettering
74
Oxford
75 71
sburg 96
74
Hillsboro
nbus
Versailles 88
50
421 Covington
Cincinnati
Florence
Newport 125
mour
50
421 127
Warsaw
Carrollton 75
42
Augusta
Ripley OHIO
Maysville KY.
125
Portsmouth
sonville
42 71
Eminence
Falmouth
Williamstown
62
Vanceburg
Flemings-burg
23 52
Russell Ironton
Carter Caves
Ashland
60 Charleston
OHIO W. VA.
Louisville
Frankfort
Cynthiana
79
Olive Hill
Morehead
Grayson
Louisa
Huntington
64 70
Lawrenceburg
Lexington
Paris
5 60
Mt. Sterling
Cave Run
7
23
Madison
138
64
Winchester
460
W. Liberty
119
Bardstown
31E 150
BLUE GRASS PKWY
Springfield
Harrodsburg
Richmond
Natural Bridge St. Res. Pk.
94
MOUNTAIN PKWY
402
Paints-ville
Dewey
Williamson
52
Tug Fk.
zabethton
150
Danville
Berea
114
Prestonsburg
23
460
Fishtrap
Hodgenville
68
Lebanon
Stanford
421
Beattyville
30
Jackson
Pikeville
W. VA.
Lincoln Birthplace NHS
61
Campbellsville
Mt. Vernon
McKee
15
23
119
Breaks Interstate Pk.
460 69 VA.
Green R.L.
Liberty
27
78
DANIEL BOONE PKWY
TOLL 15
Jenkins
Richlands
MBERLAND
55
Columbia
CUMBERLAND PKWY
122
Somerset
Lebanon
Manchester
421
Whitesburg Cumberland KY.
111
58A
45 19
TOLL 90
Cumberland Res. St. Pk.
90 127
Monticello
Corbin
Barbourville
Fork
Harlan
Big Stone Gap
81 13
163
90
Albany
Whitley City
75
Pineville
119
58
VIRGINIA
Kings-port
Bristol
81
nsville 61
Dale Hollow 53
Big S. Fork Nat'l River & Rec. Area
92
Jellico
25W
Middlesboro
Cumberland Gap NHP TENN.
23
19E
Holston
Celina 52
Livingston
Jamestown
Oneida
Tazewell
Rogersville
11W
181
Elizabethton
56
Caryville
La Follette
25E
11E
Cherokee
81
Andrew Johnson NHS
Johnson City
Gainesboro 127
Cookeville
Lake City
Rutledge
46
Morristown
Greene-ville
321
Erwin
126
Harriman
61
Oak Ridge
75
11W
35
8
Newport
25
Mt. Mitchell
162
Sparta
40
Rockwood
Lenoir City
21
411
BLUE RIDGE PKWY
705
111
Crossville
Spring City
Watts Bar L.
Maryville
54
70
Gatlinburg
40
McMinnville
127
Knoxville
Mt. Mitchell
8
Pikeville
Athens
40
Great Smoky Mts. Nat'l Pk.
Cherokee
441
26
Ashville
d Res.
8
Dayton
411
Madisonville
Clingmans Dome
BLUE
Hendersonville
26
Dunlap
TENN.
Fontana L.
Bryson City
RIDGE PKWY
64
25
Chicka-mauga
28
19
Franklin
36
S.C.
Red Bank
Benton
N. CAROLINA
GEORGIA
Spartan-burg
85
Jasper
Cleveland
127
Blairsville
GA. CAROLINA
Greenville
59
Chattanooga
74 64
5
Blue Ridge
Clayton
123
85 385
Dalton
411
19 129
S. CAROLINA
162
75 76
E 142
441 23
F

D 75 E F

Louisiana

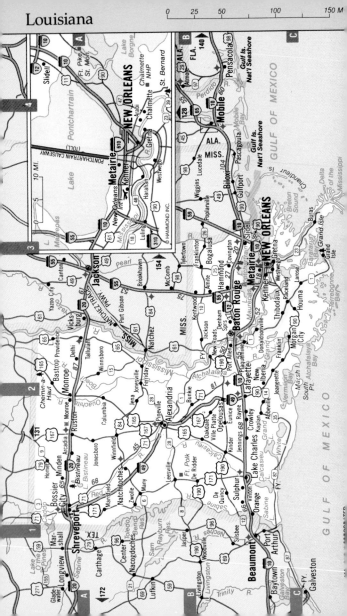

Maine 151

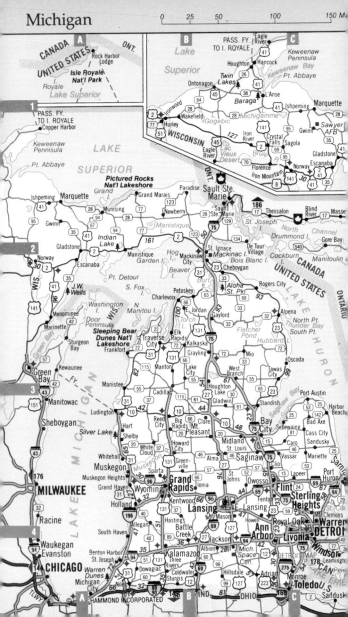

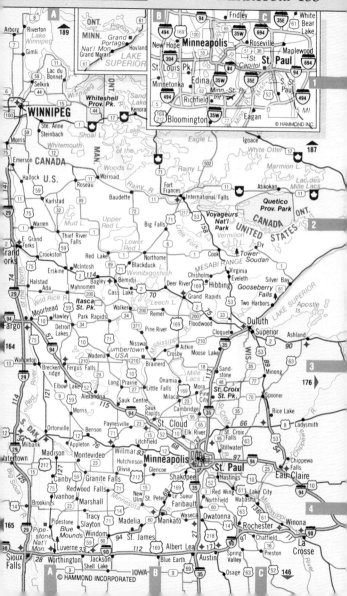

Minnesota 153

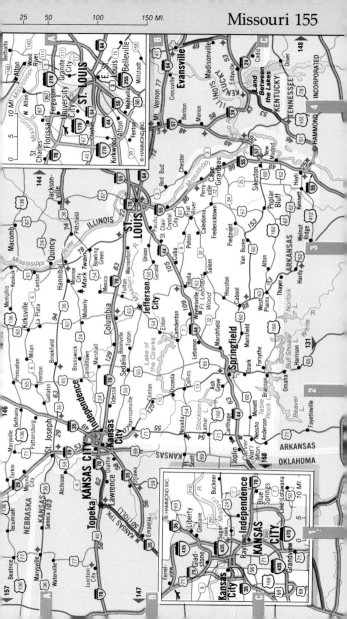

Montana

© HAMMOND

New Hampshire, Vermont

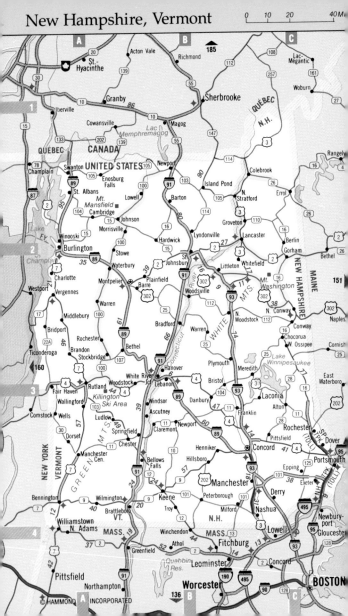

© HAMMOND INCORPORATED

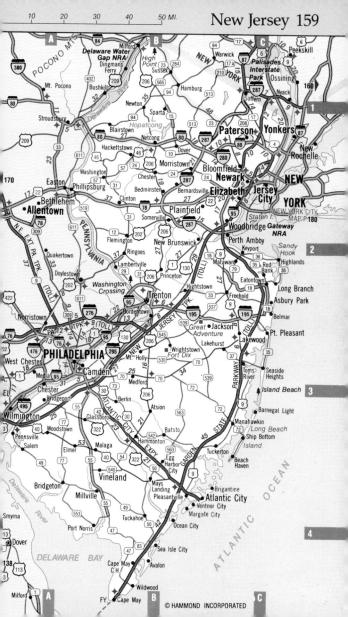

10   20   30   40   50 MI.

© HAMMOND INCORPORATED

New York

Lockport
405
429
270
31
ONT. W. NY.
Niagara Falls
Niagara Falls
St. Johnsburg
384
N. Tonawanda
Grand
62
190
263
78
Tonawanda
Island
QUEEN ELIZABETH WAY
Niagara R.
290
Buffalo Int'l.
Ridgeway
OEW
Kenmore
33
Depew
20
Fort Erie
130
Cheektowaga
3
Buffalo
190
5 MI.
LAKE ERIE
90
W. Seneca
5
219
20
400

5 MI.
© HAMMOND INC
LAKE ONTARIO
259
Windsor Beach
Sea Breeze
261
ONTARIO
18
Parma
Irondequoit
Cors.
Greece
18
Bay
386
104
404
Webster
Spencerport
390
590
259
490
Rochester
33
490
Rochester
441
252A
590
E. Rochester
Chili
Fairport
Cen.
Genesee R.
Henrietta
31
90
490
Fishers
383
390
65
90
Harri
41

Shelburne
Bradford
Peterborough
401
Scugog
115
36
Rice L.
30
Belleville
89
9
404
63
Brighton
Trenton
FY
Orangeville
400
Whitby
Newcastle
401
Cobourg
Picton
10
Brampton
18
32
Oshawa
LAKE
Fergus
6
ONTARIO
CANADA
Guelph
401
Q.E.W. 30
24
TORONTO
UNITED STATES
4
38
Mississauga
ONTARIO
Cambridge
8
Oakville
27
Burlington
Olcott
Hamlin Beach
403
Hamilton
St.
18
Branford
56
Catharines
77
Albion
104
Rochester
104
Sodu
24
Welland
104
Barge Canal
98
490
Webster
21
Palmyra
186
Niagara
Falls
42
31
Haldimand
Ft. Erie
Tonawanda
90
STATE
THWY
20
Geneva
Buffalo
20
Batavia
59
TOLL
89
Depew
98
63
FIN
Nanticoke
Lackawanna
20A
Canadaigua
24
E. Aurora
Geneseo
Long Point
90
18
Letchworth
390
43
L A K
Bay
Springville
39
Dansville
15
Keuka
LAKE ERIE
Dunkirk
59
Arcade
19
Hammondsport
Watkin
CANADA
39
Gowanda
5
Arkport
26
Glen
UNITED STATES
Fredonia
62
219
Franklinville
17
Bath
414
Hor
Erie
32
Westfield
28
Salamanca
16
Belmont
36
Andover
97
Corning
60
Jamestown
Olean
417
Bolivar
Elm
90
170
201
Allegany Res.
Allegany
St. Pk.
417

84
17
7
New Haven
95
POCONO
23
CONN STATE
684
Bridgeport
Orient Point
MTS. PK.
N.J. STATE THWY
Delaware
Suffern
White
Norwalk
Greenport
Pt.
209
Water Gap
206
Plains
Stamford
Long Island Sound
Montai
NRA
Port Jefferson
Riverhead
East Hampton
80
Netcong
Paterson
Yonkers
Huntington
25
Southampton
287
Newark
25A
495
Mineola
Babylon
Patchogue
ATLANTIC OCEA
Clinton
Elizabeth
NEW
Freeport
Long
78
YORK
Gateway NRA
Island
0 10 20 30 40 MI
202
New Brunswick
NEW YORK CITY
© HAMMOND INCORPORATE
MAP P. 180

North Carolina, South Carolina

Hazard · Jenkins · Saler
75 · DANIEL BOONE PKWY. (TOLL) · 119 · KY. · VA. · 460 · Bluefield · Blacksburg
Corbin · 23 · Norton · 460 · 80 · 77 · Wytheville · Radford · 81
Middlesboro · Cumberland · 19 · Mt. Rogers NRA · 58 · Mar
Cumberland Gap NHP · KY. · 25E · 23 · 58 · Galax · Mt. Airy · Hanging
TENN. · Kingsport · Bristol · 421 · Sparta · PKWY · 21 · Pilot Mt. · Win
104 · 148 · 54 · 81 · Johnson City · Elizabethton · 74 · Elkin · 601 · Yadkinville · Sal
Oak Ridge · 61 · Morristown · Newport · Boone · Wilkesboro · 45 · 421 · 31 · High Pc
Knoxville · 35 · 19E · RIDGE · 18 · Lenoir · 64 · 22 · 77 · Lexington
Lenoir City · Maryville · 66 · Gatlinburg · BLUE · 110 · Morganton · 103 · Hickory · Statesville · 85
129 · Great Smoky Mts. Nat'l Park · Asheville · Black Mtn. · 40 · Newton · Mooresville · Salisbury · Kannapolis · Concord
Cherokee · Waynesville · 74 · 92 · Rutherfordton · Shelby · 16 · 49 · Albemarle · Charlotte
Fontana · Franklin · 23 · Brevard · Hendersonville · Forest City · Kings Mtn. · 29 · 85 · Monroe · 601
Hiwassee · Murphy · Highlands · 11 · Chesnee · Gaffney · Kings Mtn. NMP · Rock Hill · S.C. · N.C. · Wades
N.C. · GA. · Travelers Rest · Greer · Spartanburg · Jonesville · 176 · Chester · Lancaster · Chesterfi
Walhalla · Keowee L. · Greenville · 85 · Woodruff · Union · 72 · Kershaw · McBee
Westminster · Liberty · 123 · Clinton · Whitmire · Winnsboro · 77 · Camden · Bishopville · Hartsv
Seneca · 385 · Newberry · Broad · Elgin · 521
Sidney Lanier L. · Toccoa · Anderson · 178 · Greenwood · 26 · Columbia · Sumter
Gainsville · Hartwell L. · Abbeville · 72 · Saluda · Lexington · Congaree Swp. Nat'l Mon. · 15
985 · 85 · Elberton · B. Brown L. · Greenwood · 378 · Johnston · St. Mathews · Summerton · 301
Lawrenceville · Athens · Strom Thurmond L. · McCormick · Edgefield · Swansea · Neeses · Orangeburg · Marion
Decatur · Monroe · Augusta · Aiken · Williston · Norway · Branchville · St. George · Moul
Covington · Madison · Jackson L. · Thomson · 125 · Denmark · Bamberg · Canadys · Charl
Griffin · Forsyth · Milledgeville · Waynesboro · Savannah River Plant · Allendale · Summervi · Walterboro
Thomaston · Macon · 441 · 95 · Fairfax · Hampton · 17 · 174
Perry · Dublin · Sylvania · Estill · Yemassee · Ridgeland · Beaufort · Huntin
Eastman · Vidalia · Swainsboro · Statesboro · Hardeeville · Bluffton · Hilton Head Isl
McRae · Claxton · Savannah · Parris Island · Sea Islands
Cordele · Hinesville · Fort Pulaski Nat'l Mon.
Albany · Baxley · Jesup · Douglas · 142

0 25 50 100 MI.

D 138

Lynchburg
29
360
501

Williamsburg *Colonial NHP* **Hampton**
Newport News **Norfolk** CHESAPEAKE BAY BRIDGE–TUNNEL (TOLL)
Portsmouth **Virginia Beach**
56 **Franklin** **Suffolk** **Chesapeake**
VIRGINIA
Murfreesboro N. CAROLINA
Emporia

South Boston
South Hill
Oxford
Roxboro
Buggs I.
Medoc Mtn.
Enfield
Henderson
Roanoke Rapids
Scotland Neck
Windsor
Edenton
Columbia
Elizabeth City
Kitty Hawk
Nags Head *Wright Bros. Nat'l Mem.*
Manteo
Albemarle Sound
Winton
Ahoskie

Yanceyville
Graham
Burham
Wake Forest
Falls L.
L. Gaston
Medoc Mtn.

Chapel Hill
Siler City
Apex
Raleigh
Fuquay-Varina
Smithfield
Jordan L.
Rocky Mount
Tarboro
Wilson
Farmville
Greenville
Washington
Goose Cr.
Pamlico Sound
Cape Hatteras Nat'l Seashore
Hatteras FERRY
C. Hatteras

Sanford
Dunn
Goldsboro
Kinston
New Bern
Hobucken
FERRY
Ocracoke
Fort Bragg
Fayetteville
Raeford
Clinton
Warsaw
Richlands
Morehead City
Beaufort
Cape Lookout Nat'l Seashore
Atlantic

Southern Pines
Neuse R.
Jones Lake
Wallace
Jacksonville
Camp Lejeune
New River Inlet
Onslow C. Lookout
Bay

Lumberton
Moores Cr. NBP
Wilmington
Wrightsville Beach
Carolina Beach

Rowland
Clarkton
Whiteville
Cape Fear R.
Southport FERRY
C. Fear

Dillon
Marion
Mullins
Tabor City
Conway
Loris

Myrtle Beach
North Myrtle Beach
Huntington Beach

Andrews

ATLANTIC OCEAN

SEA ISLANDS
C. Romain

Inset 3 — Charlotte
© HAMMOND INC.
0 5 MI.
Charlotte
Charlotte-Douglas Int'l
Revolution Park
Sugar Cr.
Briar Cr.

Inset 4 — Winston-Salem / Greensboro
Bethania
Winston-Salem
Lewisville
Walkertown
Kernersville
Colfax
Greensboro High Point
Guilford C.H. NMP
L. Brandt
Old Salem
Friendship
Greensboro
Clemmons
Jamestown
Wallburg
High Point
South Furn. Mkt. Ctr.
Arcadia
Eller
Sedgefield
Pleasant Garden
Welcome
Thomasville
© HAMMOND INC.
0 5 10 MI.

INCORPORATED

D E F

North Dakota, South Dakota

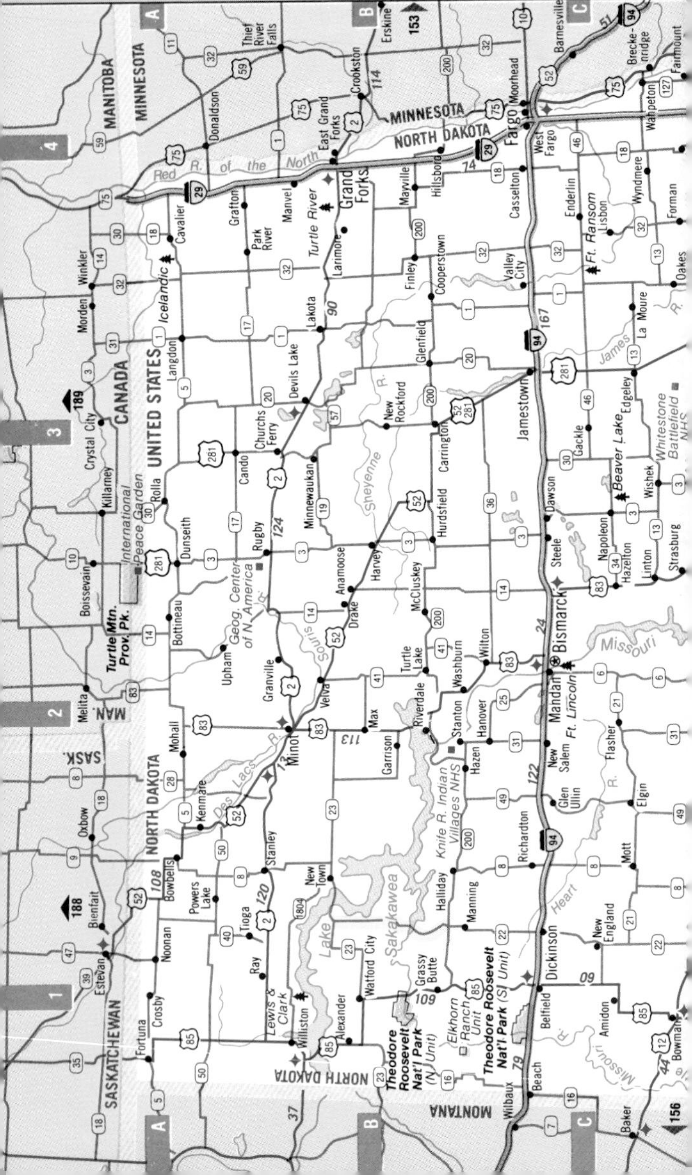

Ohio

0   25   50 MI.

© HAMMOND INC.

5 MI.

LAKE ERIE

CLEVELAND

Eastlake, Willowick, Euclid, Richmond Heights, Mayfield Heights, Lyndhurst, Shaker Heights, Maple Heights, Bedford, Cuyahoga Valley NRA, Garfield Heights, Cleveland Heights, S. Euclid, East Cleveland, Solon, N. Royalton, Strongsville, Brook Park, Parma, Parma Heights, Brooklyn, Lakewood, Rocky River, Westlake, N. Olmsted, Berea, Cleve. Hopkins Int'l, Cuyahoga R.

W. VA. KY. W. VIRGINIA

New Martinsville, W. Union, New Matamoras, St. Marys, Marietta, Belpre, Parkersburg, Ripley, Spencer, Beverly, McConnelsville, Gloucester, Athens, Nelsonville, Logan, McArthur, Wellston, Jackson, Oak Hill, Rio Grande, Gallipolis, Crown City, South Pt., Ironton, Wheelersburg, Portsmouth, Ashland, Grayson, Huntington, St. Albans, Louisa, Paintsville, Salyersville, Prestonburg, Morehead, Cave Run Lake

Hopewell Culture NHP, Circleville, Washington C.H., Greenfield, Chillicothe, Waverly, Piketon, Bainbridge, Hillsboro, Peebles, Manchester, Serpent Mound, W. Union, Ripley, Maysville, Georgetown, Bethel, New Richmond, Mt. Orab, Blanchester, Wilmington, Jamestown, Kettering, Miamisburg, Middletown, Hamilton, Oxford, Harrison, Florence, Covington

KENTUCKY OHIO IND.

CINCINNATI

Ross, Fairfield, Springdale, Wyoming, N. College Hill, Mt. Healthy, Bridgetown, Cheviot, Ft. Mitchell, Erlanger, Greater Cinc. Int'l, Loveland, Montgomery, Milford, Newtown, Forestville, Sharonville, Reading, Silverton, Norwood, Newport, Taft NHS

© HAMMOND INCORPORATED

Oklahoma

0   25   50   100 Mi

Pennsylvania

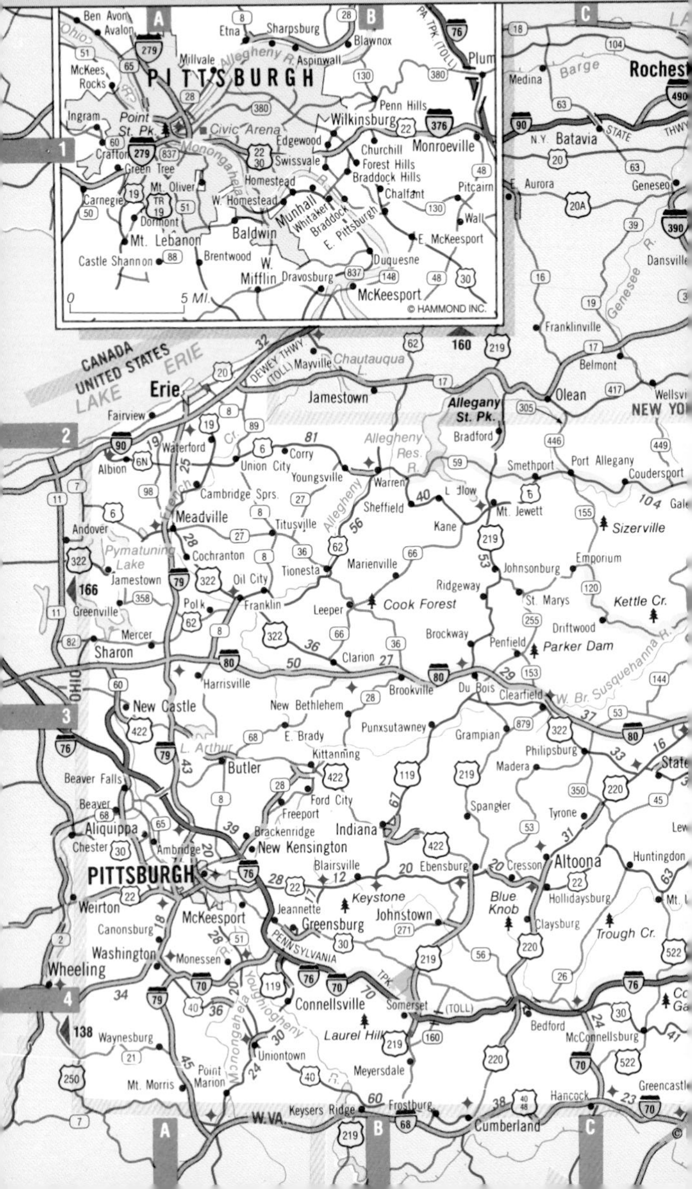

Texas

A **B** **C**

TEXAS

Clayton · Stratford
87
Dalhart
54
Perryton
83
Higgins
60
209
Canyon
60
Hereford
Tulia
287
W
Memphi
287
Prairie Dog Town
Clovis
Friona
Muleshoe
Plainview
70
206
Portales
70
Littlefield
84
124
27
70
Pa
Dumas
287
Stinnett
L. Meredith
Borger
Canadian
Pampa
273
TEX.
OKLA.
Amarillo
40
L. Meredith NRA
60
96
McLean
Wheeler
15
Shamrock
83
N.M.
TEX.
Canadian R.
40
Vega
91
Canyon
124
287
Memphis
Wellington
55
62
Lubbock
82
Slaton
G
Tatum
82
62
82
87
Hereford
97
60
Prairie Dog Town Fk.
Tulia
27
Childress
Brownfield
Post
380
Clovis
84
Friona
18
Lovington
Seminole
Tahoka
84
Snyder
Hobbs
143
Lamesa
180
© HAMMOND INC.

134
U.S.
10
54
NEW MEXICO
Carlsbad Caverns Nat'l Park
Carlsbad
Andrews
118
Big Spring
20
Colo
Cr
EL PASO
MEX
Ciudad Juárez
2
Chamizal Nat'l Mon.
62
180
Guadalupe Mountains Nat'l Park
285
Kermit
77
Midland
Odessa
385
87
Sterling City
San Ange
Rio Grande
167
Van Horn
90
20 41
Pecos
Monahans
18
Big Lake
67 385
McCamey
349
Twin Buttes Res.
E D W A R D
APACHE MTS.
72
10
STOCKTON
Ozona
78
Sonora
277
UNITED STATES
Balmorhea
17
67
Ft. Stockton
PLATEAU
Pecos R.
PLATEAU
MEXICO
DAVIS MTS.
Ft. Davis
Ft. Davis NHS
285
Sanderson
Rocks
El Sueco
10
Marfa
Alpine
Marathon
305
90
277
3
45
235
67
385
Amistad Res.
Amistad NRA
B.
Del Ric
Coyame
Presidio
Big Bend Nat'l Park
Villa Acuña
27
16
Ojinaga
170
Boquillas del Carmen
2
R. Conchos
16
Chihuahua
45
53
Piedras Negras
Cuauhtémoc
Meoqui
Zaragoza
57
Ciudad Delicias
© HAMMOND INCORPORATED
Morelos
Allende

© HAMMOND INC.
81
287
35
W
Grapevine
114
Grapevine
35
Carrollton
75
Richardson
289
Garland
Eagle Mountain Lake
Keller
377
Farmers Branch
635
635
R.
Salado
26
114
White Rock
North Richland Hills
Dallas-Fort Worth Int'l
77
TOLL HWY.
Univ. Pk
Highland Pk.
67
L. Worth
199
820
183
Haltom City
Hurst
10
Euless
360
12
183
Irving
Cotton Bowl
30
Sat
Hi
White Settlement
820
180
Arlington
180
Grand Prairie
175
Mesquite
4
Fort Worth
30
303
Arlington
12
67
35
E
45
20
Seagoville
53
Ci
20
Benbrook
287
Joe Pool L.
Duncanville
Hutchins
Trinity R.
Monterre
Benbrook Lake
35
W
0   5   10 MI.
De Soto
Lancaster
Wilmer
Cedar Hill

A **B** **C**

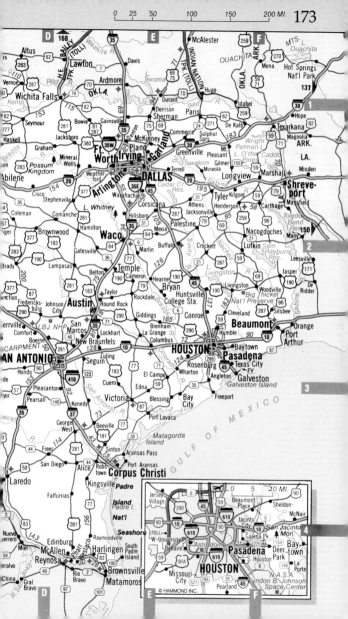

Utah

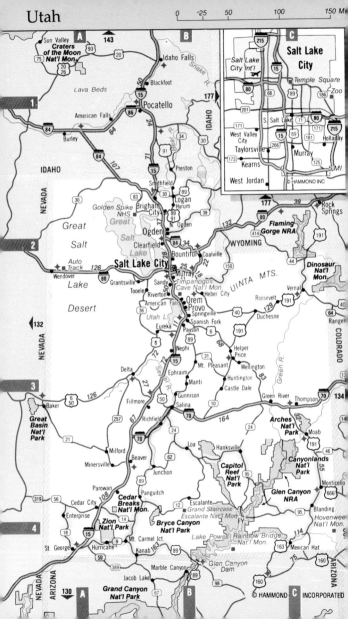

0   25   50   100   150 Mi

Salt Lake City

Salt Lake City Int'l
Temple Square
Zoo
S. Salt Lake
West Valley City
Taylorsville
Murray
Kearns
West Jordan
Holladay
© HAMMOND INC.

Sun Valley
Craters of the Moon Nat'l Mon.
Idaho Falls
Snake R.
Lava Beds
Blackfoot
Pocatello
American Falls
Burley
IDAHO
NEVADA
Preston
Smithfield
Logan
Hyrum
Brigham City
Golden Spike NHS
Great
N. Ogden
Ogden
Clearfield
Bountiful
Coalville
Salt Lake
City
Murray
Lake
Sandy
Salt
Tooele
Riverton
American Falls
Desert
Auto Track
Wendover
Grantsville
Timpanogos Cave Nat'l Mon.
Heber City
Orem
Provo
Utah L.
Springville
Spanish Fork
Payson
Eureka
Nephi
Delta
Mt. Pleasant
Ephraim
Manti
Helper
Price
Wellington
Huntington
Castle Dale
Gunnison
Salina
Green River
Thompson
Fillmore
Richfield
Baker
Great Basin Nat'l Park
Milford
Minersville
Beaver
Junction
Loa
Hanksville
Capitol Reef Nat'l Park
Arches Nat'l Park
Moab
Canyonlands Nat'l Park
Glen Canyon NRA
Monticello
Blanding
Hovenweep Nat'l Mon.
Parowan
Cedar Breaks Nat'l Mon.
Panguitch
Escalante
Grand Staircase Escalante Nat'l Mon.
Cedar City
Enterprise
Zion Nat'l Park
Bryce Canyon Nat'l Park
Lake Powell
Rainbow Bridge Nat'l Mon.
St. George
Hurricane
Mt. Carmel Jct.
Kanab
Marble Canyon
Glen Canyon Dam
Mexican Hat
Jacob Lake
Grand Canyon Nat'l Park
© HAMMOND INCORPORATED
WYOMING
Rock Springs
Flaming Gorge NRA
Dinosaur Nat'l Mon.
Vernal
Roosevelt
Duchesne
UINTA MTS.
COLORADO
Rangel
NEVADA
ARIZONA

Wisconsin

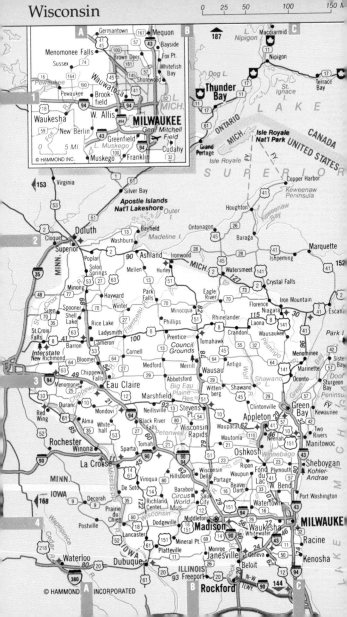

Chicago, Denver, Detroit

A **B** **C**

0 5 10 15 20 MI.

Fox Lake

31

McHenry
120
12

Grayslake
45 Illinois Beach
120
41
Waukegan

North Chicago

60
Mondelein
Wauconda
Lake Bluff

Crystal Lake
14
59
Lake Zurich
83
Deerfield
94
22
Highwood
Highland Park
41

LAKE

Algonquin
31
Barrington
12
Wheeling
Glencoe
Winnetka

Carpenters-
ville
Palatine
Arlington
Hts.
294
Wilmette

N-W TOLLWAY
90
14
Morton
Grove
Evanston

Elgin
Des
Plaines
Park
Ridge
Skokie
MICHIGAN

Streamwood
290
Chicago
Int'l
90
Norridge
14

S. Elgin
59
20
Bloomingdale
50
Wrigley Field

St. Charles
64
Villa
Park
Elmwood Park
94
CHICAGO

W
Chicago
31
Lombard
Elm-
hurst
64
Oak Park
290
The Loop

Glen Ellyn
Berwyn
Cicero
Soldier Field

E-W TOLLWAY
88
Lisle
34
Brookfield
55
Comiskey Pk.

Aurora
34
Downers
Grove
171
50
Midway

Naperville
355
Oaklawn
12
20

Des Plaines
294
Blue
Island
94
90
Whiting
E. Chicago

55
171
45
Palos
Park
TLWY
Calumet
City
Gary
Ogden Dunes

126
53
Orland Pk.
6
Hammond
80

Plainfield
Lockport
Tinley Pk.
Chicago
Hts.
Lansing
Highland
Hobart
130

Shorewood
30
Joliet
80
New Lenox
Frankfort
30
Park Forest
41
Schererville
65

52
6
52
15
57
394
ILL.
IND.
30

© HAMMOND INCORPORATED

Boulder
7
Lafayette
Brighton
Pontiac
59
Utica
53

36
287
25
85
6
Keego Hbr.
Sterling
Hts.
Mt. Clemens
59
94

Marshall
Broom-
field
North-
glenn
76
Bloomfield
Hills
24
1
Warren
696
St. Clair
Shores
Eastpointe

93
121
Thornton
Denver
Int'l
Franklin
Royal Oak
696
St. Cla

72
Westminster
Arvada
DENVER
Southfield
102
102
53
94
DETROIT

58
Wheat
Ridge
87
70
275
Livonia
10
U.S.
Windsor
CANAD

70
Golden
Lakewood
rora
Garden
City
96
39
24

Morrison
2
West-
land
Dearborn
75
3
Tecumse

Englewood
94
Allen Pk.
Lincoln
Park

285
Littleton
470
88
83
275
Detroit
Metro.
85
18
401

Fenders
85
25
Parker
75
MICH.
ONT.

0 5 MI.
0 5 MI.

A **B** **C**

© HAMMOND INC.
© HAMMOND INC.

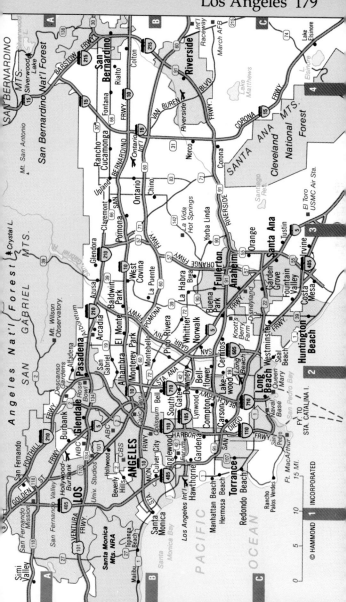

New York City, Portland, San Diego

New York City area

Wanaque Res., Mahwah, Wanaque, Ramsey, Oakland, Franklin Lakes, Pompton Lakes, Ho-Ho-Kus, Waldwick, Lincoln Park, Pompton Lakes, North Haledon, Hawthorne, Fair Lawn, Paramus, Maywood, Englewood, Paterson, Elmwood Park, Totowa, Clifton, Lodi, Teaneck, Cedar Grove, Passaic, Garfield, Caldwell, Rutherford, Montclair, Bloomfield, Nutley, Meadowlands Sports Complex, Livingston, East Orange, Kearny, Union City, Hoboken, Irvington, Harrison, Maplewood, Newark, Jersey City, Union, Newark Int'l, Elizabeth, Bayonne, Roselle, Linden, Staten Island, Woodbridge, Perth Amboy, South Amboy, Statue of Liberty, Gateway NRA, Lower Bay

Closter, Cresskill, Tenafly, Tappan, Westwood, Dobbs Ferry, Yonkers, Mount Vernon, Bronx, Yankee Stadium, La Guardia, Shea Stadium, Queens, Brooklyn, New York, Manhattan, Times Sq., Belmont Race Track, Aqueduct Race Track, Kennedy Int'l, Jamaica Bay, Gateway NRA, Interborough Pkwy., Shore Pkwy., Atlantic Ocean

Blauvelt St. Pk., Tallman Mtn. St. Pk., Valhalla, Elmsford, White Plains, Scarsdale, Rye, Harrison, Larchmont, New Rochelle, Mamaroneck, Long Island Sound, Glen Cove, Port Washington, Kings Point, Great Neck, Mineola, Floral Park, Garden City, Hempstead, Valley Stream, Woodmere, Cedarhurst, Lawrence, Inwood, Greenwich, Port Chester

10 MI.

© Hammond Incorporated

Portland area

Wash., Ore., Battle Ground, Vancouver, Camas, Portland Int'l, Hillsboro, Portland, Beaverton, Gresham, Milwaukie, Gladstone, Oregon City, Newberg, Canby, Columbia R., Pacific

© Hammond Inc.

San Diego area

Oceanside, Vista, Valley Center, Escondido, Carlsbad, San Diego State Beaches, San Marcos, San Diego Wild Animal Park, Leucadia, Encinitas, Rancho Santa Fe, San Pasqual, Ramona, Cardiff-by-the-Sea, Solana Beach, Del Mar, Poway, La Jolla, Lakeside, La Mesa, El Cajon, San Diego, San Diego Int'l, Spring Valley, National City, Coronado, Cabrillo Nat'l Mon., Chula Vista, Pacific Ocean

10 MI.

© Hammond Inc.

GULF OF MEXICO

Caribbean Sea

PACIFIC OCEAN

© HAMMOND INCORPORATED

Jacksonville
St. Petersburg
Birmingham
Mobile
New Orleans
Jackson
Galveston
Houston
Corpus Christi
San Antonio
Laredo
Brownsville
Matamoros
Dallas
Abilene
San Angelo
El Paso
Cd. Juárez
Phoenix
Tucson
Nogales
Agua Prieta
Mexicali
Tijuana
Ensenada
San Diego
La Paz
C. San Lucas
Sta. Rosalía
Hermosillo
Guaymas
Cd. Obregón
Los Mochis
Culiacán
Durango
Mazatlán
Tepic
Guadalajara
Puerto Vallarta
Colima
Las Hadas
Zihuatanejo
Acapulco
MEXICO CITY
Morelia
Querétaro
León
S. Luis Potosí
Zacatecas
Saltillo
Monterrey
Reynosa
Nvo. Laredo
Piedras Negras
Cd. Victoria
Tampico
Poza Rica
Veracruz
Orizaba
Oaxaca
Monte Albán Ruins
Mitla Ruins
Tehuantepec
Villahermosa
Tuxtla Gutiérrez
Campeche
Mérida
Uxmal Ruins
Kabab Ruins
Chichen Itzá
Cancún
Cozumel I.
Tulum Ruins
Chetumal
Belize City
BELMOPAN
BELIZE
GUATEMALA
GUAT.
HONDURAS
Lag. de Montebello Nat'l Park
Yucatán Pen.
Bay of Campeche
San Pedro Mártir Nat'l Park
Sa. de Carmen Nat'l Park
Chihuahua
Parral
Cumbres de Majalca Nat'l Park
Barranca del Cobre Nat'l Park
Torreón
Los Angeles Nat'l Park
Lower California (Baja)
GULF OF CALIFORNIA
U.S.
MEX.

Rio Grande

Inset:
MEXICO CITY
20 MI.
20 KM.
© HAMMOND INC.
Tula Ruins
Pachuca
El Chico Nat'l Park
Teotihuacan Ruins
La Malinche Nat'l Park
Puebla
Popocatépetl
Texcoco
Coacalco
Xochimilco
Tlalpan
Toluca
Cuernavaca

Atlantic Provinces

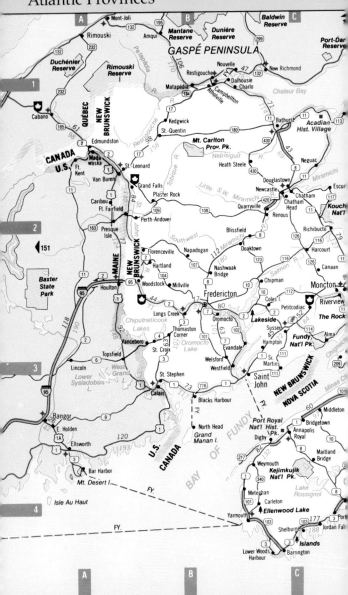

Québec

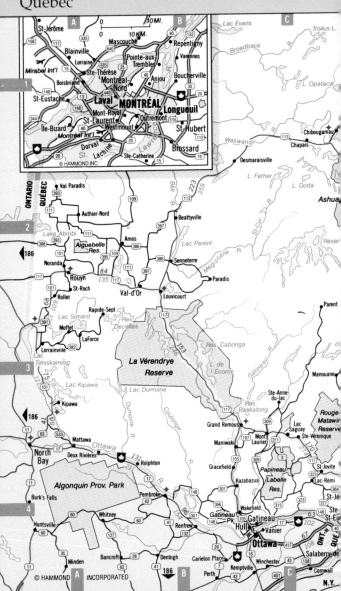

Ontario

Gatineau Park

Gatineau
148
Vanier
17
Hull
QUE.
148
Ottawa
417
OTTAWA
Kanata
417
Ottawa Int'l
31
0   5 MI.
0   5 KM.
© HAMMOND INCORPORATED

Elk Lake
101
11
Gogoma
560
New Liskeard
65
Ville-Marie
184
Lady Evelyn L.
Latchford
144
Temagami Lake
L. Timiskaming
101
Halfway Lakes
Wanapitei
Echo Bay
129
Mississagi
Chelmsford
Sudbury
Marten River
64
11
Sturgeon Falls
95
154
St. Joseph I.
548
108
Elliot Lake
Espanola
17
43
89
Estaire
80
129
North Bay
63
Thessalon
Blind River
91
146
6
Killarney Prov. Park
637
French R.
Lake Nipissing
Powassa
75
120
Drummond I.
Little Current
Gore Bay
540
Killarney
Grundy Lake
89
South River
124
11
Cockburn I.
6
GEORGIAN BAY
171
Parry Sound
Rogers City
23
Manitoulin Island
South Baymouth
Fitzwilliam I.
Huntsville
Rosseau
Mac Tier
Port Carling
Musk
32
Alpena
Tobermory
Lion's Head
Bruce Peninsula Nat'l Park
C. Croker
69
169
118
Gravenhurst
LAKE HURON
South Pt.
152
6
Georgian Bay Is. Nat'l Park
55
Orillia
Oscoda
Owen Sound
Midland
Coldwater
11
L. Simcoe
404
U.S.
CANADA
Southampton
26
Nottawasaga Bay
Barrie
48
MICHIGAN
MacGregor Point
Port Elgin
Collingwood
26
400
Port Austin
Kincardine
Walkerton
6
10
Durham
24
Cookstown
89
47
Newmarke
Osha
Bay City
25
Bad Axe
21
9
92
Shelburne
Brampton
400
TO
Saginaw
46
25
Wingham
86
4
Orangeville
401
Mississauga
Goderich
138
Listowel
86
Guelph
6
Burlington
Hamilton
75
53
Waterloo
Kitchener
Cambridge
403
St. Catherines
Flint
69
67
21
8
Stratford
36
Brantford
43
20
23
Parkhill
Woodstock
401
Buffa
Pontiac
The Pinery
21
London
35
24
3
Simcoe
59
Nanticoke
Port Huron
402
2
Sarnia
79
2
St. Thomas
Long Pt. Bay
DETROIT
94
40
Wallaceburg
Thames
58
Dunkirk
Ann Arbor
Chatham
3
LAKE ERIE
Windsor
2
401
Blenheim
Rondeau
CANADA
UNITED STATES
97
N.Y.
53
Tilbury
18
88
Leamington
166
Erie
90
17
Jamestown
Point Pelee Nat'l Pk.
Pelee I.
Toledo
75

© HAMMON

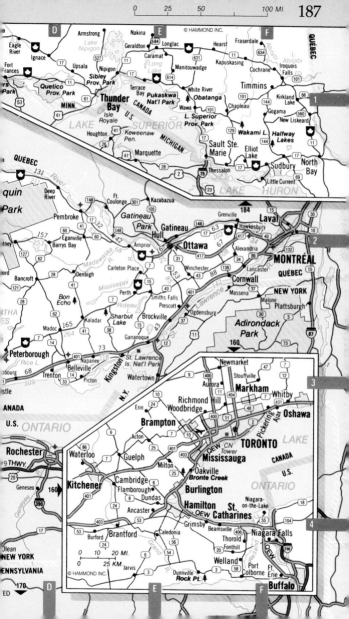

Manitoba, Saskatchewan

La Loche
955
155
Peter Pond Lake
Buffalo Narrows
155
191

Brabant Lake
905
102
Sou

Lac La Ronge Prov. Pk.
2
55

Cole Bay
965
Beauval
165
La Ronge
Lac la Ronge
904
Primrose L.
Doré L.
155
106
Meadow Lake Prov. Pk.
Medley
55
224
903
Montreal Lake
165
28
Pierceland
55
4
Green Lake
146
Nipawin Prov. Pk.
Cumber
41
26
Meadow Lake
Prince Albert Nat'l Pk.
45
Ft. Pitt Hist. Pk.
4
55
106
Tobin L.
16
17
97
Glaslyn
110
Shell Lake
Smeaton
Choiceland
Carro
Lloydminster
85
21
156
Shellbrook
6
Nipawin Wildca Wilderne
14
Maidstone
26
The Battlefords
40
Prince Albert
35
13
16
North Battleford
12
40
R
59
Melfort
3
97
Hu
Battleford
21
Blaine Lake
11
Tisdale
156
Re
40
86
16
Wakaw
20
Greenwat Prov. Pk.
Provost
13
14
139
Saskatoon
87
Humboldt
Ende
Macklin
93
Biggar
14
7
16
Viscount
174
Watson
Quill Lakes
Kelvington
49
Altario
12
Kerrobert
51
Delisle
11
Colonsay
Lanigan
16
Foam Lake
Wadena
She
Unity
21
Dundurn
Nokomis
161
Springs
Kindersley
90
Rosetown
Harris
Hanley
15
Simpson
Raymore
Alsask
7
145
Dinsmore
Kenaston
Danielson
160
15
Eatonia
Glidden
44
Elrose
42
45
Douglas
20
Ft. Qu'Appelle
116
Leader
342
Chamberlain
221
Holdfast
Melvil
Saskatchewan Landing Prov. Pk.
Lake Diefenbaker
42
2
Lumsden
10
White City
187
Qu'Appelle
107
Tuxford
Regina
48
Walsh
941
152
172
Moose Jaw
44
6
Montmartre
1
105
Gull Lake
1
Swift Current
Webb
Old Wives L.
339
39
Francis
Cypress Hills Prov. Pk.
169
37
Notukeu Cr.
2
Avonlea
334
146
Corinne
Milestone
35
33
Maple Creek
Cadillac
13
Wood
Lafleche
Assiniboia
Pangman
259
Weyburn
41
Shaunavon
13
130
34
73
18
39
501
21
Climax
Val Marie
18
Grasslands Nat'l Pk.
2
Rockglen
Big Beaver
Minton
35
Estevan
232
233
18
Killdeer
18
Opheim
511
16
Noona
CANADA
UNITED STATES
© HAMMOND INCORPORATED
242
156
24
248
5

ALBERTA
SASKATCHEWAN
Saskatchewan R.
Eagle Cr.

Alberta, British Columbia

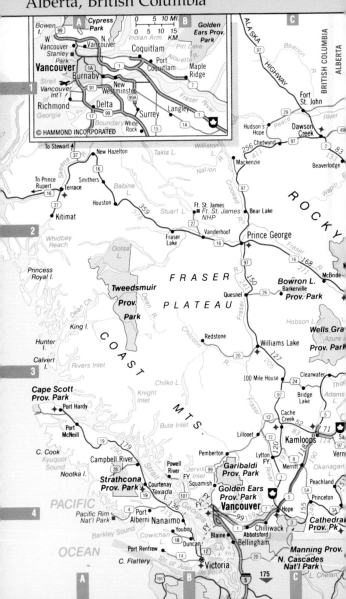

Bowen I.
W. Vancouver
Stanley Park
Vancouver
Vancouver
Burnaby
Vancouver Int'l
Richmond
Delta
Surrey
White Rock
Boundary
Strait of Georgia
© HAMMOND INCORPORATED
To Stewart
Coquitlam
Port Coquitlam
Maple Ridge
New Westminster
Langley
Indian Arm
Pitt Lake
Alouette
Fraser River
Golden Ears Prov. Park
Cypress Park
ALASKA HIGHWAY
BRITISH COLUMBIA
ALBERTA
Beatton
Fort St. John
Peace River
Dawson Creek
Hudson's Hope
Chetwynd
Mackenzie
Beaverlodge
Williston L.
Takla L.
Nation L.
Crooked R.
Wapiti R.
New Hazelton
Skeena R.
To Prince Rupert
Terrace
Smithers
Babine L.
Houston
Kitimat
Stuart L.
Ft. St. James
Ft. St. James NHP
Bear Lake
R O C K Y
Whidbey Reach
Fraser Lake
Vanderhoof
Prince George
Fraser R.
McBride
Ootsa L.
F R A S E R   P L A T E A U
Bowron L.
Barkerville **Prov. Park**
Princess Royal I.
Tweedsmuir Prov. Park
Dean Ch.
Dean R.
Quesnel
Hobson L.
Wells Gra
Azure L.
Prov. Par
King I.
Chilcotin R.
Redstone
Williams Lake
Hunter I.
Calvert I.
Rivers Inlet
Chilko L.
100 Mile House
Clearwater
Tho
Adams
Cape Scott Prov. Park
Knight Inlet
Bridge Lake
C O A S T
Port Hardy
Port McNeill
Bute Inlet
Lillooet
Cache Creek
Kamloops
Sa
C. Cook
Kyuquot Sound
Nootka I.
M T S.
Campbell River
Pemberton
Lytton
Merritt
Okanagan
Powell River
Jervis Inlet
Garibaldi Prov. Park
Peachland
Strathcona Prov. Park
Courtenay
Texada
Squamish
Golden Ears Prov. Park
Vancouver
Hope
Princeton
Cathedra Prov. Pk
PACIFIC
Pacific Rim Nat'l Park
Port Alberni
Nanaimo
Strait of Georgia
Chilliwack
Abbotsford
Barkley Sound
Youbou
Blaine
Bellingham
Manning Prov.
N. Cascades Nat'l Park
OCEAN
Cowichan L.
Duncan
Port Renfrew
C. Flattery
Str. of Juan de Fuca
Victoria
L. Chelan

© HAMMOND INC

CALGARY

Cochrane
1A
22
1
Calgary Int'l
Elbow R.
8
Olympic Park
Bragg Creek
Glenmore Res.
22X
Bow R.
22
Turner Valley
Okotoks
2A
Black Diamond

© HAMMOND INC

St. Albert
Fort Saskatchewan
15
Elk I. NP
16X
28
Spruce Grove
Sherwood Park
60
14
EDMONTON
Devon
14
21
Edmonton Int'l
39
Leduc
10 MI.
10 KM.

Cooking

Peace River
35
57
Donnelly
49
Peace River
erview
49
Lesser Slave L.
Lesser Slave L.
To Fort McMurray
Primrose L.
188
th
69
30
111
34
High Prairie
Slave Lake
234
63
Lac La Biche
Meadow Lake Prov. Park
Valleyview
2
33
380
Lac La Biche
Cold L.
Grand Centre
Smoky
Swan Hills
Athabasca
Boyle
55
Pierce-land
55
Fox Creek
43
33
44
63
36
St. Paul
28
Bonnyville
Cold Lake
200
32
Westlock
18
28
Smoky Lake
28
Two Hills
Saskatchewan
Whitecourt
Barrhead
Morinville
Gibbons
Vegreville
41
Lloydminster
40
Mayerthorpe
22
43
St. Albert
Elk I. Nat'l Pk.
155
250
Vermilion
16
225
Edson
Evansburg
16
14
Beaver hill L.
Viking
Jasper
362
Hinton
Drayton Valley
EDMONTON
Camrose
14
Wainwright
40
Nat'l
93
Breton
Wetaskiwin
Killam
14
Park
M T S
22
12
Ponoka
Battle R.
13
Provost
Macklin
31
42
Rimbey
265
266
Buffalo
41
51
Abraham
11
Lacombe
Stettler
Coronation
Consort
12
Kinbasket
Rocky Mountain House
Sylvan Lake
Red Deer
Castor
Sullivan L.
Banff
Innisfail
21
Hanna
224
Youngstown
7
Yoho NP
Nat'l
Sundre
27
361
9
Alsask
Glacier
203
Lake Louise
Park
Olds
27
Drumheller
Oyen
41
Nat'l Park
95
Cochrane
Airdrie
9
56
Golden
111
188
1
Strathmore
Bassano
184
Revelstoke
Kootenay
Canmore
Dinosaur
21
FY.
93
CALGARY
24
Brooks
Radium Hot Springs
High River
101
Bow
296
per
23
Gerrard
Vulcan
Medicine Hat
row
BR. COLUMBIA
23
36
1
Nakusp
31
Claresholm
Redcliff
Silverton
ALBERTA
135
Bow Island
Kaslo
93
Fort Macleod
Taber
Nelson
95
160
Lethbridge
Cypress Hills Prov. Park
41
6
3A
Sparwood
5
Writing-On-Stone
astlegar
Cranbrook
Fernie
25
501
22
214
Waterton Lakes Nat'l Park
Cardston
CANADA
Trail
344
Creston
93
32
MONTANA
25
195
Glacier
89
U.S.
15
WASH.
Bonners Ferry
Nat'l Park
Browning
Shelby
395
IDAHO
2
Hungry Horse Res.
89
87
Colville
43
56
56

© HAMMOND INCORPORATED

Highway Mileage Table

Highway distances (in miles) between major U.S. and Canadian cities. The table is an upper-triangular matrix; each value is the distance between the city at the left (row) and the city at the top (column).

From \ To	Bham	Boston	Buffalo	Chicago	Cincinnati	Cleveland	Dallas	Denver	Detroit	Houston	K.C.	L.A.	Mex. City	Miami	Minneapolis	Montreal	Nashville	New Orleans	New York	Okla. City	Phila.	Phoenix	Pittsburgh	Portland	St. Louis	Salt Lake	S.F.	Seattle	Wash. D.C.
Atlanta	152	1068	877	695	461	686	805	1401	810	726	814	2197	1899	665	1105	1230	256	493	855	865	766	1810	697	2736	558	1900	2523	2756	630
Birmingham		1185	902	656	476	716	653	1357	741	699	662	1916	1751	765	1016	1373	186	343	902	699	902	1470	641	2405	529	1751	2405	2716	748
Boston			449	975	840	628	1819	1991	716	1819	1470	3005	2606	1539	1385	324	1189	1543	216	1701	304	2721	598	3085	1178	2405	3163	3036	437
Buffalo				529	430	186	1357	1543	252	1459	966	2528	2245	1451	939	367	699	1470	436	1250	365	2360	217	2660	871	1958	2716	2590	359
Chicago					295	343	936	1016	282	1085	499	2095	2079	1377	412	848	475	924	821	797	762	1800	460	2112	291	1431	2189	2063	687
Cincinnati						244	943	1189	257	1040	590	2186	2079	1169	705	820	265	844	659	1063	578	1816	284	2413	338	1644	2402	2356	492
Cleveland							1187	1357	167	1357	784	2245	2188	1284	753	533	533	1096	507	1188	426	2050	125	2519	546	1772	2404	2404	351
Dallas								781	1188	242	489	1403	751	1327	956	1763	686	498	1607	212	1526	1005	1232	2082	645	1241	1806	2112	1372
Denver									1284	1029	600	1059	1403	2056	841	1845	1189	1284	1788	616	1726	858	1411	1285	843	505	1235	1377	1018
Detroit										1312	749	2420	2337	1387	685	573	555	1085	667	1068	586	1977	285	2425	543	1700	2458	2336	511
Houston											751	1553	741	1190	1242	1860	783	359	1635	458	1546	1158	1319	2282	794	1431	1955	2302	1410
Kansas City												1596	1553	1647	457	961	1242	1198	1319	350	1238	1206	838	1901	252	1116	1874	1872	1048
Los Angeles													2020	2737	1940	2920	2058	1940	2915	1353	2721	398	2533	994	1848	734	403	1145	2644
Mexico City														2177	2177	2920	2058	1744	2821	1744	2597	1327	2100	2597	1680	2280	2990	2603	2396
Miami															1744	1553	1647	2020	2737	1491	2057	1518	1230	1172	1237	2388	3414	3193	1105
Minneapolis																916	861	685	1198	457	1240	818	871	1630	546	1222	1997	1641	1097
Montreal																	1109	1324	2821	1324	1258	1253	1172	1630	1239	2603	3193	2697	600
Nashville																		1109	1320	916	861	554	861	2058	302	1670	2410	2610	686
New Orleans																			1320	1109	878	1241	1109	2144	1744	1670	2303	2610	1099
New York City																				821	1320	359	1640	321	868	2457	2459	2915	225
Oklahoma City																					530	949	1320	1109	1235	1662	868	1436	1330
Philadelphia																						1325	684	1241	388	1725	2459	2464	136
Phoenix																							1436	1099	702	868	1235	92	2274
Pittsburgh																								530	949	1325	2459	2459	230
Portland, Ore.																									2085	1273	695	92	2904
St. Louis																										559	1492	1436	807
Salt Lake City																											2113	1893	800	2111
San Francisco																												807	827	2869
Seattle																													2748

achen, Ger. 71/B3
alborg, Den. 69/B3
alst, Belg. 73/C6
arau, Switz. 80/D1
are (riv.), Switz. 80/C1
ba, Nigeria 60/C4
badan, Iran 100/F5
bakan, Russia 91/E3
bbotsford, Br. Col. 190/C4
béché, Chad 61/E3
beokuta, Nigeria 60/C4
berdeen, Md. 139/E3
berdeen, S. Dak. 165/D3
berdeen, Scot. 66/F2
berdeen, Wash. 175/B2
bidjan, Iv. Coast 60/B4
bilene, Kans. 147/B3
bilene, Texas 173/D4
bington, Pa. 171/F1
braham Lincoln Birthplace Nat'l Hist. Site, Ky. 149/D3
bruzzi (reg.), Italy 78/D3
bsaroka (range), Wyo. 177/A3
bu Dhabi (cap.), U.A.E. 95/G5
buja (cap.), Nigeria 60/C4
cadia Nat'l Pk., Maine 151/C3
capulco, Mex. 47/E5
ccra (cap.), Ghana 60/B4
chill (isl.), Ire. 67/A4
chinsk, Russia 91/E3
coma Pueblo, N. Mex. 135/D2
concagua (mt.), Arg. 58/C6
cre, Isr. 98/C2
da, Okla. 168/C3
dalia (gulf), Turkey 96/D4
dams (mt.), Wash. 175/C3
dana, Turkey 96/F4
dapazari, Turkey 96/D2
delaide, Austr. 114/C4
den, Yemen 94/F7
den (gulf) 94/F7
dige (riv.), Italy 78/C2
dirondack (mts.), N.Y. 161/F2
dmiralty (isls.), Papua N.G. 116/E6
dmiralty Island Nat'l Mon., Alaska 129/C2
drian, Mich. 152/C4
driatic (sea), Europe 64/F4
gean (sea) 65/G5
fghanistan 102/A1
frica 60-63
gadir, Morocco 60/A1
gana (cap.), Guam 116/E4
gate Fossil Beds Natl Mon., Nebr. 157/A1
gra, India 102/C2
grigento, Italy 79/D6
guascalientes, Mex. 46/D4
gulhas (cape), S. Africa 63/D8
haggar (mts.), Alg. 60/C2
hmadabad, India 102/C4
hvaz (Ahwaz), Iran 100/F5
hvenanmaa (Aland) (isls.), Fin. 69/D2
iea, Hawaii 129/A4
iken, S.C. 162/B3
insworth, Nebr. 157/A3
irdrie, Alta. 191/E3
irdrie, Scot. 66/B1
irdrie, Pa.) Eng. 67/F4
ir Force Acad., Colo. 134/B3
isne (riv.), France 74/F3
itape, Papua N.G. 112/B6
ix-en-Provence, France 75/F6
jaccio, France 75/B7

Ajanta, India 102/C2
Ajax, Ont. 187/F3
'Ajlun, Jordan 98/D3
Ajmer, India 102/C2
Akita, Japan 107/E3
Akola, India 102/C2
Akron, Ohio 166/B3
Akureyri, Ice. 64/C2
Akyab, Burma, see Sittwe
Alabama (riv.), Ala. 128/A3
Alabama (state), U.S. 128
Alajuela, C. Rica 48/C3
Alameda, Calif. 133/E1
Alamogordo, N. Mex. 135/E3
Alamosa, Colo. 134/C2
Alaska (gulf), Alaska 129/B2
Alaska (state), U.S. 129
Albacete, Spain 77/F3
Albania 65/G4
Albany (cap.), N.Y. 161/F3
Albany, Ga. 142/A4
Albany, Oreg. 169/B2
Albemarle, N.C. 162/C2
Albemarle (sound), N.C. 163/F1
Albert (lake), Africa 63/E4
Alberta (prov.), Can. 191
Albert Lea, Minn. 153/A4
Albertville, Ala. 128/B1
Albuquerque, N. Mex. 135/D2
Albury, Austr. 115/H8
Aldabra (isls.), Seychelles 63/G5
Aldan (riv.), Russia 91/O3
Alderney (isl.), Chan. Is. 67/E6
Aleppo, Syria 97/G4
Alessandria, Italy 78/B2
Ålesund, Nor. 68/A7
Aleutian (isls.), Alaska 44/C6
Alexander I (isl.), Antarc. 118
Alexander City, Ala. 128/C2
Alexandretta (gulf), Turkey 97/F4
Alexandria, Egypt 61/E1
Alexandria, La. 150/B2
Alexandria, Minn. 153/A3
Alexandria, Va. 139/D1
Algarve (reg.), Port. 76/B4
Algeciras, Spain 76/D4
Algeria 60/C2
Algiers (cap.), Alg. 60/C1
Alhambra, Calif. 179/C5
Alicante, Spain 77/F3
Alice Springs, Austr. 114/C3
Alice, Texas 173/D4
Aligarh, India 102/C2
Aliquippa, Pa. 170/A3
Alkmaar, Neth. 72/E2
Al Kuwait (cap.), Kuwait 94/F4
Allahabad, India 102/D2
Allegheny (riv.), U.S. 160/B4, 170/B2
Allegheny (riv.), Pa. 170/B2
Allen Park, Mich. 178/B4
Allenstein, Pol., see Olsztyn
Allentown, Pa. 171/F3
Allepey, India 102/C4
Aller (riv.), Ger. 70/C2
Alliance, Nebr. 157/B1
Alliance, Ohio 166/B4
Alma, Que. 185/E2
Almaty (cap.), Kazak. 102/D3
Almeria, Spain 77/E4
Alor Setar, Malaysia 111/B6
Alpena, Mich. 152/C2
Alpine, Texas 172/B2
Alps (mts.), Europe 80-81/C-F2
Alsace (prov.), France 74/G3
Altadena, Calif. 179/A2
Altai (mts.), Asia 104/B1
Alton, Ill. 144/A3
Alton, N.H. 158/C3
Altoona, Pa. 170/C4

Altun Shan (Altyn Tagh) (mts.), China 104/B2
Altus, Okla. 168/C2
Amagasaki, Japan 107/E4
Amalfi, Italy 79/E4
Amami-O-Shima (isl.), Japan 107/H3
'Amara, Iraq 100/E5
Amarillo, Texas 172/A1
Amazon (riv.), S. Amer. 57/D3
Ambato, Ecuador 56/B3
Amber (cape), Madag., see Bobaomby
Ambergris (cay), Belize 48/C1
Ambon, Indon. 113/H6
Amelia (isl.), Fla. 140/A3
American Falls, Idaho 143/B4
American Fork, Utah 174/B2
American Samoa 117/J7
Americus, Ga. 142/A3
Ames, Iowa 146/B2
Amherst, Mass. 136/C1
Amherst, N.S. 183/F3
Amiens, France 74/D3
Amman (cap.), Jordan 99/D4
Ammassalik, Greenl. 40/Q3
Amol, Iran 101/H2
Amos, Que. 184/A2
Amoy, China, see Xiamen
Amravati, India 102/C2
Amritsar, India 102/C1
Amsterdam (isl.), Fr. 35/M7
Amsterdam (cap.), Neth. 72/E3
Amsterdam, N.Y. 161/E3
Amudar'ya (riv.), Asia 92/F3
Amur (riv.), Asia 92/J3
Anaconda, Mont. 156/B1
Anacortes, Wash. 175/A2
Anadarko, Okla. 168/B2
Anadyr', Russia 91/J2
Anaheim, Calif. 179/C3
Ancaster, Ont. 187/E4
Anchorage, Alaska 129/B2
Ancona, Italy 78/D3
Andalusia (reg.), Spain 76/C4
Andalusia, Ala. 128/B3
Andaman (isls.), India 103/F3
Anderlecht, Belg. 73/D6
Anderson, Ind. 145/C2
Anderson, S.C. 162/B2
Andes (mts.), S. Amer. 56/B3, C5/58
Andijon, Uzbek. 90/D3
Andorra 77/G1
Andorra la Vella (cap.), Andorra 77/G1
Andover, Mass. 137/D1
Andrews A.F.B., Md. 139/E1
Andros (isl.), Bah. 50/B1
Androscoggin (riv.), U.S. 151/A3
Anegada (isl.), U.K. 51/F3
Angara (riv.), Russia 91/F3
Angarsk, Russia 91/F3
Angel (falls), Ven. 56/C2
Angers, France 74/C4
Angkor Wat (ruins), Camb. 111/D4
Anglesey (isl.), Wales 67/D4
Angola 62-63/D6
Angoulême, France 75/C5
Anguilla (isl.) 51/F3
Anhui (Anhwei) (prov.), China 105/E2
Aniakchak Nat'l Mon., Alaska 129/A2
Anjou, Que. 184/B1
Ankara (cap.), Turkey 96/E3
Ankeny, Iowa 146/B2
Ann (cape), Mass. 137/E1
Annaba, Alg. 60/C1

Index

An Najaf, Iraq 100/D4
Annandale, Va. 139/D1
Annapolis (cap.), Md. 139/C2
Annapolis Royal, N.S. 182/C3
Ann Arbor, Mich. 152/C4
An Nasiriya, Iraq 100/D5
Annecy, France 75/G5
Anniston, Ala. 128/C3
Annobón (isl.), Equat. Guinea 62/C5
Anshan, China 105/F1
Antakya, Turkey 97/G4
Antalya, Turkey 96/D4
Antananarivo (cap.), Madag. 63/G6
Antarctica 118
Antibes, France 75/G6
Anticosti (isl.), Que. 43/K6
Antigonish, N.S. 183/E3
Antigua (isl.), 55/V
Antigua and Barbuda 51/G3
Antigua, Guat. 48/B2
Antilles (isls.), W. Indies 50-51/B-F4
Antofagasta, Chile 58/B5
Antsiranana, Madag. 63/G6
Antwerp, Belg. 73/D5
Anuradhapura, Sri Lanka 102/D4
Anyang, China 105/E2
Anzio, Italy 79/D4
Aomori, Japan 107/F2
Aosta, Italy 78/A2
Apache (mts.), Texas 172/B2
Apalachee (bay), Fla. 136/B2
Apalachicola, Fla. 140/B1
Apataki (isl.), Fr. Poly. 117/M7
Apeldoorn, Neth. 72/G3
Apennines (mts.), Italy 78-79/C-E3-4
Apia (cap.), Samoa 117/J7
Apo (vol.), Phil. 109/E7
Appalachian (mts.), U.S. 45/K-L3-4 .,
Appenzell, Switz. 81/E1
Appleton, Wis. 176/C3
Appomattox Court House Nat'l Hist. Pk., Va. 139/D4
Apulia (reg.), Italy 79/F4
Apurímac (riv.), Peru 56/B4
Aqaba (gulf), Asia 94/C4
'Aqaba, Jordan 99/D6
Aqtaū, Kazak. 90/C3
Aqtöbe, Kazak. 90/C3
Araba, Wadi (valley), Asia 99/D5
Arabian (des.), Egypt 94/C4
Arabian (sea), Asia 93/F5
Aracaju, Braz. 57/F4
Arad, Rom. 84/C2
Arafura (sea) 116/D6
Aragón (reg.), Spain 77/F2
Araguaia (riv.), Braz. 57/E3
Arak, Iran 100/F3
Arakan Yoma (mts.), Burma 110/A3
Araks (riv.), Asia 89/G7
Aral (sea) 90/C3
Aran (isls.), Ire. 67/A4
Aranjuez, Spain 77/E3
Aransas Pass, Texas 173/E3
Ararat (mt.), Turkey 97/L3
Arauca (riv.), S. Amer. 56/C2
Arbutus, Md. 139/E1
Arcadia, Calif. 179/B2
Archangel (Arkhangel'sk), Russia 88/F2
Arches Nat'l Pk., Utah 174/C3
Arco, Idaho 143/B3
Arctic Ocean 33
Ardabil, Iran 100/F1
Ardmore, Okla. 168/C3
Ardmore, Pa. 171/E1

Arecibo, P. Rico 54/B1
Arequipa, Peru 56/B4
Argenteuil, France 74/A1
Argentina, Newf. 183/F2
Argentina 58-59/B-D5-8
Árgos, Greece 85/C4
Århus, Den. 69/B3
Arima, Trin. & Tob. 55/T
Aripuanã (riv.), Braz. 56/C3
Arizona (state), U.S. 130
Arkadelphia, Ark. 131/C2
Arkansas (riv.), U.S. 44/F3
Arkansas (state), U.S. 131
Arkansas City, Kans. 147/D3
Arles, France 75/F6
Arlington Hts., Ill. 178/A1
Arlington, Texas 172/B4
Arlington, Va. 139/D1
Arlon, Belg. 73/G8
Armavir, Russia 89/F6
Armenia 89/F6
Armenia, Col. 56/B2
Arnhem, Neth. 72/G4
Arno (riv.), Italy 78/C3
Arnprior, Ontario 187/E2
Arosa, Switz. 81/E2
Arran (isl.), Scot. 66/D3
Arras, France 74/E2
Artesia, N. Mex. 135/E3
Aru (isls.), Indon. 113/J7
Aruba (isl.) 50/D4, 55/O
Arusha, Tanz. 63/F5
Arvada, Colo. 178/A4
Arzamas, Russia 89/F3
Asahikawa, Japan 107/F2
Asansol, India 103/D2
Asbury Park, N.J. 159/C2
Ascension (isl.), St. Helena 62/A5
Ashanti (reg.), Ghana 60/B4
Ashdod, Isr. 99/B4
Asheboro, N.C. 163/D2
Asheville, N.C. 162/B2
Ashgabat (cap.), Turkmen. 90/C4
Ashland, Ky. 149/F2
Ashland, Oreg. 169/C2
Ashland, Wis. 176/B2
Ashqelon, Isr. 99/B4
Ashtabula, Ohio 166/F4
Asia 92-93
Asmara (cap.), Eritrea 61/F3
Aspen, Colo. 134/B2
Assiniboine (riv.), Man. 189/D4
Assisi, Italy 78/D3
Astana, Kazak. 90/D3
Astoria, Oreg. 169/A2
Astrakhan', Russia 89/G5
Asturias (reg.), Spain 76/D1
Asunción (cap.), Par. 59/D5
Aswān, Egypt 61/F2
Asyūt, Egypt 61/F2
Atacama (des.), Chile 58/B5
Atar, Maur. 60/A2
Atbara, Sudan 61/F3
Atchafalaya (riv.), La. 150/B2
Atchison, Kans. 147/A4
Athabasca (lake), Can. 42/E4
Athabasca (riv.), Alta. 42/E4
Athens, Ala. 128/C3
Athens, Ga. 142/C2
Athens (cap.), Greece 85/C4
Athens, Ohio 167/F3
Athlone, Ire. 67/C4
Áthos (mt.), Greece 85/D3
Atitlán (lake), Guat. 48/B2
Atka (isl.), Alaska 130/M4
Atlanta (cap.), Ga. 142/B1
Atlantic Beach, Fla. 140/A3
Atlantic City, N.J. 159/B4
Atlantic Ocean, see North Atlantic, South Atlantic
Atlas (mts.), Africa 60/B1

Atrak (riv.), Iran 101/J2
Attleboro, Mass. 137/D2
Atyraū, Kazak. 90/C3
Au Sable Forks, N.Y. 161/F1
Auburn, Ala. 128/C2
Auburn, Maine 151/A4
Auburn, N.Y. 161/D3
Auburn, Wash. 175/C1
Auckland, N.Z. 115/F3
Augsburg, Ger. 71/D4
Augusta (cap.), Maine 151/B3
Augusta, Ga. 142/C2
Aurangabad, India 102/C3
Aurora, Colo. 178/B4
Aurora, Ill. 178/A2
Aurora, Ont. 187/F3
Auschwitz, Pol., see Oświęcim
Austin (cap.), Texas 173/D2
Austin, Minn. 153/D4
Austral (isls.), Fr. Poly. 117/M8
Australia 114-115
Australian Alps (mts.), Austr. 115/D4
Australian Cap. Terr., Austr. 115/D4
Austria 82/BC3
Auvergne (mts.), France 75/E5
Avignon, France 75/F6
Ávila, Spain 76/D2
Avondale, Ariz. 130/A1
Ayacucho, Peru 56/B4
Ayr, Scot. 66/D3
Azerbaijan 89/G6
Azores (isls.), Port. 35/J4
Azov (sea), Eur. 89/E5
Aztec Ruins Nat'l Mon., N. Mex 134/C2
Azuero (pen.), Panama 49/D4
Azusa, Calif. 179/A3

B

Ba'albek, Leb. 97/G5
Bab el Mandeb (str.) 94/E7
Babol, Iran 101/H2
Babruysk, Belarus 89/C4
Babuyan (isls.), Phil. 108/C1
Babylon (ruins), Iraq 100/D4
Bacău, Rom. 84/D2
Bacolod, Phil. 109/D5
Badajos, Spain 76/C3
Badalona, Spain 77/H2
Baden, Switz. 81/D1
Baden-Baden, Ger. 71/C4
Baden-Württemberg (state), Ge 71/C4
Badgastein, Austria 82/B3
Bad Kissingen, Ger. 71/D3
Badlands Nat'l Pk., S. Dak. 165/E1
Bad Nauheim, Ger. 71/C3
Baffin (isl.), N.W.T. 43/J3
Baghdad (cap.), Iraq 101/D4
Baguio, Phil. 108/C2
Bahamas 50/C1
Bahawalpur, Pak. 102/C2
Bahia, Braz., see Salvador
Bahía Blanca, Arg. 58/C6
Bahrain 95/G4
Baia Mare, Rom. 84/C2
Baie Comeau, Que. 185/D1
Bainbridge (isl.), Wash. 175/B1
Bairiki (cap.), Kiribati 117/H5
Baker (isl.), U.S. 117/J5
Baker, Oreg. 169/B4
Bakersfield, Calif. 133/E3
Bakhtaran, Iran 100/E3
Baku (cap.), Azer. 89/H6
Balashov, Russia 89/F4
Balaton (lake), Hung. 83/D3

Balcones Escarpment (plat.), Texas 173/D3
Baldwin, Pa. 170/A1
Baldwin Park, Calif. 179/B2
Balearic (isls.), Spain 77/G3
Bali (isl.), Indon. 112/E7
Balikesir, Turkey 96/C3
Balikpapan, Indon. 112/F6
Balkan (mts.), Bulg. 84/D3
Balkhash (lake), Kazakh. 90/D3
Ballarat, Austri. 115/D4
Balleny (isls.), Antarc. 118
Ballymena, N. Ire. 66/C3
Balmorhea, Texas 172/B2
Balqash, Kazakh. 90/D3
Bălți, Moldova 89/C5
Baltic (sea), Europe 64/F3
Baltimore, Md. 139/F1
Bamako (cap.), Mali 60/B3
Bambari, Cent. Afr. Rep. 61/E4
Bamberg, Ger. 71/D4
Banaba (isl.), Kiribati 116/G7
Banda, India, see Machilipatnam
Banda (sea), Indon. 113/H6
Bandar, India, see Machilipatnam
Bandar 'Abbas, Iran 101/K7
Bandar-e Anzali, Iran 100/F2
Bandar Seri Begawan, (cap.), Brunei 112/E4
Bandelier Nat'l Mon., N. Mex. 135/D2
Bandundu, Zaire 63/D5
Bandung, Indon. 113/H2
Banff Nat'l Pk., Alta. 191/D3
Bangalore, India 102/C3
Bangkok (cap.), Thai. 111/C4
Bangladesh 103/G2
Bangor, Maine 151/B3
Bangor, Wales 67/D4
Bangui (cap.), Cent. Afr. Rep. 60/D4
Banja Luka, Bos. & Herc. 84/B2
Banjarmasin, Indon. 112/E6
Banjul (cap.), Gambia 60/A3
Banks (isl.), N.W.T. 42/D1
Ban Me Thuot, Viet. 111/E4
Banngka (isl.), Indon. 112/D6
Baoding, China 105/E2
Baotou, China 104/D1
Baraboo, Wis. 176/B4
Barahona, Dom. Rep. 52/R7
Baranavichy, Belarus 89/B4
Barataria (bay), La. 150/C3
Barbados 51/G4, 55/S
Barberton, Ohio 166/B3
Barbuda (isl.), Ant. & Barb. 51/G3
Barcelona, Spain 77/H2
Barcelona, Ven. 56/C2
Bardstown, Ky. 149/D2
Bareilly, India 102/D2
Barents (sea), Europe 90/BC2
Bari, Italy 79/F4
Barisol, Bang. 103/G3
Barkley (lake), U.S. 148/B3
Barnaul, Russia 90/E3
Barnegat Light, N.J. 159/C3
Barnet, Eng. 67/B5
Barnstable, Mass. 137/F3
Baroda, India 102/C2
Barquisimeto, Ven. 56/C1
Barranquilla, Col. 56/B1
Barre, Vt. 158/B2
Barrie, Ont. 186/C3
Barrow, Alaska 129/A1
Barrow (pt.), Alaska 129/B1
Barrow (riv.), Ire. 67/C4
Barrow-in-Furness, Eng. 67/E3
Barstow, Calif. 133/C3
Bartlesville, Okla. 168/A4
Barysaw, Belarus 89/C4
Basel, Switz. 80/C1

Basilan (isl.), Phil. 109/D7
Basilicata (reg.), Italy 79/F4
Basra, Iraq 100/F3
Bass (str.), Austri. 115/D5
Bassas da India, Reunion 63/F7
Bassein, Burma 110/A3
Basse-Terre (cap.), Guad. 51/F4, 55/H
Basseterre (cap.), St. Kitts & Nevis 51/F3, 55/W
Bastogne, Belg. 73/G7
Bastrop, La. 150/A2
Bata, Equat. Guinea 60/C4
Bataan (pen.), Phil. 108/C3
Batangas, Phil. 108/C4
Batavia, N.Y. 160/B3
Batdambang, Camb. 111/C4
Batsto, N.J. 159/B3
Battambang, Camb. 111/C4
Battle (riv.), Can. 191/F3
Battle Creek, Mich. 152/B4
Battleford, Sask. 188/A3
Battle Mountain, Nev. 132/B3
Bat'umi, Georgia 89/F6
Bat Yam, Isr. 99/B3
Bavaria (state), Ger. 71/D4
Bayamo, Cuba 53/J4
Bayamón, P. Rico 54/C1
Bay City, Mich. 152/C3
Bay City Texas 173/E3
Bayeux, France 74/C3
Baykal (lake), Russia 91/F3
Bayonne, France 75/C6
Bayonne, N.J. 180/B3
Bayreuth, Ger. 71/D4
Bay Roberts, Newf. 183/F1
Bay St. Louis, Miss. 154/B4
Baytown, Texas 173/F4
Beach Haven, N.J. 159/C3
Bear (isl.), Nor. 33
Beardstown, Ill. 144/A2
Beatrice, Nebr. 157/C4
Beaufort (sea), N. Amer. 40/CD2
Beaufort, S.C. 162/C4
Beaumont, Texas 173/F3
Beaver (isl.), Mich. 152/B2
Beaver Dam, Wis. 176/B4
Beaver Falls, Pa. 170/A3
Beaver Lodge, Alta. 190/C2
Beaverton, Oreg. 180/A4
Béchar, Alg. 60/B1
Beckley, W. Va. 138/B3
Bedford, Eng. 67/F4
Bedford, Ind. 145/B3
Bedford, Pa. 170/C4
Beersheba, Isr. 99/B5
Beeville, Texas 173/E4
Beihai, China 104/D3
Beijing (cap.), China 105/E1
Beira, Moz. 63/F6
Beirut (cap.), Leb. 94/C3
Bejaïa, Alg. 60/C1
Békéscsaba, Hung. 83/F3
Belarus 89/C4
Belau, see Palau
Belém, Braz. 57/E3
Belfast, Maine 151/B3
Belfast (cap.), N. Ire. 67/D3
Belgaum, India 102/C3
Belgium 73
Belgorod, Russia 89/E4
Belgrade (cap.), Yugo. 84/C2
Belize 48/B1
Belize City, Belize 48/B1
Bellary, India 102/C3

Belle Fourche, S. Dak. 165/D1
Belle Glade, Fla. 141/D4
Belleville, Ill. 144/B3
Belleville, Ont. 187/D3
Bellevue, Nebr. 157/B4
Bellevue, Wash. 175/B1
Bellflower, Calif. 179/C2
Bellingham, Wash. 175/A2
Bellingshausen (sea), Antarc. 118
Bellinzona, Switz. 81/D2
Bellows Falls, Vt. 158/B4
Belmopan (cap.), Belize 48/B1
Belogorsk, Russia 91/G3
Belo Horizonte, Braz. 57/E4
Beloit, Wis. 176/C4
Belvidere, Ill. 144/B1
Bemidji, Minn. 153/B2
Ben Nevis (mt.), Scot. 66/D2
Benares, see Varanasi
Bend, Oreg. 169/B2
Bendigo, Austri. 115/D4
Bene Beraq, Isr. 99/B3
Bengal (bay), Asia 93/G5
Bengbu, China 105/E2
Benghazi, Libya 61/D1
Benguela, Angola 62/D6
Beni (riv.), Bol. 56/C4
Beni Suef, Egypt 61/F2
Benin 60/C4
Benin City, Nigeria 60/C4
Bennington, Vt. 158/A4
Benton, Ark. 131/B2
Benton Harbor, Mich. 152/A4
Benue (riv.), Africa 60/C4
Benxi, China 105/F1
Beppu, Japan 106/C4
Berbera, Somalia 61/G3
Berberati, Cent. Afr. Rep. 60/D4
Berchtesgaden, Ger. 71/E5
Berea, Ky. 149/E2
Berea, Ohio 167/F3
Berezniki, Russia 88/J3
Bergamo, Italy 78/B2
Bergen, Nor. 68/A2
Bergisch Gladbach, Ger. 71/B3
Bering (sea) 34/CD3
Bering (str.) 34/D2
Berkeley, Calif. 133/E1
Berlin (cap.), Ger. 70/E2
Berlin, N.H. 158/C2
Bermejo (riv.), Arg. 58/C5
Bermuda 41/M6, H3/51
Bern (cap.), Switz. 80/C2
Bernardsville, N.J. 159/B2
Berwick, Pa. 171/E3
Berwyn, Ill. 178/B2
Besançon, France 74/G4
Beskids (mts.), Europe 87/E4
Bessemer, Ala. 128/B2
Bethany, Okla. 168/B3
Bethel, Alaska 129/A2
Bethel, Conn. 136/A3
Bethesda, Md. 139/D1
Bethlehem, Pa. 171/F3
Bethlehem, West Bank 99/C4
Bettendorf, Iowa 146/B4
Beverly, Mass. 137/E1
Beverly Hills, Calif. 179/B2
Beyoğlu, Turkey 96/D6
Béziers, France 75/E6
Bhagalpur, India 102/F2
Bhatpara, India 103/D2
Bhavnagar, India 102/C2
Bhopal, India 102/C2
Bhutan 103/D2
Biak (isl.), Indon. 113/K6
Bialystok, Pol. 87/F2
Biarritz, France 75/C6
Biddeford, Maine 151/A4
Biel, Switz. 80/C1
Bielefeld, Ger. 70/C2

Index

Bielsko-Biala, Poland 86/D4
Bien Hoa, Viet. 111/D5
Big Bend Nat'l Pk., Texas 172/B3
Biggar, Sask. 188/B3
Bighorn (mts.), Wyo. 177/A2
Bighorn (riv.), U.S. 177/A3
Big Spring, Texas 172/C2
Big Sur, Calif. 133/D1
Bikaner, India 102/C2
Bikini (atoll), Marshall Is. 116/G4
Bilbao, Spain 77/E1
Billings, Mont. 156/C3
Billiton (is.), Indon. 112/D6
Biloxi, Miss. 154/C4
Biminis, The (isls.), Bah. 50/B1
Binghamton, N.Y. 161/D4
Bioko (isl.), Equat. Guin. 60/C4
Birkenhead, Eng. 67/C4
Birmingham, Ala. 128/B2
Birmingham, Eng. 67/E4
Birobidzhan, Russia 91/G3
Bisbee, Ariz. 130/C4
Biscay (bay), Europe 64/D4
Biscayne Nat'l Pk., Fla. 141/F4
Bishkek (cap.), Kyrgyz. 90/D3
Bismarck (cap.), N. Dak. 164/C2
Bismarck (arch.), Papua N.G. 116/E6
Bissau (cap.), Guinea-Bissau 60/A3
Bitola, Macedonia 85/C3
Bitterroot (range), U.S. 143/B2
Biysk, Russia 90/F2
Bizerte, Tun. 60/C1
Black (for.), Ger. 71/B4
Black (sea) 65/H4
Blackburn, Eng. 66/G4
Black Canyon of the Gunnison Nat'l Mon., Colo. 134/B2
Blackfoot, Idaho 143/C4
Black Hills (mts.), U.S. 165/C1
Blackpool, Eng. 66/F1
Blacksburg, Va. 138/C4
Blackwater (riv.), Ire. 67/B4
Blagoveshchensk, Russia 91/G3
Blainville, Que. 184/A1
Blanc (cape), Africa 60/A2
Blanc (mt.), Europe 80/B3
Blanco (cape), Oreg. 169/A4
Blanding, Utah 174/C4
Blantyre, Malawi 63/F6
Blida, Alg. 60/D1
Block (isl.), R.I. 137/D3
Bloemfontein, S. Africa 63/E7
Bloomfield, N.J. 180/A2
Bloomfield Hills, Mich. 178/B3
Bloomington, Ill. 144/B2
Bloomington, Ind. 145/B3
Bloomington, Minn. 153/B1
Bloomsburg, Pa. 171/D3
Blue (mts.), Jam. 53/W9
Blue (mts.), Oreg. 169/A3
Bluefield, W. Va. 138/B4
Blue Nile (riv.), Africa 61/F3
Blue Ridge (mts.), U.S. 162/A2, 138/C4
Blue Springs, Mo. 155/C1
Blytheville, Ark. 131/A4
Boa Vista, Braz. 56/C2
Bobaomby (cape), Madag. 63/G6
Bobo-Dioulasso, Burkina Faso 60/B3
Boca Raton, Fla. 141/F4
Bochum, Ger. 70/B2
Bodélé (depr.), Chad 61/D3
Bodensee (lake), see Constance
Boerne, Texas 173/D3
Bogalusa, La. 150/B3
Bogor, Indon. 113/H2
Bogotá (cap.), Col. 56/B2

Bohemian (for.) 82/B2
Bohol (isl.), Phil. 109/E6
Bois Blanc (isl.), Mich. 152/B2
Bolton, Eng. 66/G1
Bolivia 56/C4
Bologna, Italy 78/C1
Bolton, Eng. 66/G1
Bolzano, Italy 78/C1
Boma, D.R. Congo 62/D5
Bombay, India 102/C3
Bomu (riv.), Africa 61/E4
Bon (cape), Tun. 60/D1
Bonaire (isl.), Neth. Ant. 51/E4, 55/M
Bonin (isls.), Japan 107/G2
Bonita Springs, Fla. 141/E3
Bonn, Ger. 71/B3
Bonneville (dam), U.S. 169/A2
Bonnyville, Alta. 191/F2
Bontoc, Phil. 108/C2
Boone, Iowa 146/B2
Boone, N.C. 162/B1
Boothbay Harbor, Maine 151/B4
Bootle, Eng. 66/F2
Bora Bora (isl.), Fr. Poly. 117/L7
Borås, Swed. 69/C3
Bordeaux, France 75/C5
Borden, P.E.I. 183/D2
Bordentown, N.J. 159/B2
Borger, Texas 172/A1
Borneo (isl.), Asia 112/E5
Bornholm (isl.), Den. 69/C3
Borujerd, Iran 100/F4
Bosnia & Herzegovina 84/B2
Bosporus (str.), Turkey 96/C2
Bossier City, La. 150/A1
Boston, Eng. 67/F4
Boston (cap.), Mass. 137/F4
Bothnia (gulf), Europe 65/G2
Botswana 63/E7
Bottineau, N. Dak. 164/A2
Bouaké, Iv. Coast 60/B4
Bouar, Cent. Afr. Rep. 60/D4
Boucherville, Que. 184/B1
Bougainville (isl.), Papua N.G. 116/F6
Boulder, Colo. 178/A3
Boulder City, Nev. 133/D4
Boulogne, France 74/D2
Bountiful, Utah 174/B2
Bourges, France 74/E4
Bournemouth, Eng. 67/F3
Bouvet (isl.), Nor. 35/K8
Bow (riv.), Alta. 191/E3
Branco (riv.), Braz. 56/C2
Brandenburg (state), Ger. 70/E2
Brandon, Man. 189/D4
Brantford, Ont. 187/E4
Bras d'Or (lake), N.S. 183/F3
Brasília (cap.), Braz. 57/E4
Braşov, Rom. 84/D2
Bratislava (cap.), Slovakia 83/D2
Bratsk, Russia 91/F3
Brattleboro, Vt. 158/A4
Bray, Ire. 67/C4
Brazil 56-57,59
Brazos (riv.), Texas 173/E2

Brazzaville (cap.), Congo 62/D5
Breda, Neth. 72/E4
Bregenz, Austria 82/A3
Bremen, Ger. 70/C2
Bremerhaven, Ger. 70/C2
Bremerton, Wash. 175/C1
Brenner (pass), Europe 82/A3
Brescia, Italy 78/C2
Breslau, Pol., see Wroclaw
Brest, France 74/A3
Brest, Belarus 89/B4
Breton (sound), La. 150/C3
Brewer, Maine 151/B3
Bridgeport, Conn. 136/A3
Bridgeport, Nebr. 157/B1
Bridgeton, N.J. 159/A4
Bridgetown (cap.), Barbados 51/G4, 55/S
Bridgewater, N.S. 182/C4
Brigantine, N.J. 159/C4
Brigham City, Utah 174/B2
Brighton, Colo. 178/B3
Brighton, Eng. 67/F5
Brindisi, Italy 79/G4
Brisbane, Austr. 115/E3
Bristol (bay), Alaska 129/A2
Bristol, Conn. 136/B3
Bristol, Eng. 67/E5
Bristol, R.I. 137/D3
Bristol, Tenn. 149/F3
Bristol (chan.), U.K. 67/D5
Bristol, Va. 138/B4
British Columbia (prov.), Can. 19
British Indian Ocean Terr. 93/F6
Brittany (prov.), France 74/B3
Brno, Czech Rep. 82/D2
Brockton, Mass. 137/E2
Brockville, Ont. 187/E3
Broken Bow, Nebr. 157/B3
Broken Hill, Austr. 115/D4
Bromley, Eng. 67/B6
Bronx (borough), N.Y. 180/B2
Brookfield, Wis. 176/A1
Brookhaven, Miss. 154/B3
Brookings, Oreg. 169/C1
Brookings, S. Dak. 165/E4
Brookline, Mass. 137/F4
Brooklyn (borough), N.Y. 180/B3
Brooks (range), Alaska 129/A1
Brooks, Alta. 191/F3
Broomfield, Colo. 178/A3
Brossard, Que. 184/B1
Brownfield, Texas 172/C1
Brownsville, Tenn. 148/A4
Brownsville, Texas 173/E4
Brownwood, Texas 173/D2
Bruges, Belg. 73/B5
Brunei 112/E5
Brunswick, Ga. 142/C4
Brunswick (Braunschweig), Ger. 70/D2
Brunswick, Maine 151/A4
Brunswick, Ohio 166/B3
Brussels (cap.), Belg. 73/E6
Bryan, Texas 173/E2
Bryansk, Russia 89/D4
Bryce Canyon Nat'l Pk., Utah 174/B4
Bryn Mawr, Pa. 171/D1
Bubiyan (isl.), Kuwait 100/F6
Bucaramanga, Col. 56/B2
Bucharest (cap.), Rom. 84/D2
Bucksport, Maine 151/B3
Budapest (cap.), Hung. 83/E3
Buena Park, Calif. 179/C2
Buenaventura, Col. 56/B2
Buenos Aires (cap.), Arg. 58/C6
Buenos Aires (lake), S. Amer. 58/B7
Buffalo, N.Y. 160/B3

Buffalo, Wyo. 177/A2
Bug (riv.), Europe 87/F2
Bujumbura (cap.), Burundi 63/F5
Bukavu, D.R. Congo 63/E5
Bukhoro, Uzbek. 90/D4
Bulawayo, Zim. 63/E7
Bulgaria 84/D3
Bull Shoals (lake), U.S. 131/A2
Bunbury, Austr. 114/A4
Bundaberg, Austr. 115/E3
Buraida, S. Arabia 94/E4
Burbank, Calif. 179/A2
Burdwan, India 102/D2
Burgas, Bulg. 83/D3
Burgos, Spain 76/E1
Burkina Faso 60/B3
Burley, Idaho 143/B4
Burlingame, Calif. 133/F1
Burlington, Iowa 146/C4
Burlington, N.C. 163/D1
Burlington, Vt. 158/A2
Burma 110/A2
Burnaby, Br. Col. 190/A1
Burnley, Eng. 66/G1
Burns, Oreg. 169/B3
Bursa, Turkey 96/C2
Buru (isl.), Indon. 113/H6
Burundi 63/F5
Bushehr (Bushire), Iran 100/G6
Busuanga (isl.), Phil. 108/B4
Butler, Pa. 170/A3
Butte, Mont. 156/C1
Butuan, Phil. 109/E6
Buzău, Rom. 84/D2
Buzzards (bay), Mass. 137/E3
Bydgoszcz, Pol. 86/C2
Bytom, Pol. 86/A3

C

Cabanatuan, Phil. 108/C3
Cabimas, Ven. 56/B1
Cabinda (reg.), Angola 62/D5
Cabot (str.), Can. 183/E2
Cache Creek, Br. Col. 190/C3
Caddo (lake), U.S. 150/A1
Cadiz, Phil. 109/D5
Cádiz, Spain 76/C4
Caen, France 74/C2
Caernarvon, Wales 67/D4
Cagayan de Oro, Phil. 109/E6
Cagliari, Italy 79/B5
Caguas, P. Rico 54/C1
Caicos (isls.), Turks & Caicos Is.
  50/D2
Cairns, Austr. 115/D2
Cairo (cap.), Egypt 61/F1
Cairo, Ill. 144/B4
Cajamarca, Peru 56/B3
Calabar, Nigeria 60/C4
Calabria (reg.), Italy 79/F5
Calais, France 74/D2
Calais, Maine 151/C3
Calcasieu (lake), La. 150/C1
Calcutta, India 103/D2
Caldwell, Idaho 143/A4
Calgary, Alta. 191/E1
Cali, Col. 56/B2
Calicut, India, see Kozhikode
California (gulf), Mex. 46/B-C2-3
California (state), U.S. 132-133
Callao, Peru 56/B4
Calumet City, Ill. 178/B3
Camagüey, Cuba 50/B2, 53/G3
Cambodia 111/D4
Cambridge, Eng. 66/F4
Cambridge, Md. 139/F3

Cambridge, Mass. 137/F4
Cambridge, Ont. 187/E4
Camden, Ark. 131/C2
Camden, Maine 151/B3
Camden, N.J. 159/A3
Camden, S.C. 162/C3
Cameroon 60/D4
Cameroon (mt.), Cam. 60/C4
Campania (reg.), Italy 79/E4
Campbell River, Br. Col. 190/A4
Campbellsville, Ky. 149/D3
Campbellton, N. Br. 182/B1
Campeche (bay), Mex. 47/G4
Campina Grande, Braz. 57/F3
Campinas, Braz. 59/E5
Campo Grande, Braz. 57/D4
Campos, Braz. 59/E5
Cam Ranh (bay), Viet. 111/E5
Camrose, Alta. 191/E2
Canada 42-43
Canadian (riv.), U.S. 168/B3
Canandaigua, N.Y. 160/C3
Canary (isls.), Spain 76/B4, 35/J4
Canaveral (cape), Fla. 140/C4
Canberra (cap.), Austr. 115/E4
Cancún (isl.), Mex. 47/H4
Canmore, Alta. 191/D3
Cannanore (isls.), India 102/C3
Cannes, France 75/G6
Canon City, Colo. 134/B3
Canso, N.S. 183/F3
Cantabrian (mts.), Spain 76/CD1
Canterbury, Eng. 67/G5
Can Tho, Viet. 111/D5
Canton (Guangzhou), China
  105/E3
Canton, Mass. 154/B3
Canton, Ohio 166/B4
Canyon de Chelly Nat'l Mon.,
  Ariz. 130/C2
Canyonlands Nat'l Pk., Utah
  174/C4
Cap-de-la-Madeleine, Que.
  185/D1
Cape (prov.), S. Africa 63/D8
Cape Breton (isl.), N.S. 183/E2
Cape Breton Highlands Nat'l Pk.,
  N.S. 183/F1
Cape Charles, Va. 139/F4
Cape Coast, Ghana 60/B4
Cape Coral, Fla. 141/D3
Cape Fear (riv.), N.C. 163/D2
Cape Girardeau, Mo. 155/C4
Cape Krusenstern Nat'l Mon.,
  Alaska 129/A1
Cape May, N.J. 159/B4
Cape Town (cap.), S. Africa
  63/D8
Cape Verde 35/J5
Cape York (pen.), Austr. 115/D2
Cap-Haïtien, Haiti 52/P6
Capitol Reef Nat'l Pk., Utah
  174/B4
Capri (isl.), Italy 79/E4
Caprivi Strip (reg.), Namibia
  63/E6
Capulin Vol. Nat'l Mon., N. Mex.
  134/C3
Caquetá (riv.), Col. 56/B2
Caracas (cap.), Ven. 56/C1
Caratasca (lag.), Hond. 49/D2
Carbondale, Ill. 144/B4
Carbondale, Pa. 171/F2
Carcassonne, France 75/D6
Cardiff (cap.), Wales 67/E5
Cardigan (bay), Wales 67/D4
Caribbean (sea) 50-51
Caribou, Maine 151/C1
Carleton Place, Ont. 187/E2

Carlisle, Eng. 66/E3
Carlisle, Pa. 171/D4
Carlow, Ire. 67/C4
Carlsbad, N. Mex. 135/F3
Carlsbad Caverns Nat'l Pk., N.
  Mex. 135/F3
Carman, Man. 189/E4
Carmel, Calif. 133/D1
Carmel (mt.), Isr. 98/C2
Carmichael, Calif. 132/C2
Caroline (isls.), Micronesia
  116/EF5
Caroni (riv.), Ven. 56/C2
Carpentaria (gulf), Austr. 114/C2
Carrara, Italy 78/C2
Carrington, N. Dak. 164/B3
Carson, Calif. 179/C2
Carrollton, Texas 172/B4
Carson (sink), Nev. 132/B3
Carson City (cap.), Nev. 132/C2
Cartagena, Col. 56/B1
Cartagena, Spain 77/F4
Carúpano, Ven. 56/C1
Carver Nat'l Mon., Mo. 155/C2
Casablanca, Mor. 60/B1
Casa Grande, Ariz. 130/B4
Cascade (range), U.S. 44/B2
Casper, Wyo. 177/B2
Caspian (sea) 92/E3
Cassino, Italy 79/D4
Castellón de la Plana, Spain
  77/G3
Castile (reg.), Spain 76-77/D-E2
Castillo de San Marcos Nat'l
  Mon., Fla. 140/A3
Castlegar, Br. Col. 191/D4
Castries (cap.), St. Lucia 51/G4,
  55/L
Castro Valley, Calif. 133/E1
Catalonia (reg.), Spain 77/G2
Catamarca, Chile 58/C5
Catanduanes (isl.), Phil. 108/E4
Catania, Italy 79/E6
Cataño, P. Rico 54/C1
Catanzaro, Italy 79/F5
Catonsville, Md. 139/F3
Catskill (mts.), N.Y. 161/E4
Cauca (riv.), Col. 56/B2
Caucasus (mts.) 90/C3
Cavite, Phil. 108/C3
Cawnpore, India, see Kanpur
Caxias do Sul, Braz. 59/D5
Cayce, S.C. 162/C3
Cayenne (cap.), Fr. Guiana 57/D2
Cayey, P. Rico 54/C1
Cayman Islands 50/B3
Cayuga (lake), N.Y. 160/C3
Cebu, Phil. 109/E5
Cebu (isl.), Phil. 109/D5
Cedar Breaks Nat'l Mon., Utah
  174/A4
Cedar City, Utah 174/A4
Cedar Falls, Iowa 146/B3
Cedar Key, Fla. 140/B2
Cedar Rapids, Iowa 146/B3
Celebes, Asia 113/G5
Celebes (isl.), Indon. 113/G6
Celle, Ger. 70/D2
Central African Republic 61/DE4
Central America 48-49
Centralia, Ill. 144/B3
Centralia, Wash. 175/B2
Ceram (isl.), Indon. 113/H6
Cerritos, Calif. 179/C2
Cerro de Pasco, Peru 56/B4
Česke Budějovice, Czech Rep.
  82/C2
Ceuta, Spain 76/D5
Ceylon, see Sri Lanka
Chad 60-61/D3
Chad (lake), Africa 60/D3

Index

Chadron, Nebr. 157/A1
Chamberlain, S. Dak. 165/E3
Chambersburg, Pa. 170/C4
Chambery, France 75/G5
Champaign, Ill. 144/C2
Champlain (lake), N. Amer. 158/A2
Chandigarh, India 102/C1
Chandler, Ariz. 130/B1
Chandleur (isls.), La. 150/C3
Changchun, China 105/F1
Chang Jiang (Yangtze) (riv.), China 104/D2
Changsha, China 105/E3
Channel Islands 67/E6
Channel Isls. Nat'l Pk., Calif. 133/A2
Channel-Port-aux-Basques, Newf. 183/E1
Chapaevsk, Russia 89/G4
Chapel Hill, N.C. 163/D1
Chàrjew, Turkmen. 90/D3
Charleroi, Belg. 73/D7
Charleston (cap.), W. Va. 138/B3
Charleston, S.C. 162/C4
Charles Town, W. Va. 139/D2
Charlevoix, Mich. 152/B2
Charlotte, N.C. 162/C2
Charlotte Amalie (cap.), V.I. (U.S.) 51/F3, 54/F
Charlottesville, Va. 139/D3
Charlottetown (cap.), P.E.I. 183/D2
Chartres, France 74/D3
Château-Thierry, France 74/E3
Chatham, Eng. 67/G5
Chatham, N. Br. 182/C2
Chatham (isls.), N.Z. 117/J9
Chatham, Ont. 186/A4
Chattahoochee, Fla. 140/A1
Chattahoochee (riv.), U.S. 142/A4
Chattanooga, Tenn. 149/D4
Cheboksary, Russia 88/G3
Cheboygan, Mich. 152/B2
Chedabucto (bay), N.S. 183/F3
Cheektowaga, N.Y. 160/B1
Chefoo, China, see Yantai
Chehalis, Wash. 175/C2
Cheju, S. Korea 106/B4
Cheju (isl.), S. Korea 106/B4
Chekiang, China, see Zhejiang
Chelan (lake), Wash. 175/B3
Chelm, Pol. 87/F3
Cheltenham, Eng. 67/E5
Chelyabinsk, Russia 90/D3
Chelyuskin (cape), Russia 91/F2
Chemnitz, Ger. 71/E3
Cheney, Wash. 175/B4
Chengchow, China, see Zhengzhou
Chengde, China 105/E1
Chengdu (Chengtu), China 104/D2
Cherbourg, France 74/C3
Cherepovets, Russia 88/E3
Cherkasy, Ukraine 89/D5
Cherkessk, Russia 89/F6
Chernihiv, Ukraine 89/D4
Chernivtsi, Ukraine 89/C5
Cherokee (lake), Tenn. 149/E3
Chesapeake (bay), U.S. 139/F3
Chesapeake, Va. 138/A2
Chester, Eng. 67/E4
Chester, Pa. 171/F4
Chesterfield, Eng. 67/F4
Chevy Chase, Md. 139/D1
Cheyenne (cap.), Wyo. 177/C1
Cheyenne (riv.), U.S. 165/E2
Chiang Mai, Thai. 110/B3
Chiba, Japan 107/F4

Chibougamau, Que. 184/C1
Chicago, Ill. 178/B2
Chicago Hts., Ill. 178/B3
Chichén-Itza (ruins), Mex. 47/H4
Chickamauga (lake), Tenn. 149/D4
Chickasha, Okla. 168/B3
Chiclayo, Peru 56/B3
Chico, Calif. 132/B1
Chicopee, Mass. 136/A3
Chicoutimi, Que. 185/E2
Chihuahua, Mex. 46/D2
Chile 56/B4, 58/B-C5-8
Chillicothe, Ohio 167/D2
Chilliwack, Br. Col. 190/C4
Chiloé (isl.), Chile 58/B7
Chimborazo (mt.), Ecua. 56/B3
Chimbote, Peru 56/B3
Chin (hills), Burma 110/A2
China, People's Rep. of 104-105
China, Rep. of (Taiwan) 105/F3
Chinandega, Nic. 48/C2
Chincoteague, Va. 139/F3
Chindwin (riv.), Burma 110/A1
Chingola, Zambia 63/E6
Chinju, S. Korea 106/B4
Chino, Calif. 179/B3
Chippewa (riv.), Wis. 176/A3
Chiricahua Nat'l Mon., Ariz. 130/C4
Chiriqui (lag.), Pan. 49/D3
Chisholm, Minn. 153/B2
Chisimayu, Somalia 63/G5
Chişinǎu (cap.), Moldova 89/C5
Chita, Russia 91/F3
Chittagong, Bang. 103/E2
Choluteca, Hond. 48/C2
Chŏngjin, N. Korea 106/C2
Ch'ŏngju, S. Korea 106/B3
Chongqing (Chungking), China 104/D3
Chŏnju, S. Korea 106/B3
Chonos (arch.), Chile 58/B7
Chornobyl', Ukraine 89/C4
Ch'ŏrwŏn, S. Korea 106/B3
Chorzów, Poland 86/B4
Christchurch, N.Z. 115/F4
Christiansburg, Va. 138/C4
Christiansted, V.I. (U.S.) 54/G3
Christmas (isl.), Austr. 93/H6
Christmas (Kiritimati) (isl.), Kiribati 117/L5
Chubut (riv.), Arg. 58/C7
Chukchi (pen.), Russia 91/K2
Chu Lai, Viet. 110/E4
Chula Vista, Calif. 180/C4
Ch'unch'on, S. Korea 106/C3
Chur, Switz. 81/D2
Churchill, Man. 42/G4
Cicero, Ill. 178/B4
Cienfuegos, Cuba 52/E2
Cimarron (riv.), U.S. 168/A2
Cincinnati, Ohio 167/F1
Circleville, Ohio 167/D2
Cirebon, Indon. 113/H2
Citlaltépetl (mt.), Mex. 47/G2
Citrus Heights, Calif. 132/C2
Ciudad Bolívar, Ven. 57/C2
Ciudad Guayana, Ven. 56/C2
Ciudad Juárez, Mex. 46/C1
Ciudad Madero, Mex. 47/F3
Ciudad Obregón, Mex. 46/C2
Civitavecchia, Italy 78/C3
Claremont, Calif. 179/B3
Claremont, N.H. 158/A3
Clarion, Pa. 170/B3
Clarksburg, W. Va. 138/C3
Clarksdale, Miss. 154/B1
Clarksville, Tenn. 148/C3

Clayton, Mo. 155/A4
Clear (cape), Ire. 67/B5
Clear Lake, Iowa 146/A2
Clearfield, Pa. 170/C3
Clearfield, Utah 174/B2
Clearwater, Fla. 140/C4
Clearwater (mts.), Idaho 143/AB2
Clermont-Ferrand, France 75/E5
Cleveland, Miss. 154/A2
Cleveland, Ohio 167/F3
Cleveland, Tenn. 149/D4
Cleveland Hts., Ohio 167/F4
Clifton, N.J. 180/A2
Clinton, Iowa 146/B4
Clinton, Miss. 154/B3
Clinton, Okla. 168/B3
Clipperton (isl.), Fr. 41/H8
Clonmel, Ire. 67/C4
Clovis, Calif. 133/B2
Clovis, N. Mex. 135/D4
Cluj-Napoca, Rom. 84/C2
Clyde, Scot. 66/E3
Clydebank, Scot. 66/B1
Coast (mts.), Br. Col. 190/A3
Coast (ranges), U.S. 169, 175/C1
Coatbridge, Scot. 66/B1
Coatesville, Pa. 171/E4
Cobán, Guat. 48/B2
Cóbh, Ire. 67/B5
Coblenz, Ger., see Koblenz
Cobourg, Ont. 187/D3
Cochabamba, Bol. 56/C4
Cochinos (bay), Cuba 52/E3
Cockburn (isl.), Ont. 186/A2
Coco (riv.), Cent. Amer. 49/D2
Cocoa, Fla. 140/C4
Cocos (isls.), Austr. 93/G6
Cod (cape), Mass. 137/C4
Cody, Wyo. 177/A3
Coeur d'Alene, Idaho 143/A1
Coffeyville, Kans. 147/C4
Cohoes, N.Y. 161/F3
Coiba (isl.), Panama 49/D4
Coimbatore, India 102/C3
Coimbra, Port. 76/B2
Colchester, Eng. 67/G5
Cold Lake, Alta. 191/F2
Colebrook, N.H. 158/C1
Coleraine, N. Ire. 66/C3
College Park, Ga. 142/B1
College Park, Md. 139/E1
College Station, Texas 173/E2
Collingwood, N.J. 171/F2
Collingwood, Ont. 186/C3
Colmar, France 74/G3
Cologne, Ger. 71/B3
Colombia 56/B2
Colombo (cap.), Sri Lanka 102/C4
Colón, Pan. 49/D3
Colorado (riv.), Arg. 58/C6
Colorado (riv.), Ariz.-Calif. 44/D4
Colorado (riv.), Texas 173/E3
Colorado (state), U.S. 134
Colorado Nat'l Mon., Colo. 134/B1
Colorado Sprs., Colo. 134/B3
Columbia (riv.), S.C. 162/C3
Columbia (riv.), N. Amer. 44/B1
Columbia, Mo. 155/B2
Columbia, Pa. 171/D4
Columbia, Tenn. 148/C4
Columbus, Ga. 142/A4
Columbus, Ind. 145/B3
Columbus, Miss. 154/C2
Columbus, Nebr. 157/B4
Columbus (cap.), Ohio 166/C2
Colville (riv.), Alaska 129/A1
Communism (peak), Tajik. 90/D4
Como (lake), Italy 78/B4

omorin (cape), India 102/C4
omoros 63/G6
ompiègne, France 74/E3
ompton, Calif. 179/C2
onakry (cap.), Guinea 60/A4
oncepción, Chile 58/B6
oncepción, Par. 58/D5
oncord, Calif. 133/E1
oncord (cap.), N.H. 158/C3
oncord, N.C. 162/C2
ongaree Swamp Nat'l Mon.,
  S.C. 162/C3
ongo, Dem. Rep. of the 63/E5
ongo, Rep. of the 62/D5
ongo (riv.), Africa 62/D5
onnecticut (riv.), U.S. 136/C3,
  158/B3
onnecticut (state), U.S. 136
onnellsville, Pa. 170/B4
onnersville, Ind. 145/C3
onstance (lake), Europe 81/E1
onstanța, Rom. 81/D1
onstantine, Alg. 60/C1
onway, Ark. 131/B2
onway, N.H. 158/C3
onway, S.C. 163/D3
ook (str.), N.Z. 115/F4
ook Islands 117/K7
ookeville, Tenn. 149/D3
ooper (riv.), S.C. 162/C3
ooperstown, N.Y. 161/E3
oos Bay, Oreg. 169/C1
opiapó, Chile 58/B5
opper Harbor, Mich. 152/A1
oquitlam, Br. Col. 190/B1
oral (sea) 116/F7
orbin, Ky. 149/E3
ordele, Ga. 142/B3
órdoba, Arg. 58/C4
óroba, Spain 76/D4
orfu, Greece, see Kérkira
orinth, Greece 85/C4
orinth, Miss. 154/C1
ork, Ire. 67/B5
orn (isls.), N.H. 49/D2
orner Brook, Newf. 183/E1
orning, N.Y. 160/C3
ornwall, Ont. 187/F2
oro, Ven. 56/C1
orona, Calif. 179/C4
oronado, Calif. 180/C4
orpus Christi, Texas 173/E4
orregidor (isl.), Phil. 108/C3
orrib, Lough (lake), Ire. 67/B4
orrientes, Arg. 58/D5
orsica (isl.), France 75/B7
orsicana, Texas 173/E2
ortez, Colo. 134/C2
ortina d'Ampezzo, Italy 78/D1
ortland, N.Y. 161/D3
orum, Turkey 96/E2
orvallis, Oreg. 169/B2
osenza, Italy 79/F5
oshocton, Ohio 166/D3
osta Brava (reg.), Spain 77/H2
osta del Sol (reg.), Spain 76/D4
osta Mesa, Calif. 179/C3
osta Rica 48/C3
ôte d'Ivoire 60/B4
ôte-d'Or (mts.), France 74/F4
otonou, Benin 60/C4
ottage Grove, Oreg. 169/B2
ouncil Bluffs, Iowa 146/C1
ouncil Grove, Kans. 147/B3
ourantyne (riv.), S. Amer. 57/D2
ourtenay, Br. Col. 190/B4
ourtrai, Belg. 73/B6

Coventry, Eng. 67/F4
Covington, Ky. 149/D2
Coyoacan, Mex. 47/F1
Cozumel (isl.), Mex. 47/H4
Craigavon, N. Ire. 67/C3
Craiova, Rom. 84/C2
Cranbrook, Br. Col. 191/D4
Cranston, R.I. 137/D2
Crater Lake Nat'l Pk., Oreg.
  169/C2
Craters of the Moon Nat'l Mon.,
  Idaho 143/B3
Crawford, Nebr. 157/A1
Crawfordsville, Ind. 145/B2
Creston, Br. Col. 191/D4
Crete (isl.), Greece 85/D5
Crewe, Eng. 67/E4
Crimea (pen.), Ukraine 89/D5
Crisfield, Md. 159/A3
Cristóbal Colón (mt.), Col. 56/B1
Croatia 84/A2
Crowley, La. 150/C2
Crown Point, Ind. 145/A1
Crown Point, N.Y. 161/F2
Croydon, Eng. 67/B6
Crozet (isls.), Fr. 35/L8
Ctesiphon (ruins), Iraq 100/D4
Cuba 50/B2, 52-53
Cúcuta, Col. 56/B2
Cudahy, Wis. 176/B1
Cuenca, Ecua. 56/B3
Cuernavaca, Mex. 47/F2
Cuiabá, Braz. 57/D4
Culebra (isl.), P. Rico 51/G1,
  54/E1
Culiacán, Mex. 46/C3
Cullman, Ala. 128/B1
Culver City, Calif. 179/B1
Cumaná, Ven. 56/C1
Cumberland, Md. 159/D2
Cumberland (riv.), U.S. 149/D3
Cunene (riv.), Angola 62/D6
Curaçao (isl.), Neth. Ant. 50/E4,
  55/N
Curitiba, Braz. 59/E5
Cusco, Peru 56/B4
Cushing, Okla. 168/B3
Custer, S. Dak. 165/E1
Custer Battlfld. Nat'l Mon., Mont.
  156/C3
Cuttack, India 102/D2
Cuxhaven, Ger. 70/C2
Cuyahoga Falls, Ohio 166/B3
Cuyuni (riv.), S. Amer. 56/C2
Cyclades (isls.), Greece 85/D4
Cyprus 96/E5
Cyrenaica (reg.), Libya 61/E1
Czech Republic 82/C2
Czestochowa, Pol. 86/D3

D

Dacca (Dhaka) (cap.), Bang.
  103/D2
Dachau, Ger. 71/D4
Dahlak (arch.), Eth. 94/E6
Dahlonega, Ga. 142/A2
Daito (isls.), Japan 105/G3
Dakar (cap.), Sen. 60/A3
Dakhla (oasis), Egypt 94/B4
Dakhla, W. Sahara 60/A2
Da Lat, Viet. 111/E5
Dale Hollow (lake), U.S. 149/D3
Dalhousie, N. Br. 182/B1
Dalian, China 105/F2
Dallas, Texas 173/E2
Daloa, Iv. Coast 60/B4
Dalton, Ga. 142/A2
Daly City, Calif. 133/E1

Damascus (cap.), Syria 97/G6
Damavand (mt.), Iran 101/H3
Damietta, Egypt 61/F1
Da Nang, Viet. 110/E3
Danbury, Conn. 136/A3
Dandong, China 105/F1
Danli, Hond. 48/C2
Danube (riv.), Europe 64/F4
Danville, Ill. 144/C2
Danville, Ky. 149/D2
Danville, Va. 138/C4
Danzig, Pol., see Gdansk
Darbhanga, India 102/D2
Darby, Pa. 171/E2
Dardanelles (str.), Turkey 96/B6
Dar es Salaam (cap.), Tanz.
  63/F5
Darien, Conn. 136/A4
Darién (mts.), Pan. 49/E3
Darjeeling, India 103/E2
Darling (riv.), Austr. 115/D4
Darlington, Eng. 67/F3
Darmstadt, Ger. 71/C4
Dartmouth, N.S. 183/D4
Darwin, Austr. 114/C2
Dasht-e Kavir (des.), Iran 101/J3
Dasht-e Lut (des.), Iran 101/K5
Datong, China 105/E2
Daugavpils, Latvia 88/C3
Dauphin River, Man. 189/E3
Dauphin, Man. 189/D3
Davao, Phil. 109/E7
Davenport, Iowa 146/B4
David, Panama 49/D3
Davis (sea), Antarc. 118
Davis, Calif. 132/C1
Davis (str.), N. Amer. 40/N3
Davis (mts.), Texas 172/B2
Davos, Switz. 81/E2
Dawson, Yukon 42/C3
Dawson Creek, Br. Col. 190/C1
Dayton, Ohio 167/D3
Daytona Bch., Fla. 140/B3
De Kalb, Ill. 144/B1
De Land, Fla. 140/B3
De Ridder, La. 150/B1
Dead Sea, Asia 99/C4
Dearborn, Mich. 178/A4
Death Valley Nat'l Park, U.S.
  133/D3
Debra Markos, Eth. 61/F3
Debrecen, Hung. 83/F3
Decatur, Ala. 128/B1
Decatur, Ga. 142/C1
Decatur, Ill. 144/B3
Deccan (plat.), India 102/C3
Decorah, Iowa 146/A3
Dedham, Mass. 137/F4
Dee (riv.), Eng. 66/F2
Dee (riv.), Scot. 66/E2
Deep River, Ont. 187/D2
Deerfield, Ill. 178/A3
Defiance, Ohio 166/B1
Dehra Dun, India 102/C1
Deir ez Zor, Syria 97/H5
Del Mar, Calif. 180/C4
Del Rio, Texas 172/C3
Delaware, Ohio 166/C2
Delaware (bay), U.S. 159/A4
Delaware (riv.), U.S. 159/A1
Delaware (state), U.S. 139/E2
Delft, Neth. 72/D3
Delgado (cape), Moz. 63/G6
Delhi, India 102/C2
Delray Beach, Fla. 141/E4
Delta, Br. Col. 190/A1
Delta, Colo. 134/B2
Deming, N. Mex. 135/F2
Den Helder, Neth. 72/E2
Denali Nat'l Pk., Alaska 129/B1
Denison, Texas 173/E1

Index

Denizli, Turkey 96/C4
Denmark 69/B3
Denmark (str.) 40/R3
Denton, Texas 169/F3
Denver (cap.), Colo. 178/B4
Depew, N.Y. 160/B3
Der'a, Syria 97/G6
Derby, Eng. 67/F4
Derg, Lough (lake), Ire. 67/B4
Derna, Libya 61/E1
Derry, N.H. 158/E4
Des Moines (cap.), Iowa 146/B2
Des Moines (riv.), Iowa 146/C3
Des Plaines, Ill. 178/B1
Deschutes (riv.), Oreg. 169/A3
Deseado (riv.), Arg. 58/C7
Dessau, Ger. 70/E3
Dessye, Eth. 61/G3
Detroit, Mich. 178/C4
Deventer, Neth. 72/H3
Devil's (isl.), Fr. Guiana 57/D2
Devils Lake, N. Dak. 164/B3
Devils Tower Nat'l Mon., Wyo.
177/N1
Devon (isl.), N.W.T. 43/H1
Dewsbury, Eng. 66/H2
Dezful, Iran 100/F4
Dezhnev (cape), Russia 91/K2
Dhahran, S. Arabia 94/F4
Dhaka (cap.), Bang. 103/D2
Dhofar (reg.), Oman 95/G6
Dhulia, India 102/C2
Diamond (head), Hawaii 129/B4
Dickinson, N. Dak. 164/C1
Diefenbaker (lake), Sask. 188/B4
Diego Garcia (isls.), Br. Ind. Oc.
Terr. 93/F6
Diégo Suarez, Madag., see
Antsiranana
Dien Bien Phu, Viet. 110/C2
Dieppe, France 74/D3
Dieppe, N. Br. 182/C2
Digby, N.S. 182/C4
Dijon, France 74/F4
Dili, Indon. 113/H7
Dillon, Mont. 156/C2
Dimona, Isr. 99/C5
Dinagat (isl.), Phil. 109/E5
Dinant, Belg. 73/E7
Dinaric Alps (mts.), Eur. 84/B3
Dingle (bay), Ire. 67/A4
Dinosaur Nat'l Mon., U.S.
134/A1, 174/C2
Diomede Mounds (site), Ill. 144/B2
Dixon, Ill. 144/B1
Diyarbakır, Turkey 97/H4
Djakarta, see Jakarta
Djibouti 61/G3
Djibouti (cap.), Djibouti 61/G3
Djokjakarta, Indon., see
Yogyakarta
Dnieper (riv.), Eur. 89/D5
Dniester (riv.), Eur. 89/C5
Dnipropetrov'sk, Ukr. 89/D5
Dobbs Ferry, N.Y. 180/B1
Dodecanese (isls.), Greece 85/D5
Dodge City, Kans. 147/C2
Dodoma, Tanz. 63/F5
Dogo (isl.), Japan 106/D3
Doha (cap.), Qatar 95/G4
Dolomite Alps (mts.), Italy 78/C1
Dominica 51/G4, 54-55/K
Dominican Republic 50/D3,
52-53/Q-S7
Don (riv.), Russia 89/F4
Doncaster, Eng. 67/F4
Donegal (bay), Ire. 67/B3

Donets'k, Ukraine 89/E5
Dongala, Sudan 61/E3
Door (pen.), Wis. 176/C3
Dordogne (riv.), France 75/D5
Dordrecht, Neth. 72/E4
Dornbirn, Austria 82/A3
Dortmund, Ger. 70/B3
Dorval, Que. 184/A1
Dothan, Ala. 128/C3
Douai, France 74/E2
Douala, Cameroon 60/D4
Douglas, Ariz. 130/C4
Douglas (cap.), I. of Man 67/E3
Douglas, Wyo. 177/B2
Douro (riv.), Port. 76/C2
Dover (cap.), Del. 139/F2
Dover, Eng. 67/G5
Dover (str.), Europe 67/G5
Dover, N.H. 158/E4
Dover, N.J. 159/B1
Dover-Foxcroft, Maine 151/B3
Downers Grove, Ill. 178/A2
Downey, Calif. 179/B2
Doylestown, Pa. 171/F4
Drammen, Nor. 69/B3
Dráva (riv.), Europe 84/B2
Drayton Valley, Alta. 191/D2
Dresden, Ger. 71/E3
Drin (riv.), Alb. 84/C3
Drogheda, Ire. 67/C4
Drumheller, Alta. 191/E3
Drummond (isl.), Mich. 152/C2
Drummondville, Que. 185/D4
Druz, Jebel ed (mts.), Syria
97/G6
Dubai, U.A.E. 95/G4
Dubbo, Austr. 115/D4
Dublin, Ga. 142/B3
Dublin (cap.), Ire. 67/C4
Dubois, Pa. 170/B3
Dubrovnik, Croatia 84/B3
Dubuque, Iowa 146/B4
Dudinka, Russia 90/E2
Dudley, Eng. 67/E4
Duero (riv.), Spain 76/D2
Dufourspitze (mt.), Switz. 80/C3
Duisburg, Ger. 70/B3
Duluth, Minn. 153/C3
Dumfries, Scot. 66/E3
Duncan, Br. Col. 190/B4
Duncan, Okla. 168/C3
Duncanville, Texas 172/B4
Dundalk, Ire. 67/C3
Dundalk, Md. 139/F1
Dundas, Ont. 187/D14
Dundee, Scot. 66/E2
Dunedin, Fla. 140/C1
Dunedin, N.Z. 115/F4
Dunfermline, Scot. 66/E2
Dunkirk (Dunkerque), France
74/E2
Dunkirk, N.Y. 160/A3
Dún Laoghaire, Ire. 67/D4
Dunmore, Pa. 171/F3
Durance (riv.), France 75/F6
Durango, Colo. 134/C2
Durango, Mex. 46/D3
Durant, Okla. 168/C3
Durban, S. Africa 63/F7
Durham, N.C. 163/D1
Durrës (Durazzo), Alb. 85/B3
Düsseldorf, Ger. 71/B3
Dvina, Northern (riv.), Russia
88/F2
Dvina, Western (riv.), Eur. 88/C3
Dzerzhinsk, Russia 88/F3

E

Eagan, Minn. 153/C1

Eagle Pass, Texas 172/C3
Ealing, Eng. 67/B5
Eastbourne, Eng. 67/G5
East Chicago, Ind. 145/A1
East China (sea), Asia 105/F3
E. Cleveland, Ohio 167/E4
E. Detroit, Mich. 178/C4
Easter (isl.), Chile 117/Q8
E. Hampton, N.Y. 160/C4
E. Hartford, Conn. 136/C4
Eastlake, Ohio 167/E4
E. Lansing, Mich. 152/B4
E. Liverpool, Ohio 166/C4
E. London, S. Africa 63/E8
Easton, Pa. 171/F3
E. Orange, N.J. 180/A2
E. Peoria, Ill. 144/B2
East Point, Ga. 142/C1
Eastport, Maine 151/C3
E. St. Louis, Ill. 144/B3
East Siberian (sea), Russia 91/N
Eau Claire, Wis. 176/A3
Ebro (riv.), Spain 77/F2
Ech Cheliff, Alg. 60/C1
Ecuador 56/B3
Eddystone (rocks), Eng. 67/D5
Eden, N.C. 163/D1
Edenton, N.C. 163/F1
Edina, Minn. 153/B1
Edinburg, Texas 173/D4
Edinburgh (cap.), Scot. 66/E3
Edirne, Turkey 96/B2
Edmonds, Wash. 175/B1
Edmonton (cap.), Alta. 191/F1
Edmundston, N. Br. 182/A1
Edson, Alta. 191/D2
Edward (lake), Africa 63/E5
Edwards (plat.), Texas 172/C2
Edwardsville, Ill. 144/B3
Eel (riv.), Calif. 132/B1
Effigy Mounds, Nat'l Mon., Iowa
146/A4
Effingham, Ill. 144/C3
Eger, Hung. 83/F3
Egypt 61/F2, 82/94
Eindhoven, Neth. 73/F5
El Asnam, Alg., see Ech Cheliff
Elat (Elath), Isr. 99/D6
Elazığ, Turkey 97/H3
Elba (isl.), Italy 78/C3
Elbasan, Alb. 85/B3
Elbe (riv.), Ger. 70/C2
El'brus (mt.), Russia 89/F6
Elburz (mts.), Iran 100/G3
El Cajon, Calif. 180/C4
El Centro, Calif. 133/F4
Elche, Spain 77/F3
El Dorado, Ark. 131/C2
Eldoret, Kenya 63/F4
Eleuthera (isl.), Bah. 50/C1
Elgin, Ill. 178/A1
Elgon (mt.), Uganda 63/F4
Elista, Russia 89/F6
Elizabeth, N.J. 180/A2
Elizabeth City, N.C. 163/F1
Elizabethton, Tenn. 149/F3
Elizabethtown, Ky. 149/D2
El Karak, Jordan 99/E4
El Karnak, Egypt 94/C4
Elk City, Okla. 168/B2
El Kharga, Egypt 61/E2
Elkhart, Ind. 145/B1
Elkins, W. Va. 138/C2
Elk Island Nat'l Pk., Alta. 191/E2
Elko, Nev. 132/A4
Elkton, Md. 139/F2
Ellensburg, Wash. 175/B3

Ellesmere (isl.), N.W.T. 35/G1
Ellesmere Port, Eng. 66/G2
Elliot Lake, Ont. 186/B4
Ellsworth, Maine 151/B3
Elmhurst, Ill. 178/A2
El Minya, Egypt 61/F2
Elmira, N.Y. 160/C4
El Monte, Calif. 179/B2
El Morro Nat'l Mon., N. Mex. 135/D1
Elmwood Park, Ill. 178/B2
El Obeid, Sudan 61/E3
El Paso, Texas 172/A2
El Progreso, Hond. 48/C2
El Rashid, Syria 97/H4
El Reno, Okla. 168/B2
El Salvador 48/B2
Elsinore, Den., see Helsingør
Eluru, India 102/D3
Elwood, Nebr. 157/C2
Ely, Nev. 132/B4
Elyria, Ohio 166/B3
Emden, Ger. 70/B2
Emi Koussi (mt.), Chad 61/D3
Emilia-Romagna (reg.), Italy 78/C2
Emporia, Kans. 147/B4
Ems (riv.), Ger. 70/B2
Encarnación, Par. 59/D5
Enderbury (isl.), Kiribati 117/K6
Enewetak (atoll), Marshall Is. 116/G4
Enfield, Conn., see Thompsonville
Enfield, Eng. 67/B5
Engadine (valley), Switz. 81/E2
Engaño (cape), Phil. 108/D1
Engel's, Russia 89/G4
England 66-67
Englewood, Colo. 178/A4
Englewood, N.J. 180/B1
English (chan.), Europe 64/D4
Enid, Okla. 168/A3
Ennis, Ire. 67/B4
Enniskillen, N. Ire. 67/C3
Enschede, Neth. 72/J3
Ensenada, Mex. 46/A1
Entebbe, Uganda 63/F5
Enterprise, Ala. 128/C3
Enugu, Nigeria 60/C4
Ephrata, Pa. 171/H4
Epsom and Ewell, Eng. 67/B6
Equatorial Guinea 60/C4
Erbil, Iraq 100/D2
Ereğli, Turkey 96/F4
Erfurt, Ger. 71/D3
Erie (lake), N. Amer. 45/K2, H7/43
Erie, Pa. 170/A2
Eritrea 61/F3
Erivan, Armenia, see Yerevan
Erlangen, Ger. 71/D4
Erne, Lough (lake), N. Ire. 67/C3
Erzgebirge (mts.), Europe 71/E3
Erzurum, Turkey 97/J3
Esbjerg, Den. 69/B3
Escanaba, Mich. 152/A2
Esch-sur-Alzette, Lux. 73/G8
Escondido, Calif. 180/C4
Esfahan, Iran, see Isfahan
Esher, Eng. 67/B6
Eskilstuna, Swed. 69/C3
Eskişehir, Turkey 96/D3
Espanola, Ont. 186/B1
Espiritu Santo (isl.), Vanuatu 116/G7
Es Salt, Jordan 99/D3
Essen, Ger. 70/B3
Essequibo (riv.), Guyana 56/D2
Essex, Md. 139/F1
Estados (isl.), Arg. 58/C5

Estevan, Sask. 188/C4
Estonia 88/B3
Estremadura (reg.), Spain 76/C3
Ethiopia 61/F3
Etna (vol.), Italy 79/E6
Etorofu (isl.), Japan 107/G1
Etosha (salt pan), Namibia 62/D6
Euboea (isl.), Greece 85/C4
Euclid, Ohio 167/E4
Eufaula, Ala. 128/C3
Eugene, Oreg. 169/B2
Eunice, La. 150/B2
Euphrates (riv.), Asia 94/D2
Eureka, Calif. 132/B1
Eureka Springs, Ark. 131/A2
Europa (isl.), Reunion 63/G7
Europe 64-65
Evanston, Ill. 178/B1
Evanston, Wyo. 177/C4
Evansville, Ind. 145/A4
Everest (mt.), Asia 103/D2
Everett, Wash. 175/B4
Everglades Nat'l Pk., Fla. 141/E4
Évora, Port. 76/C3
Évvoia (isl.), see Euboea
Ewa Beach, Hawaii 129/A4
Exeter, Eng. 67/E5
Exeter, N.H. 158/C4
Eyre (lake), Austr. 114/C3
Ez Zarqa', Jordan 99/E3

F

Fairbanks, Alaska 129/B1
Fairborn, Ohio 166/C1
Fairfield, Ala. 128/B2
Fairfield, Calif. 132/C1
Fairfield, Conn. 136/A3
Fairfield, Ohio 167/E1
Fair Lawn, N.J. 180/A1
Fairmont, W. Va. 138/C2
Fairweather (mt.), N. Amer. 42/C4
Faisalabad, Pak. 102/C1
Faiyûm, Egypt, see El Faiyûm
Fajardo, P. Rico 54/D1
Falkirk, Scot. 66/B1
Falkland Islands 58-59/D8
Fallon, Nev. 132/B3
Fall River, Mass. 137/D3
Falls Church, Va. 139/D1
Falmouth, Mass. 137/E3
Famagusta, Cyprus 96/F5
Fanning (isl.), see Tabuaeran
Farewell (cape), Greenl. 40/P4
Farghona, Uzbek. 90/C3
Fargo, N. Dak. 164/C4
Faribault, Minn. 153/B4
Farmers Branch, Texas 172/B4
Farmington, Maine 151/A3
Farmington, N. Mex. 134/C2
Faro, Port. 76/C4
Faroe (isls.), Den. 64/D2
Fayetteville, Ark. 131/A1
Fayetteville, N.C. 163/D2
Fear (cape), N.C. 163/E3
Fehmarn (isl.), Ger. 70/D1
Fergus Falls, Minn. 153/A3
Ferguson, Mo. 155/A4
Fernandina Bch., Fla. 140/A3
Fernando Po, see Bioko
Fernie, Br. Col. 191/E4
Ferrara, Italy 78/C2
Ferro (Hierro) (isl.), Spain 76/A5
Fès (Fez), Mor. 60/B1
Fezzan (reg.), Libya 60/D2
Fianarantsoa, Madag. 63/G7
Fichtelgebirge (range), Ger. 71/D3
Fiji 116/H7
Findlay, Ohio 166/B2

Finger (lakes), N.Y. 160-161/C-D3
Finisterre (cape), Spain 76/B1
Finland 68-69/E2
Finland (gulf), Europe 65/G3
Firenze (Florence), Italy 78/C3
Fitchburg, Mass. 137/D1
Fiume, Croatia, see Rijeka
Flagstaff, Ariz. 130/B3
Flamborough (head), Eng. 67/G3
Flamborough, Ont. 187/E4
Flaming Gorge (res.), U.S. 174/C2, 177/C3
Flanders (prov.), Belg. 73/A-B5-6
Flathead (lake), Mont. 156/A1
Flattery (cape), Wash. 175/A1
Flemington, N.J. 159/B2
Flensburg, Ger. 70/C1
Flin Flon, Man. 189/D2
Flint, Mich. 152/D4
Floral Park, N.Y. 180/C2
Florence, Ala. 128/A1
Florence, Italy 78/C3
Florence, Ky. 149/D2
Florence, Oreg. 169/B2
Florence, S.C. 163/D3
Flores (isl.), Indon. 113/G7
Flores, Guat. 48/B1
Florianópolis, Braz. 59/E5
Florida (bay), Fla. 141/F4
Florida (state), U.S. 140-141
Florida Keys (isls.), Fla. 141/F4
Florissant, Mo. 155/A4
Florissant Fossil Beds Nat'l Mon., Colo. 134/B3
Flushing, Neth. 73/C4
Fly (riv.), Papua N.G. 112/A7
Foggia, Italy 79/E4
Folkestone, Eng. 67/G5
Fond du Lac, Wis. 153/C2
Fonseca (gulf), Cent. Amer. 48/C2
Fontainebleau, France 74/E3
Fontana, Calif. 179/B4
Fontana (lake), N.C. 162/A2
Foochow, see Fuzhou
Fordyce, Ark. 131/C2
Forest Park, Ga. 142/C1
Forillon Nat'l Pk., Que. 185/F1
Forli, Italy 78/C2
Formentera (isl.), Spain 77/G3
Formosa, Arg. 58/D5
Forrest City, Ark. 131/B3
Forsyth, Mont. 156/E4
Fortaleza, Braz. 57/F3
Ft. Assiniboine, Mont. 156/A3
Ft. Belvoir, Va. 139/E3
Ft. Benton, Mont. 156/A3
Ft. Bridger, Wyo. 177/C4
Ft. Chaffee, Ark. 131/B1
Ft. Collins, Colo. 134/A3
Ft-de-France (cap.), Martinique 51/G4, 55/J
Ft. Dodge, Iowa 146/A2
Ft. Erie, Ont. 187/F4
Ft. Eustis, Va. 138/A1
Ft. Frances, Ont. 187/D1
Forth (firth), Scot. 66/F2
Ft. Kent, Maine 151/B1
Ft. Knox, Ky. 149/D2
Ft. Lauderdale, Fla. 141/D1
Ft. Leonard Wood, Mo. 155/B3
Ft. Macleod, Alta. 191/E4
Ft. Madison, Iowa 146/C4
Ft. McArthur, Calif. 179/C3
Ft. McClellan, Ala. 128/C2
Ft. McHenry Nat'l Mon., Md. 139/F1
Ft. McMurray, Alta. 42/E4
Ft. Monroe, Va. 138/A1
Ft. Myers, Fla. 141/D3

Ft. Niobrara, Nebr. 157/A2
Ft. Peck Lake (res.), Mont. 156/A3
Ft. Pierce, Fla. 141/F1
Ft. Pierre, S. Dak. 165/E2
Ft. Polk, La. 150/B1
Ft. Pulaski Nat'l Mon., Ga. 142/C3
Ft. Qu'Appelle, Sask. 188/C3
Ft. St. James, Br. Col. 190/B2
Ft. St. John, Br. Col. 190/C1
Ft. Saskatchewan, Alta. 191/H1
Ft. Smith, Ark. 131/B1
Ft. Smith, N.W.T. 42/E3
Ft. Stockton, Texas 172/B2
Ft. Story, Va. 138/B1
Ft. Sumter Nat'l Mon., S.C. 163/D4
Ft. Walton Bch., Fla. 141/F1
Ft. Wayne, Ind. 145/C2
Ft. William, Scot. 66/D2
Ft. Worth, Texas 172/A4
Fossil Butte Nat'l Mon., Wyo. 177/C4
Fostoria, Ohio 166/B2
Fountain Valley, Calif. 179/B4
Foxe (basin), N.W.T. 43/J3
Foyle, Lough (inlet), Ire. 66/C3
Framingham, Mass. 137/D2
France 74-75
Francis Case (lake), S. Dak. 165/E2
Frankfort, Ind. 145/B2
Frankfort (cap.), Ky. 149/D2
Frankfort, Mich. 152/B3
Frankfurt-am-Main, Ger. 71/C3
Frankfurt-an-der-Oder, Ger. 70/F2
Franklin, Pa. 170/A3
Franklin, Tenn. 148/C4
Franklin, Va. 139/E4
Franklin, Wis. 176/B1
Franklin D. Roosevelt (lake), Wash. 175/E4
Franz Josef Land (isls.), Russia 90/C1
Fraser (riv.), Br. Col. 190/C3
Fraserburgh, Scot. 66/E2
Frederica, Den. 69/B3
Frederick, Md. 139/E2
Fredericksburg, Texas 173/D2
Fredericksburg, Va. 139/E3
Fredericton (cap.), N. Br. 182/B2
Frederik VI Coast, Greenl. 40/P3
Frederikshavn, Den. 69/B3
Freehold, N.J. 159/C2
Freeport, Ill. 144/B1
Freeport, N.Y. 160/B4
Freeport, Texas 173/F3
Freetown (cap.), S. Leone 60/A4
Freiburg im Breisgau, Ger. 71/B5
Fremantle, Austr. 114/A4
Fremont, Calif. 133/D2
Fremont, Nebr. 157/B4
Fremont, Ohio 166/B2
French Guiana 57/D2
French Polynesia 117/M8
Fresno, Calif. 133/D2
Fria (cape), Namibia 62/D6
Fribourg, Switz. 80/C2
Fridley, Minn. 153/C1
Friedrichshafen, Ger. 71/C5
Friesland (prov.), Neth. 72/G1
Frio (cape), Braz. 59/E5
Frisian (isls.), Ger. 70/C1
Friuli-Venezia Giulia (reg.), Italy 78/D1
Frome (lake), Austr. 115/D4
Front Royal, Va. 139/D2
Frontenac Prov. Pk., Que. 185/E4

Fuerteventura (isl.), Spain 76/C4
Fuji (mt.), Japan 107/E4
Fujian (Fukien) (prov.), China 105/E3
Fukui, Japan 106/D3
Fukuoka, Japan 106/C4
Fukushima, Japan 107/F3
Fukuyama, Japan 106/D4
Fulda, Ger. 71/C3
Fullerton, Calif. 179/C3
Fulton, Mo. 155/B3
Fulton, N.Y. 161/D2
Funabashi, Japan 107/H2
Funafuti (cap.), Tuvalu 116/J6
Funchal, Port. 76/A2
Fundy (bay), N. Amer. 182/B3
Fundy Nat'l Pk., N. Br. 182/C3
Furneaux Group (isls.), Austr. 115/D4
Fürth, Ger. 71/D4
Fushun, China 105/F2
Füssen, Ger. 71/D5
Fuxin, China 105/F1
Fuzhou, China 105/E3

G

Gabès, Tun. 60/D1
Gabon 62/D5
Gaborone (cap.), Bots. 63/E7
Gabrovo, Bulg. 84/D3
Gadsden, Ala. 148/C1
Gaffney, S.C. 162/C2
Gainesville, Fla. 140/B2
Gainesville, Ga. 142/B3
Gairdner (lake), Austr. 114/C4
Gaithersburg, Md. 139/E2
Galápagos (isls.), Ecua. 34/F6
Galați, Rom. 84/D2
Galena, Ill. 144/A1
Galesburg, Ill. 144/A2
Galicia (reg.), Spain 76/B1
Galilee, Sea of (lake), Isr. 98/D2
Gallatin, Tenn. 148/C3
Galle, Sri Lanka 102/D3
Gallipoli, see Gelibolu
Gallipolis, Ohio 167/D3
Gallup, N. Mex. 135/D2
Galveston, Texas 173/F3
Galway, Ire. 67/B4
Galway (bay), Ire. 67/B4
Gambia 60/A3
Gambier (isls.), Fr. Poly. 117/N8
Gananoque, Ont. 187/E3
Gäncä, Azer. 89/G6
Gander, Newf. 183/F1
Ganges (riv.), Asia 102/D2
Gangtok, India 103/D2
Gansu (prov.), China 104/D2
Gao, Mali 60/C1
Garabogazköl (gulf), Turkmen. 89/H6
Garagum (des.), Turkmen. 90/C3
Garda (lake), Italy 78/C2
Garden City, Kans. 147/B1
Garden City, Mich. 178/B4
Garden City, N.Y. 160/B4
Garden Grove, Calif. 179/C3
Gardena, Calif. 179/B1
Garfield, N.J. 180/A2
Garfield Hts., Ohio 167/F4
Garland, Texas 172/C4
Garmisch-Partenkirchen, Ger. 71/D5
Garonne (riv.), France 75/C5
Gary, Ind. 145/A1
Gaspé, Que. 185/F1
Gaspé (pen.), Que. 185/E1
Gastonia, N.C. 162/C2

Gates of the Arctic Nat'l Pk., Alaska 129/H1
Gateshead, Eng. 66/F3
Gatineau, Que. 184/C4
Gatineau Pk., Que. 184/B4
Gatlinburg, Tenn. 149/E4
Gauhati, India 103/E2
Gävle, Swed. 69/C2
Gaya, India 102/D2
Gaza, Gaza Strip 94/43, 99/A4
Gaza Strip 99/A4
Gaziantep, Turkey 97/G4
Gdańsk, Pol. 86/D1
Gdańsk (gulf), Pol. 86/D1
Gdynia, Pol. 86/D1
Gedaref, Sudan 61/F3
Geelong, Austr. 115/D4
Gejiu, China 104/D3
Gelibolu, Turkey 96/C6
Gelsenkirchen, Ger. 70/B3
Genesee (riv.), N.Y. 160/B3
Geneva (lake), Europe 80/B2
Geneva, N.Y. 160/C3
Geneva, Switz. 80/B2
Genk, Belg. 73/G6
Genoa (Genova), Italy 78/B2
Georgetown (cap.), Cayman Is. 50/A3
Georgetown (cap.), Guyana 57/D2
George Town, Malaysia 112/B4
Georgetown, S.C. 163/D4
George Washington Birthplace Nat'l Mon., Va. 139/E3
G.W. Carver Nat'l Mon., Mo. 155/C2
Georgia 89/F6
Georgia (str.), Br. Col. 190/B4
Georgia (state), U.S. 142
Georgian (bay), Ont. 186/B2
Georgian Bay Is. Nat'l Pk., Ont. 186/B2
Gera, Ger. 71/D3
Geraldton, Austr. 114/A3
Gerlachovka (mt.), Slvk. 83/F2
Germany 70-71
Germiston, S. Africa 63/E7
Gettysburg, Pa. 171/D4
Ghana 60/B4
Ghazni, Afghan. 102/B1
Ghent, Belg. 73/C5
Gibraltar 76/D4
Gibraltar (str.) 76/D5
Gibson (des.), Austr. 114/B3
Gifu, Japan 106/E4
Gijón, Spain 76/C1
Gila (riv.), U.S. 135/D2
Gila Cliff Dwellings Nat'l Mon., N Mex. 135/E1
Gilbert Is., see Kiribati
Gillette, Wyo. 177/A2
Girona (Gerona), Spain 77/H1
Gironde (riv.), France 75/C5
Giza, Egypt 94/C4
Glace Bay, N.S. 183/F2
Glacier Bay Nat'l Pk., Alaska 129/G3
Glacier Nat'l Pk., Br. Col. 191/D3
Glacier Nat'l Pk., Mont. 156/A1
Gladstone, Mich. 152/A2
Gladstone, Mo. 155/C1
Glarus, Switz. 81/D1
Glasgow, Ky. 149/D3
Glasgow, Mont. 156/A4
Glasgow, Scot. 66/E3
Glassboro, N.J. 159/A3
Glastonbury, Conn. 136/B3
Glazov, Russia 88/H3
Glencoe, Ill. 178/B1
Glen Cove, N.Y. 180/C1

Glendale, Ariz. 130/A1
Glendale, Calif. 179/A2
Glens Falls, N.Y. 161/F2
Glenwood Springs, Colo. 134/A2
Gliwice, Pol. 86/C2
Globe, Ariz. 130/C3
Gloucester, Eng. 67/F5
Gloucester, Mass. 137/E1
Gloversville, N.Y. 161/E3
Gniezno, Pol. 86/C2
Gobi (des.), Asia 104/D1
Godavari (riv.), India 102/D3
Goderich, Ont. 186/B3
Godthåb (Nuuk) (cap.), Greenl. 40/N3
Godwin Austen (K2) (mt.), India 102/C1
Goiânia, Braz. 57/E4
Golan Heights 98/D1
Golden, Br. Col. 191/D3
Golden, Colo. 178/A4
Goldsboro, N.C. 163/E2
Golmud, China 104/C2
Gomera (isl.), Spain 76/A5
Gonaïves, Haiti 52/P6
Gonâve (isl.), Haiti 50/D3, 52/N7
Gondar, Eth. 61/F3
Good Hope (cape), S. Africa 63/D8
Goodland, Kans. 147/A1
Goose (lake), U.S. 132/A2
Goose Bay, Newf. 43/L5
Gorakhpur, India 102/D2
Gorgan, Iran 101/J2
Gorham, N.H. 158/C2
Goshen, Ind. 145/B1
Goslar, Ger. 70/D3
Gosport, Eng. 67/F5
Göta (canal), Swed. 69/C3
Göteborg, Swed. 69/B3
Gotland (isl.), Swed. 69/D3
Göttingen, Ger. 70/D3
Gouda, Neth. 72/E3
Gough (isl.), U.K. 35/J8
Gouin (res.), Que. 184/C2
Gracias a Dios (cape), Cent. Amer. 49/D2
Grafton, N. Dak. 164/A4
Graham Land, Antarc. 118
Grahamstown, S. Africa 63/E8
Granada, Nic. 48/C3
Granada, Spain 76/E4
Granby, Que. 185/D4
Gran Canaria (isl.), Spain 76/B5
Gran Chaco (reg.), S. Amer. 58/C5
Grand (canal), China 105/E2
Grand (isl.), N.Y. 160/A1
Grand Bahama (isl.), Bah. 50/B1
Grand Canyon Nat'l Pk., Ariz. 130/B2
Grand Cayman (isl.), Cayman Is. 50/B3
Grand Coulee (dam), Wash. 175/B4
Grande (riv.), Braz. 59/E5
Grande (riv.), Nic. 48/C2
Grande, Rio (riv.), N. Amer. 41/J7
Grande Cache, Alta. 190/C2
Grande Prairie, Alta. 191/D2
Grand Erg Occidental (des.), Africa 60/C1
Grand Erg Oriental (des.), Africa 60/C1
Grande-Rivière, Que. 185/F1
Grand Falls, N. Br. 182/A2
Grand Forks, N. Dak. 164/B4
Grand Island, Nebr. 157/B3
Grand Isle, La. 150/C3
Grand Junction, Colo. 134/A2
Grand Manan (isl.), N. Br. 182/B4

Grand Marais, Minn. 153/A1
Grand Portage Nat'l Mon., Minn. 153/B1
Grand Prairie, Texas 172/B4
Grand Rapids, Mich. 152/B4
Grand Teton Nat'l Pk., Wyo. 177/A4
Grandview, Mo. 155/C1
Granite City, Ill. 144/A3
Grants, N. Mex. 135/D2
Grants Pass, Oreg. 169/C1
Grasslands Nat'l Pk., Sask. 188/B4
'sGravenhage (The Hague) (cap.), Neth. 72/D3
Gravenhurst, Ont. 186/B2
Gravesend, Eng. 67/C6
Graz, Austria 82/C3
Great Abaco (isl.), Bah. 50/C1
Great Australian (bight), Austr. 114/B4
Great Barrier (reef), Austr. 115/D-E2-3
Great Basin Nat'l Pk., Nev 132/C4
Great Bear (lake), N.W.T. 42/D2
Great Bend, Kans. 147/B2
Great Britain & Northern Ireland (United Kingdom) 86/B
Great Dividing (range), Austr. 115/D3
Great Exuma (isl.), Bah. 50/C2
Great Falls, Mont. 156/B2
Great Inagua (isl.), Bah. 50/D2
Great Miami (riv.), Ohio 166/C1
Great Neck, N.Y. 180/C2
Great Salt (lake), Utah 174/A2
Great Salt Lake (des.), Utah 174/A2
Great Sand Dunes Nat'l Mon., Colo. 134/C3
Great Sandy (des.), Austr. 114/B3
Great Slave (lake), N.W.T. 42/E3
Great Smoky Mts. Nat'l Pk., U.S. 149/E4, 162/A2
Great Victoria (des.), Austr. 114/B3
Great Wall, China 104-105/D-E1-2
Great Yarmouth, Eng. 67/G4
Greece 85/C4
Greece, N.Y. 160/B1
Greeley, Colo. 134/A3
Green (riv.), U.S. 177/C4
Green (mts.), Vt. 158/A4
Green Bay, Wis. 176/C3
Greenbelt, Md. 139/E1
Greeneville, Tenn. 149/E3
Greenfield, Mass. 136/B1
Greenfield, Wis. 176/A1
Greenland 40/P2
Greenland (sea) 35/J2
Greenock, Scot. 66/A1
Green River, Utah 174/C3
Green River, Wyo. 177/C3
Greensboro, N.C. 163/F4
Greensburg, Pa. 170/B4
Greenville, Miss. 154/A2
Greenville, N.C. 163/E2
Greenville, S.C. 162/B2
Greenville, Texas 173/E1
Greenwich, Conn. 136/A4
Greenwich, Eng. 67/B5
Greenwood, Ind. 145/B3
Greenwood, Miss. 154/B2
Greenwood, S.C. 162/B3
Greer, S.C. 162/B2
Grenada 51/F4, 55/R
Grenada, Miss. 154/B2
Grenadines (isls.), see St. Vincent & the Grenadines
Grenoble, France 75/F5

Gresham, Oreg. 180/B5
Gretna, La. 150/B4
Greybull, Wyo. 177/A3
Griffin, Ga. 142/A3
Grimsby (Great Grimsby), Eng. 67/G4
Grimsby, Ont. 187/E4
Grindelwald, Switz. 80/C2
Groningen, Neth. 72/H1
Groote Eylandt (isl.), Austr. 114/C2
Gros Morne Nat'l Pk., Newf. 183/E1
Grossglockner (mt.), Austria 82/B3
Groton, Conn. 136/C3
Groznyy, Russia 89/G6
Grudziądz, Pol. 86/D2
Gruyères, Switz. 80/B2
Gstaad, Switz. 80/C2
Guadalajara, Mex. 46/D4
Guadalajara, Spain 77/E2
Guadalcanal (isl.), Sol. Is. 116/F7
Guadalquivir (riv.), Spain 76/C4
Guadalupe Mts. Nat'l Pk., Texas 172/B2
Guadeloupe 51/F3, 54-55/H
Guadiana (riv.), Europe 76/D3
Guainía (riv.), S. Amer. 56/C2
Guajira (pen.), S. Amer. 56/B1
Guam, U.S. 116/E4
Guanabacoa, Cuba 50/A2, C1/52
Guangdong (prov.), China 105/E3
Guangxi Zhuangzu (reg.), China 104/D3
Guangzhou (Canton), China 105/E3
Guantánamo, Cuba 53/K5
Guantánamo (bay), Cuba 53/K5
Guaporé (riv.), S. Amer. 56/C4
Guardafui, Somalia, see Ras Asèr
Guatemala 48/B2
Guatemala (cap.), Guat. 48/B2
Guaviare (riv.), Col. 56/B2
Guayaquil, Ecua. 56/A3
Guaynabo, P. Rico 54/C1
Guelph, Ont. 187/E4
Guernsey (isl.), Chan. Is. 67/E6
Guiana (highlands), S. Amer. 56-57/C-D2
Guilford, Conn. 136/B3
Guinea 60/A4
Guinea (gulf), Africa 60/C4
Guinea-Bissau 60/A3
Guiyang, China 104/D3
Guizhou (prov.), China 104/D3
Gulbarga, India 102/C3
Gulfport, Miss. 154/C4
Guntur, India 102/C3
Guri (res.), Ven. 56/C2
Guthrie, Okla. 168/B3
Guyama, P. Rico 54/C1
Guyana 56/D2
Guymon, Okla. 168/C1
Gwalior, India 102/C2
Gweru, Zimb. 63/F6
Gyangzê, China 104/D3
Győr, Hung. 83/D3
Gyumri, Armenia 89/F6

H

Haarlem, Neth. 72/E3
Habomai (isls.), Japan 107/G2
Hachinohe, Japan 107/F3
Hachioji, Japan 107/H2
Haddonfield, N.J. 171/F2
Hadhramaut (reg.), Yemen 94-95/F-G6-7

Index

Haeju, N. Korea 106/B3
Hagen, Ger. 70/B3
Hagerstown, Md. 139/E2
Haifa, Isr. 98/B2
Haikou, China 105/E4
Hail, S. Arabia 94/E4
Hainan (isl.), China 104-105/D4
Haines City, Fla. 140/C3
Haiphong, Viet. 110/D2
Haiti 50/D3, 52/P6
Hakodate, Japan 107/F2
Haleakala Nat'l Pk., Hawaii 129/C3
Haleb (Aleppo), Syria 97/G4
Halifax, Eng. 66/G1
Halifax (cap.), N.S. 183/D4
Hallandale, Fla. 141/D1
Halle, Ger. 70/E3
Halmahera (isl.), Indon. 113/H5
Hälsingborg, Swed. 69/C3
Haltom City, Texas 172/A4
Hama, Syria 97/G5
Hamadan, Iran 100/F3
Hamamatsu, Japan 107/E4
Hamburg, Ger. 70/D2
Hamden, Conn. 136/B3
Hamhŭng, N. Korea 106/B3
Hamilton (cap.), Bermuda 51/G3
Hamilton, N.Z. 115/F3
Hamilton, Ohio 167/D1
Hamilton, Ont. 187/E4
Hamilton, Scot. 66/B1
Hamm, Ger. 70/B3
Hammerfest, Nor. 68/D1
Hammond, Ind. 145/A1
Hammond, La. 150/B3
Hammondsport, N.Y. 160/C3
Hampton, Va. 138/V1
Han (riv.), S. Korea 106/B3
Hana, Hawaii 129/C3
Handan, China 105/E2
Hanford, Calif. 133/D2
Hangzhou (Hangchow), China 105/E2
Hannibal, Mo. 155/A3
Hannover, Ger. 70/C2
Hanoi (cap.), Viet. 110/D2
Hanover, N.H. 158/B3
Hanover, Pa. 171/D4
Harar, Eth. 61/G4
Harare (cap.), Zim. 63/F6
Harbin, China 105/F1
Hardanger (fjord), Nor. 69/B2
Hargeysa, Somalia 61/G4
Harlan, Ky. 149/E3
Harlingen, Texas 173/E4
Harriman, Tenn. 149/D4
Harris (dist.), Scot. 66/C2
Harrisburg (cap.), Pa. 171/D4
Harrison, N.Y. 180/C1
Harrisonburg, Va. 139/D3
Harrodsburg, Ky. 149/D2
Harrogate, Eng. 67/B5
Harrow, Eng. 67/B5
Hartford (cap.), Conn. 136/B2
Harz (mts.), Ger. 70/D3
Hasa (reg.), S. Arabia 94/F4
Hasselt, Belg. 73/F6
Hastings, Eng. 67/G5
Hastings, Minn. 153/C4
Hastings, Nebr. 157/C3
Hastings, N.Z. 115/F3
Hatteras (cape), N.C. 163/F2
Hattiesburg, Miss. 154/C4
Havana (cap.), Cuba 50/A2, 52/C1
Havel (riv.), Ger. 70/E2
Haverford, Pa. 171/E1
Haverhill, Mass. 137/D1
Havre, Mont. 156/A3
Havre de Grace, Md. 139/F2

Hawaii (isl.), Hawaii 129/C4
Hawaii (state), U.S. 129
Hawaii Volcanoes Nat'l Pk., Hawaii 129/C4
Hawaiian (isls.), U.S. 117/K3
Hawkesbury, Ont. 187/F2
Hawthorne, Calif. 179/B1
Hawthorne, Nev. 132/C3
Hawthorne, N.J. 180/A1
Hay River, N.W.T. 42/E3
Hays, Kans. 147/B2
Hayward, Calif. 133/E1
Hayward, Wis. 176/A2
Hazleton, Pa. 171/E3
Heard (isl.), Austr. 35/M8
Hearst, Ont. 187/F1
Hebei (prov.), China 105/E2
Hebrides, Outer (isls.), Scot. 66/C1-2
Hebron, West Bank 99/C4
Heerlen, Neth. 73/G6
Hefei, China 105/E2
Hegang, China 105/G1
Heidelberg, Ger. 71/C4
Heilbronn, Ger. 71/C4
Heilongjiang (prov.), China 105/F1
Hejaz (reg.), Saudi Arabia 94/D4-5
Helena (cap.), Mont. 156/B2
Helgoland (isl.), Ger. 70/C1
Helmand (riv.), Afghan. 102/B1
Helsingør, Den. 69/C3
Helsinki (cap.), Fin. 69/D2
Henan (prov.), China 105/E2
Henderson, Ky. 148/C2
Henderson, Nev. 133/D4
Henderson, N.C. 163/D1
Hengelo, Neth. 72/J3
Hengyang, China 105/E3
Henzada, Burma 110/A3
Herat, Afghan. 102/B1
Herbert Hoover Nat'l Hist. Site, Iowa 146/B4
Hereford, Eng. 67/E4
Hereford, Texas 172/A1
Hermon (mt.), Asia 98/D1
Hermosillo, Mex. 46/B2
Hershey, Pa. 171/D4
Hertford, Eng. 67/G5
's Hertogenbosch, Neth. 72/F4
Herzeliyya, Isr. 98/B3
Hesse (state), Ger. 71/C3
Hever City, Utah 174/B2
Hialeah, Fla. 141/D1
Hibbing, Minn. 153/B2
Hickory, N.C. 162/C2
Hierro (isl.), Spain 76/A5
Higashiosaka, Japan 107/E4
Highland Park, Ill. 178/B1
High Point, N.C. 163/E4
High River, Alta. 191/E3
Hildesheim, Ger. 70/D2
Hilla, Iraq 100/D4
Hillcrest Hts., Md. 139/E1
Hillsboro, N.H. 158/B4
Hillsboro, Oreg. 180/A1
Hilo, Hawaii 129/C4
Hilton Head Island, S.C. 162/C4
Hilversum, Neth. 72/F3
Himalaya (mts.), Asia 102-103/C1-E1-2
Himeji, Japan 106/D4
Hindu Kush (mts.), Asia 102/C1
Hingham, Mass. 137/E2
Hinton, Alta. 191/D2
Hirakata, Japan 107/E4
Hiroshima, Japan 106/C4
Hispaniola (isl.), W. Indies 52-53
Hitachi, Japan 107/F3
Hivaoa (isl.), Fr. Poly. 117/N6

Hobart, Austr. 115/D5
Hobart, Ind. 145/A1
Hobbs, N. Mex. 135/F4
Hoboken, N.J. 180/B2
Ho Chi Minh City, Viet. 111/D5
Hocking (riv.), Ohio 167/D3
Hodeida, Yemen 94/E7
Hofuf, Saudi Arabia 94/F4
Hohhot, China 105/E1
Hokkaido (isl.), Japan 107/G2
Holbrook, Ariz. 130/C3
Holguín, Cuba 50/C2, J4/53
Holladay, Utah 174/C1
Holland, Mich. 152/A4
Holland, see Netherlands
Hollidaysburg, Pa. 170/C4
Hollywood, Calif. 179/B1
Hollywood, Fla. 141/D1
Holon, Isr. 98/B3
Holyoke, Mass. 136/B2
Homer, Alaska 129/A2
Homestead, Fla. 141/E4
Homestead, Pa. 170/B1
Homestead Nat'l Mon., Nebr. 157/C4
Homewood, Ala. 128/B2
Homs, Libya 60/D1
Homs, Syria 97/G5
Homyel', Belarus 89/D4
Honan, China, see Henan
Honduras 48/C2
Honduras (gulf), Cent. Amer. 48/B1
Honesdale, Pa. 171/F2
Hong Kong 105/E3
Honiara (cap.), Sol. Is. 116/G6
Honolulu (cap.), Hawaii 129/B4
Honshu (isl.), Japan 107/F3
Hood (mt.), Oreg. 169/A2
Hood River, Oreg. 169/A2
Hoover (dam), U.S. 133/D4
Hopatcong (lake), N.J. 159/B1
Hope, Ark. 131/C3
Hope, Br. Col. 190/C4
Hopei, China, see Hebei
Hopewell, Va. 139/E4
Hopewell Culture Nat'l Hist. Pk., Ohio 167/D2
Hopkinsville, Ky. 148/C3
Hoquiam, Wash. 175/B22
Horlivka, Ukraine 89/E5
Hormuz (str.), Asia 101/K7
Horn (cape), Chile 58/C8
Horsens, Den. 69/B3
Horseshoe Bend Nat'l Mil. Pk., Ala. 128/C2
Hospitalet, Spain 77/H2
Hoste (isl.), Chile 58/B8
Hot Springs, Ark. 131/B2
Hot Springs, S. Dak. 165/E1
Hot Springs Nat'l Pk., Ark. 131/B2
Houghton, Mich. 152/C1
Houlton, Maine 151/C2
Houma, La. 150/C3
Houston, Texas 173/F4
Hove, Eng. 67/F5
Hovenweep Nat'l Mon., U.S. 174/C4
Howland (isl.), U.S. 117/J5
Howrah, India 103/D2
Hradec Králové, Czech Rep. 82/D1
Hrodna, Belarus 89/B4
Huainan, China 105/E2
Huallaga (riv.), Peru 56/B3
Huambo, Angola 62/D6
Huancayo, Peru 56/B4
Huang (Hwang) He (Yellow) (riv.) China 105/E2
Huánuco, Peru 56/B3

Huaráz, Peru 56/B3
Huascarán (mt.), Peru 56/B3
Hubei (prov.), China 105/E2
Hubli, India 102/C3
Huddersfield, Eng. 66/G1
Hudson (bay), Can. 43/H3
Hudson (str.), Can. 43/J3
Hudson, N.Y. 161/F3
Hudson (riv.), U.S. 161/F4
Hue, Viet. 110/D3
Huelva, Spain 76/C4
Huesca, Spain 77/F1
Hull, Eng. 67/F4
Hull, Que. 184/C4
Humacao, P. Rico 54/D1
Humboldt, Tenn. 148/B4
Hunan (prov.), China 105/E3
Hungary 83/EF3
Húngnam, N. Korea 106/B3
Hunsrück (mts.), Ger. 71/B4
Huntington, Pa. 170/C2
Huntington, Ind. 145/C2
Huntington, N.Y. 161/G1
Huntington, W. Va. 130/B3
Huntington Bch., Calif. 179/C2
Huntsville, Ala. 128/B1
Huntsville, Ark. 131/A2
Huntsville, Ont. 186/C2
Huntsville, Texas 173/E2
Huon (gulf), Papua N.G. 112/C7
Hupei, China, see Hubei
Huron (lake), N. Amer. 43/H7, 45/K2
Huron, S. Dak. 165/E3
Hurst, Texas 172/B4
Hutchinson, Kans. 147/B3
Hwange, Zimb. 63/E6
Hyannis, Mass. 137/F3
Hyannis, Nebr. 157/B2
Hyattsville, Md. 139/E1
Hyde, Eng. 66/G2
Hyderabad, India 102/C3
Hyderabad, Pak. 102/B2

Iaşi, Rom. 84/D2
Ibadan, Nigeria 60/C4
Ibagué Col. 56/B2
Ibiza (isl.), Spain 77/G3
Ica, Peru 56/B4
Iceland 64/C2
Ichang, China, see Yichang
Ichikawa, Japan 107/H2
Idabell, Okla. 168/C4
Idaho (state), U.S. 143
Idaho City, Idaho 143/A3
Idaho Falls, Idaho 143/C3
Iguaçu (riv.), S. Amer. 59/D5
Iguazú (falls), S. Amer. 59/D5
IJsselmeer (lake), Neth. 72/F2
Iligan, Phil. 109/E6
Illinois (riv.), Ill. 144/A3
Illinois (state), U.S. 144
Iloilo, Phil. 109/D5
Ilorin, Nigeria 60/C4
Imphal, India 103/E2
Inarijärvi (lake), Fin. 68/E1
Inch'ŏn, S. Korea 106/B3
Independence, Kans. 147/C4
Independence, Mo. 155/C1
India 102-103
Indiana (lake), Mich. 152/A2
Indiana, Pa. 170/B3
Indiana (state), U.S. 145
Indiana Dunes Nat'l Lakeshore, Ind. 145/A1

Indianapolis (cap.), Ind. 145/B3
Indian Ocean 93/F-G6
Indigirka (riv.), Russia 91/H2
Indio, Calif. 133/F4
Indochina (reg.), Asia 110-111/D2-5
Indonesia 112-113/C-H6-7
Indore, India 102/C2
Indus (riv.), Asia 102/B2
Inglewood, Calif. 179/B1
Inhambane, Moz. 63/F7
Inn (riv.), Europe 82/B2
Inner Mongolia (reg.), China 104-105/D-E1
Innisfail, Alta. 191/E3
Innsbruck, Austria 82/A3
In Salah, Alg. 60/C2
Insein, Burma 110/A3
Interlaken, Switz. 80/C2
International Falls, Minn. 153/B2
International Peace Garden, N. Amer. 164/A3, 189/D4
Inuvik, N.W.T. 42/C2
Invercargill, N.Z. 115/F4
Inverness, Scot. 66/D2
Ionian (isls.), Greece 85/C4
Iowa (state), U.S. 146
Iowa City, Iowa 146/B3
Ipoh, Malaysia 112/C5
Ipswich, Eng. 67/G4
Iqaluit, N.W.T. 43/K3
Iquique, Chile 56/B5
Iquitos, Peru 56/B3
Iráklion, Greece 85/D5
Iran 100-101
Irapuato, Mex. 46/E4
Iraq 100
Irbid, Jordan 98/D2
Ireland 67/BC4
Ireland, Northern, U.K. 67/C3
Iringa, Tanz. 63/F5
Irish (sea), Europe 67/D4
Irkutsk, Russia 91/F3
Irondequoit (bay), N.Y. 160/C1
Iron Mountain, Mich. 152/C1
Ironton, Ohio 167/E3
Iroquois Falls, Ont. 187/F1
Irrawaddy (riv.), Burma 110/A2
Irtysh (riv.), Asia 90/D3
Irvine, Calif. 179/D2
Irving, Texas 172/B4
Irvington, N.J. 180/A2
Isar (riv.), Ger. 71/D4
Ischia (isl.), Italy 79/D4
Ise, Japan 106/E4
Ise (bay), Japan 106/E4
Isère (riv.), France 75/F5
Isfahan, Iran 101/G4
Ishim (riv.), Asia 90/D3
Ishpeming, Mich. 152/C1
Iskenderun, Turkey 97/G4
Islamabad (cap.), Pak. 102/C1
Islamorada, Fla. 141/F5
Isle of Man 67/D3
Isle Royale Nat'l Pk., Mich. 152/A1
Isparta, Turkey 96/D4
Israel 98-99
Istanbul, Turkey 96/C2
Itaipú (res.), S. Amer. 59/D5
Italy 78-79
Ithaca, N.Y. 161/D3
Itháki (Ithaca) (isl.), Greece 85/C4
Ivano-Frankiv'sk, Ukr. 89/B5
Ivanovo, Russia 88/F3
Ivory Coast, see Côte d'Ivoire
Iwaki, Japan 107/F3
Iwo (isl.), Japan 107/G3
Izabal (lake), Guat. 48/B2
Izhevsk, Russia 88/H3
Izmayil, Ukraine 89/C5

İzmir, Turkey 96/B3
Izmit, Turkey 96/C2
Izu (isls.), Japan 107/E4

J

Jabalpur, India 102/D2
Jackman, Maine 151/A2
Jackson, Mich. 152/B4
Jackson (cap.), Miss. 154/A4
Jackson, Tenn. 148/B4
Jackson, Wyo. 177/B4
Jackson (lake), Wyo. 177/A4
Jacksonville, Ark. 131/B2
Jacksonville, Fla. 140/A3
Jacksonville, Ill. 144/A3
Jacksonville, N.C. 163/E2
Jacksonville Bch., Fla. 140/A3
Jaén, Spain 76/D4
Jaffa, Isr., see Tel Aviv-Jaffa
Jaffna, Sri Lanka 102/D4
Jaipur, India 102/C2
Jakarta (cap.), Indon. 113/H1
Jalalabad, Afgh. 102/B1
Jalapa, Mex. 47/H1
Jamaica 50,53
Jambi, Indon. 112/C6
James (bay), Can. 43/H5
James (riv.), N. Dak.-S. Dak. 164/C3, 165/E4
James (riv.), Va. 139/D3
Jamestown, N.Y. 160/A4
Jamestown, N. Dak. 164/C3
Jammu, India 102/C1
Jamnagar, India 102/B2
Jamshedpur, India 102/D2
Janesville, Wis. 176/B4
Jan Mayen (isl.), Nor. 35/J2
Japan 106-107
Japan (sea), Asia 92/A4
Japurá (riv.), Braz. 56/C3
Jarash, Jordan 98/D3
Jars (plain), Laos 110/C3
Jarvis (isl.), Pacific 117/L6
Jasper Nat'l Park, Alta. 191/D2
Java (isl.), Indon. 112/DE6
Java (sea), Indon. 112/DE6
Jaworzno, Pol. 87/D3
Jayapura, Indon. 113/K6
Jefferson City (cap.), Mo. 155/B3
Jeffersontown, Ky. 149/F1
Jeffersonville, Ind. 145/C4
Jena, Ger. 71/D3
Jerez de la Frontera, Spain 76/D4
Jericho, West Bank 99/C4
Jersey (isl.), Chan. Is. 67/E6
Jersey City, N.J. 180/B2
Jerusalem (cap.), Isr. 99/C4
Jewel Cave Nat'l Mon., S. Dak. 165/E1
Jhansi, India 102/C2
Jiamusi, China 105/F1
Jiangsu (prov.), China 105/F2
Jiangxi (prov.), China 105/E3
Jidda, Saudi Arabia 94/D5
Jilin, China 105/F1
Jilin (prov.), China 105/F1
Jimma, Eth. 61/F4
Jinan, China 105/E2
Jingdezhen, China 105/E3
Jinja, Uganda 63/F4
Jinmen (isl.), China 105/E3
Jinzhou, China 105/F1
Jixi, China 105/G1
João Pessoa, Braz. 57/F3
Jodhpur, India 102/C2
Johannesburg, S. Africa 63/E7
John Day (riv.), Oreg. 169/B3
John Day Fossil Beds Nat'l Mon., Oreg. 169/B3

Index

John Muir Nat'l Hist. Site, Calif. 133/E1
Johnson City, N.Y. 161/D3
Johnson City, Tenn. 149/F3
Johnson Space Center, Texas 173/H4
Johnston (atoll), U.S. 117/K4
Johnstown, N.Y. 161/E3
Johnstown, Pa. 170/B4
Johore Baharu, Malaysia 111/C7
Joinvile, Braz. 59/E5
Joliet, Ill. 178/A3
Joliette, Que. 185/D4
Jolo (isl.), Phil. 109/C8
Jonesboro, Ark. 131/A3
Jönköping, Swede. 69/B3
Jonquière, Que. 185/E2
Joplin, Mo. 155/C2
Jordan 98-99
Jordan (riv.), Asia 98/D3
Jos, Nigeria 60/C3
Joshua Tree Nat'l Park, Calif. 133/C4
Juan de Fuca (str.), N. Amer. 175/A2, 190/B4
Juan de Nova, Réunion 63/G6
Juan Fernández (isls.), Chile 58/B4
Juba, Sudan 61/F4
Jubbulpore, India, see Jabalpur
Judaea (dist.) 98/C4-5
Juiz de Fora, Braz. 59/E5
Jujuy, Arg. 58/C5
Julesburg, Nebr. 157/B1
Julianehåb, Greenl., see Qaqortoq
Jullundur, India 102/C1
Jumna (riv.), India 102/B2
Junagadh, India 102/B2
Junction City, Kans. 147/B3
Juneau (cap.), Alaska 129/C2
Jungfrau (mt.), Switz. 80/D2
Jupiter, Fla. 141/F4
Jura (mts.), Europe 74-75/F-G4
Juruá (riv.), Braz. 56/C3
Juventud (isl.), Cuba 50/A2, C2/52
Jyväskylä, Fin. 69/E2

K

K2 (mt.), Asia 102/C1
Kabul (cap.), Afghan. 102/B1
Kabwe, Zambia 63/E6
Kadiköy, Turkey 96/D6
Kadoma, Zimb. 63/E6
Kaduna, Nigeria 60/C3
Kaédi, Maur. 60/A3
Kaesŏng, N. Korea 106/B3
Kagoshima, Japan 106/C5
Kahoolawe (isl.), Hawaii 129/B4
Kahului, Hawaii 129/B4
Kaifeng, China 105/E2
Kailua, Hawaii 129/B4
Kaiserslautern, Ger. 71/B4
Kakinada, India 102/D3
Kalaallit Nunaat (Greenland) 40/P2
Ka Lae (cape), Hawaii 129/C4
Kalahari (des.), Africa 63/E7
Kálamai, Greece 85/C4
Kalamazoo, Mich. 152/B4
Kalaupapa Nat'l Hist. Pk., Hawaii 129/B3
Kalemie, Congo, Rep. of the 63/E5
Kalgan, China, see Zhangjiakou
Kalimantan (reg.), Indon. 112/E5
Kaliningrad, Russia 88/B4
Kalispell, Mont. 156/A1
Kalisz, Pol. 86/D3

Kaloko-Honokohau Nat'l Hist. Pk., Hawaii 129/B4
Kaluga, Russia 89/E4
Kama (riv.), Russia 88/H2
Kamakura, Japan 107/H2
Kamaran (isl.), Yemen 94/E6
Kamchatka (pen.), Russia 91/H3
Kam'yanets-Podil's'kyy, Ukr. 89/C5
Kamina, Congo, Rep. of the 63/E5
Kamloops, Br. Col. 190/C3
Kampala (cap.), Uganda 63/F4
Kampuchea, see Cambodia
Kamyshin, Russia 89/F4
Kananga, Congo, Rep. of the 63/E5
Kanata, Ont. 186/A1
Kanawha (riv.), W. Va. 138/B3
Kanazawa, Japan 106/E3
Kanchipuram, India 102/D3
Kandahar, Afghan., see Qandahar
Kandy, Sri Lanka 102/C4
Kaneohe, Hawaii 129/B3
Kangaroo (isl.), Austr. 114/C4
Kanin (pen.), Russia 90/C2
Kankakee, Ill. 144/C2
Kankan, Guinea 60/B3
Kannapolis, N.C. 162/C2
Kano, Nigeria 60/C3
Kanpur, India 102/C2
Kansas (state), U.S. 147
Kansas City, Kans. 147/A4
Kansas City, Mo. 155/C1
Kansk, Russia 91/E3
Kansu, China, see Gansu
Kanton (isl.), Kiribati 117/J6
Kaohsiung, Taiwan 105/F3
Kaolack, Sen. 60/A3
Kapingamarangi, Micronesia 116/E5
Kaposvár, Hung. 83/D2
Kapuas (riv.), Indon. 112/E6
Kapuskasing, Ont. 187/F1
Kara (sea), Russia 90/D2
Karachi, Pak. 102/B2
Karaj, Iran 100/C3
Karak, Jordan, see El Karak
Karakoram (mts.), Asia 102/C1
Karakorum (ruins), Mong. 104/D1
Karbala, Iraq 100/C4
Kariba (lake), Africa 63/E6
Karimata (str.), Indon. 112/D6
Karlsruhe, Ger. 71/C4
Karnak, Egypt, see El Karnak
Kárpathos (isl.), Greece 85/D5
Karun (riv.), Iran 100/F5
Karviná, Czech Rep. 83/E2
Kasai (riv.), Africa 63/D5
Kasama, Zambia 63/F6
Kashan, Iran 101/C3
Kashi (Kashgar), China 104/A2
Kassala, Sudan 61/F3
Kassel, Ger. 70/C3
Katahdin (mt.), Maine 151/B2
Katanga (reg.), Congo, Rep. of the 63/E5
Kathmandu (cap.), Nepal 102/D2
Katmai Nat'l Pk., Alaska 129/A2
Katowice, Pol. 86/B4
Katsina, Nigeria 60/C4
Kattegat (str.), Europe 69/B3
Kauai (isl.), Hawaii 129/A3
Kaunas, Lith. 88/C3
Kavála, Greece 85/D3
Kawaguchi, Japan 107/H2
Kawartha (lakes), Ont. 187/D3
Kawasaki, Japan 107/H2
Kayenta, Ariz. 130/C2
Kayes, Mali 60/A3
Kayseri, Turkey 97/F3
Kazakhstan 90/C3
Kazan', Kazak. 88/G3

Kearney, Nebr. 157/C3
Kearny, N.J. 180/A2
Kecskemét, Hung. 83/E3
Kediri, Indon. 113/K2
Keelung, Taiwan 105/F3
Keene, N.H. 158/B4
Keetmanshoop, Namibia 63/D7
Kefallinía (isl.), Greece 85/B4
Kefar Sava, Isr. 98/B3
Kejimkujik Nat'l Pk., N.S. 182/C2
Kelang, Malaysia 111/C7
Kelantan (state), Malaysia 111/C6
Kellys (isl.), Ohio 166/A3
Kelowna, Br. Col. 190/C4
Kelso, Wash. 175/C2
Kemerovo, Russia 90/E3
Kemmerer, Wyo. 177/C1
Kenai, Alaska 129/B2
Kenai Fjords Nat'l Pk., Alaska 129/B2
Kenitra, Mor. 60/B1
Kenmore, N.Y. 160/A1
Kennebec (riv.), Maine 151/A3
Kennebunk, Maine 151/A4
Kenner, La. 150/A3
Kennewick, Wash. 175/C2
Kenora, Ont. 187/D1
Kenosha, Wis. 176/C4
Kent, Ohio 166/B4
Kent, Wash. 175/C1
Kentucky (lake), U.S. 148/B3
Kentucky (state), U.S. 148-149
Kentville, N.S. 182/C3
Kentwood, Mich. 152/B4
Kenya 63/F4
Kenya (mt.), Kenya 63/F4
Keokuk, Iowa 146/C4
Kerch, Ukr. 89/E5
Kérkira (isl.), Greece 85/B4
Kerkrade, Neth. 73/H6
Kermadec (isls.), N.Z. 117/J9
Kerman, Iran 101/K5
Kermit, Texas 173/D3
Ketchikan, Alaska 129/C2
Kettering, Eng. 67/F4
Kettering, Ohio 267/D1
Keuka (lake), N.Y. 160/C3
Kewaunee, Wis. 176/C3
Keweenaw (pen.), Mich. 152/C1
Key Biscayne, Fla. 141/E1
Key Largo, Fla. 141/F4
Key West, Fla. 141/F3
Khabarovsk, Russia 91/G3
Khalkís, Greece 85/C4
Khanty-Mansiysk, Russia 90/D3
Khan Yunis, Gaza Strip 99/A5
Kharagpur, India 102/D2
Khârga (oasis), Egypt 94/C4
Khartoum (cap.), Sudan 61/F3
Khartoum North, Sudan 61/F3
Kharkiv, Ukr. 89/E5
Khaskovo, Bulg. 84/D3
Kherson, Ukr. 89/D5
Khíos (isl.), Greece 85/D4
Khirbet Qumran, West Bank 99/C4
Khmel'nyts'kyy, Ukr. 89/C5
Khon Kaen, Thai. 110/C3
Khorramabad, Iran 100/F4
Khorramshahr, Iran 100/F5
Khvoy, Iran 100/D1
Khyber (pass), Asia 102/C1
Kiangsi, China, see Jiangxi
Kiangsu, China, see Jiangsu
Kiel (Nord Ostsee) (canal), Ger. 70/C1
Kiel, Ger. 70/C1
Kielce, Pol. 87/E3
Kiev (cap.), Ukr. 89/D4
Kigali (cap.), Rwanda 63/F5
Kigoma, Tanz. 63/F5

Kikwit, Congo, Rep. of the 63/D5
Kilgore, Texas 173/F2
Kilimanjaro (mt.), Tanz. 63/F5
Kilkenny, Ire. 67/C4
Killarney, Ire. 67/B4
Kilmarnock, Scot. 66/D3
Kimball, Nebr. 157/B1
Kimberley, S. Africa 63/E7
Kinabalu (mt.), Malaysia 113/F4
Kinbasket (lake), Br. Col. 191/D3
Kincardine, Ont. 186/B3
Kindersley, Sask. 188/A3
Kindia, Guinea 60/A3
Kineshma, Russia 88/F3
King (isl.), Austr. 114/D5
King Christian IX Land, Greenl. 40/Q3
King Christian X Land, Greenl. 40/Q2
Kingman, Ariz. 130/A3
Kings Canyon Nat'l Pk., Calif. 133/D3
King's Lynn, Eng. 67/G4
Kings Mountain, N.C. 162/C2
Kings Mountain Nat'l Mil. Pk., S.C. 162/C2
Kings Point, N.Y. 180/C2
Kingsport, Tenn. 149/F1
Kingston (cap.), Jam. 50/C3, 53/W10
Kingston, N.Y. 161/F4
Kingston, Ont. 187/E3
Kingston, Pa. 171/E4
Kingston upon Thames, Eng. 67/B6
Kingstown (cap.), St. Vinc. & Grens. 50/G4, 55/P
Kingsville, Texas 173/D4
Kinshasa (cap.), Congo, Rep. of the 62/B5
Kinston, N.C. 163/E2
Kiribati 117/J6
Kirikkale, Turkey 96/E3
Kirin, China, see Jilin
Kiritimati (isl.), Kiribati 117/L5
Kirkcaldy, Scot. 66/E2
Kirkland, Wash. 175/B1
Kirkland Lake, Ont. 187/F1
Kirksville, Mo. 155/A2
Kirkuk, Iraq 100/D3
Kirkwall, Scot. 66/E1
Kirkwood, Mo. 155/B4
Kirovohrad, Ukraine 89/D5
Kiryu, Japan 107/F3
Kisangani, Congo, Rep. of the 63/E4
Kishiwada, Japan 107/E5
Kisimayu, Somalia, see Chisimayu
Kissimmee, Fla. 140/C3
Kistna (riv.), India 102/C3
Kisumu, Kenya 63/F5
Kitakyushu, Japan 106/C4
Kitchener, Ont. 186/D3
Kitimat, Br. Col. 190/A2
Kittery, Maine 151/A4
Kitty Hawk, N.C. 163/F1
Kitwe, Zambia 63/E6
Kitzbühel, Austria 82/B3
Kivu (lake), Africa 63/E5
Kızılırmak (riv.), Turkey 96/E2
Kjölen (mts.), Europe 68/C-D1-2
Klagenfurt, Austria 82/C3
Klaipėda, Lith. 88/B3
Klamath (riv.), U.S. 132/A1, 169/C2
Klamath Falls, Oreg. 169/C2
Klosters, Switz. 81/E2
Kluane Nat'l Pk., Yukon 129/B2
Knife River Indian Villages Nat'l Hist. Site, N. Dak. 164/B2

Knoxville, Tenn. 149/E4
Kobe, Japan 106/D4
Koblenz, Ger. 71/B3
Kobuk Valley Nat'l Pk., Alaska 129/A1
Kochi, Japan 106/D4
Kodiak, Alaska 129/B2
Kodiak (isl.), Alaska 129/A2
Kofu, Japan 107/E4
Kōje (isl.), S. Korea 106/C4
Kōkshetaū, Kazak. 90/D3
Kokomo, Ind. 145/B2
Kola (pen.), Russia 88/E1
Kolar Gold Fields, India 102/C3
Kolhapur, India 102/C3
Kolomna, Russia 89/E4
Kolwezi, Congo, Rep. of the 63/E6
Kolyma (range), Russia 91/H2
Kolyma (riv.), Russia 91/H2
Kompong Cham, Camb. 111/D5
Komsomol'sk, Russia 91/G3
Königsberg (Kaliningrad), Russia 88/B4
Königssee (lake), Ger. 71/E5
Konotop, Ukr. 89/D4
Kontum, Viet. 110/E4
Konya, Turkey 96/E3
Kootenay (lake), Br. Col. 191/D3
Kootenay Nat'l Pk., Br. Col. 191/D3
Korçë, Alb. 85/C3
Korea, North 106/C2
Korea, South 106/C3
Korea (str.), Asia 106/C4
Koriyama, Japan 107/F3
Koror (cap.), Palau 113/J5
Kortrijk, Belg., see Courtrai
Koryak (range), Russia 91/J2
Kos (isl.), Greece 85/D4
Košice, Slvk. 83/F2
Kosovo (aut. reg.), Yugo. 84/C3
Kosti, Sudan 61/F3
Kostroma, Russia 88/F3
Koszalin, Pol. 86/C1
Kota, India 102/C2
Kota Baharu, Malaysia 111/C6
Kota Kinabalu, Malaysia 112/F4
Kotka, Fin. 69/E2
Kottbus, Ger. 70/F3
Kouchibouguac Nat'l Pk., N. Br. 182/C2
Kozhikode, India 102/C3
Kra (isth.), Thai. 111/B5
Kragujevac, Yugo. 84/C2
Krakatau (isl.), see Rakata
Krakow, Poland 87/E3
Kralendijk, Neth. Ant. 55/M
Krasnodar, Russia 89/E4
Krasnoyarsk, Russia 91/E3
Krefeld, Ger. 70/B3
Kremenchuk, Ukraine 89/D5
Kristiansand, Nor. 69/E2
Krung Thep, Thai., see Bangkok
Kryvyy Rih, Ukraine 89/D5
Kuala Lumpur (cap.), Malaysia 111/C7
Kuala Terengganu, Malaysia 111/C6
Kuantan, Malaysia 111/C7
Kuching, Malaysia 112/D5
Kudymkar, Russia 88/H3
Kufra (oasis), Libya 61/E2
Kumamoto, Japan 106/D4
Kumasi, Ghana 60/B4
Kunashiri (isl.), Japan 107/G1
Kunlun Shan (mts.), Asia 104/AC2
Kunming, China 104/D3
Kunsan, S. Korea 106/B4
Kuopio, Fin. 68/E2
Kurdistan (reg.), Asia 94/EF2

Kure, Japan 106/D4
Kurgan, Russia 90/D3
Kuria Muria (isls.), Oman 95/H6
Kuril (isls.), Asia 91/H3
Kurnool, India 102/C3
Kursk, Russia 89/E4
Kushiro, Japan 107/G2
Kuskokwim (mts.), Alaska 129/A2
Kut, Iraq 100/E4
Kütahya, Turkey 96/C3
K'ut'aisi, Georgia 89/F6
Kutch, Rann of (salt marsh), India 102/C2
Kutztown, Pa. 171/E4
Kuwait 94/F4
Kuwait (cap.), Kuwait 94/F4
Kuznetsk, Russia 89/G4
Kwajalein (atoll), Marshall Is. 116/G5
Kwangju, S. Korea 106/B4
Kwangsi Chuang, China, see Guangxi Zhuangzu
Kwangtung, China, see Guangdong
Kweichow, China, see Guizhou
Kwekwe, Zimb. 63/E6
Kyoto, Japan 107/E4
Kyrgyzstan 90/D3
Kyushu (isl.), Japan 106/D4
Kyzyl, Russia 91/E3

L

Laayoune, W. Sahara 60/A2
La Baie, Que. 185/E2
Labrador (dist.), Newf. 40/M4
Labuan (isl.), Malaysia 112/E4
Lac-Mégantic, Que. 185/E4
Laccadive, India, see Cannanore
La Ceiba, Hond. 48/C2
La Chaux-de-Fonds, Switz. 80/B1
Lachine, Que. 184/A1
La Chorrera, Panama 49/D3
Lackawanna, N.Y. 160/B3
Lacombe, Alta. 191/E3
Laconia, N.H. 158/C3
La Coruña, Spain 76/B1
La Crosse, Wis. 176/A4
Ladoga (lake), Russia 88/D2
Lae, Papua N.G. 116/E6
Lafayette, Ind. 145/B2
Lafayette, La. 150/C2
La Follette, Tenn. 149/E3
Laghouat, Alg. 60/C1
Lagos, Nigeria 60/C4
La Grande, Oreg. 169/A4
La Grange, Ga. 142/A3
La Guaira, Ven. 56/C1
La Habra, Calif. 179/B3
Lahaina, Hawaii 129/D4
Lahn (riv.), Ger. 71/C3
Lahore, Pak. 102/C1
Lahti, Fin. 69/E2
Laie, Hawaii 129/A4
La Jolla, Calif. 180/C4
La Junta, Colo. 134/C4
Lake Bluff, Ill. 178/B1
Lake Buena Vista, Fla. 140/B4
Lake Charles, La. 150/C1
Lake Chelan Nat'l Rec. Area, Wash. 175/A3
Lake Clark Nat'l Pk., Alaska 129/A2
Lake Forest, Ill. 178/B1
Lake George, N.Y. 161/F3
Lake Havasu City, Ariz. 130/A3
Lakeland, Fla. 140/C3
Lake Louise, Alta. 191/D3
Lake Mead Nat'l Rec. Area, U.S. 130/A2, 133/D4

Index

Lake Placid, N.Y. 161/E2
Lakeview, Oreg. 169/C3
Lake Wales, Fla. 140/C3
Lakewood, Calif. 179/C3
Lakewood, Colo. 178/A4
Lakewood, N.J. 159/C3
Lakewood, Ohio 167/F3
Lake Worth, Fla. 141/D4
Lakshadweep, India, see
　Cannanore
Lalitpur, Nepal 102/D2
La Louvière, Belg. 73/D7
La Manche (English) (chan.),
　Europe 74/A1
La Mauricie Nat'l Pk., Que.
　185/C3
Lambaréné, Gabon 62/D5
La Mesa, Calif. 180/C4
La Mesa, Texas 172/C2
Lamon (bay), Phil. 108/D3
Lamèque (isl.), N. Bruns. 182/C1
Lanai (isl.), Hawaii 129/B3
Lancaster, Calif. 133/C3
Lancaster, Eng. 67/E3
Lancaster, N.H. 158/B3
Lancaster, Ohio 167/D3
Lancaster, Pa. 171/E4
Lancaster, S.C. 162/C2
Land's End (prom.), Eng. 67/D5
Lander, Wyo. 177/B3
Langley, Br. Col. 190/B1
Lansing, Ill. 178/B3
Lansing (cap.), Mich. 152/B4
Lanzarote (isl.), Spain 76/C4
Lanzhou (Lanchow), China
　104/D2
Laos 110/D3
La Palma (isl.), Spain 76/A4
La Paz (cap.), Bol. 56/C4
Lapland (reg.), Europe 68/CF1
La Plata, Arg. 58/D6
LaPorte, Ind. 145/B1
Lappeenranta, Fin. 69/E2
Laptev (sea), Russia 91/G2
La Puente, Calif. 179/B3
Laramie (mts.), U.S. 177/C2
Laramie, Wyo. 177/C2
Laredo, Texas 173/D4
Largo, Fla. 140/C1
La Rioja, Arg. 58/C5
Lárisa, Greece 85/C4
Larnaca, Cyprus 96/E5
Larne, N. Ire. 67/D3
La Rochelle, France 75/C4
La Romana, Dom. Rep. 53/T7
La Ronge, Sask. 188/C1
Las Cruces, N. Mex. 135/F2
La Serena, Chile 58/B5
Las Palmas, Spain 76/B4
La Spezia, Italy 78/B2
Lassen Volcanic Nat'l Pk., Calif.
　132/B2
Las Vegas, Nev. 133/C3
Las Vegas, N. Mex. 135/D3
Latakia, Syria 97/G5
Latium (reg.), Italy 78/D3
La Tuque, Que. 185/D3
Latvia 88/C3
Launceston, Austr. 115/D5
Laurel, Del. 139/F3
Laurel, Md. 139/F2
Laurel, Miss. 154/C3
Lausanne, Switz. 80/B2
Lava Beds Nat'l Mon., Calif.
　132/A2
Laval, Que. 184/A1
La Vega, Dom. Rep. 52/R6
Lawrence, Kans. 147/B4
Lawrence, Mass. 137/D1
Lawrenceburg, Tenn. 148/C4
Lawton, Okla. 168/C2

Lead, S. Dak. 165/E1
Leadville, Colo. 134/B2
Leamington, Ont. 186/A4
Leavenworth, Kans. 147/A4
Lebanon 96/F6
Lebanon, N.H. 158/B3
Lebanon, Pa. 171/E4
Lebanon, Tenn. 148/C3
Leduc, Alta. 191/F1
Leech (lake), Minn. 153/B3
Leeds, Eng. 67/F4
Leesburg, Fla. 140/B3
Leeuwarden, Neth. 72/G1
Leeward (isls.), W. Indies 51/F3
Leghorn, Italy 78/C3
Legnica (Liegnitz), Pol. 86/B3
Le Havre, France 74/C3
Leicester, Eng. 67/F4
Leiden, Neth. 72/E3
Leipzig, Ger. 71/E3
Leizhou Bandao (pen.), China
　105/E3
Lelystad, Neth. 72/F3
Le Mans, France 74/D3
Lena (riv.), Russia 91/G2
Leningrad (St. Petersburg), Rus.,
　88/D3
Leninsk, Russia 90/D3
Leninsk-Kuznetskiy, Russia
　90/E3
Lenox, Mass. 136/A1
Lens, France 74/E2
Leominster, Mass. 137/D1
León, Mex. 46/E4
León, Nic. 48/C2
León, Spain 76/D1
Lérida (Lléida), Spain 77/G2
Lerwick, Scot. 66/B2
Les Cayes, Haiti 52/N7
Leskovac, Yugo. 84/C3
Lesotho 63/E7
Lesser Antilles (isls.), W. Indies
　51/EF4
Lesser Slave (lake), Alta. 191/D1
Lésvos (Lesbos) (isl.), Greece
　85/D4
Lethbridge, Alta. 191/F4
Letterkenny, Ire. 66/B3
Leverkusen, Ger. 71/B3
Lewes, Del. 139/F3
Lewis (dist.), Scot. 66/C1
Lewis and Clark (lake), Nebr.
　157/A3
Lewis and Clark Mem., Mont.
　156/C2
Lewisburg, Pa. 171/D3
Lewisburg, Tenn. 148/C4
Lewisburg, W. Va. 138/C3
Lewiston, Idaho 143/A2
Lewiston, Maine 151/A3
Lewiston, Mont. 156/B3
Lewistown, Pa. 170/C3
Lexington, Ky. 149/E2
Lexington, N.C. 162/C2
Leyte (gulf), Phil. 109/E5
Leyte (isl.), Phil. 109/E5
Lhasa, China 104/C3
Lianyungang, China 105/E2
Liaodong Bandao (pen.), China
　105/F2
Liaoning (prov.), China 105/F1
Liaoyuan, China 105/F1
Libby, Mont. 156/A1
Liberal, Kans. 147/C1
Liberec, Czech Rep. 82/C1
Liberia 60-61/D2
Liberty, Mo. 155/B1
Libreville (cap.), Gabon 62/C4
Libya 60-61/D2
Libyan (des.), Africa 61/E2
Liechtenstein 81/E1

Liège, Belg. 73/G6
Liepāja, Latvia 88/B3
Liguria (reg.), Italy 78/B2
Ligurian (sea), Italy 78/A2
Lihue, Hawaii 129/A3
Likasi, Congo, Rep. of the 63/E6
Lille, France 74/E2
Lilongwe (cap.), Malawi 63/F6
Lima, Ohio 166/B1
Lima (cap.), Peru 56/B4
Limassol, Cyprus 97/E5
Limerick, Ire. 67/B4
Limnos (isl.), Greece 85/D4
Limoges, France 75/D4
Limón, C. Rica 49/D3
Limpopo (riv.), Africa 63/E7
Lincoln (sea), Arctic 40/M1
Lincoln, Eng. 67/F4
Lincoln, Ill. 144/B2
Lincoln (cap.), Nebr. 157/B4
Lincoln Boyhood Nat'l Mem., Ind.
　145/B3
Lincoln Park, Mich. 178/C4
Lindau, Ger. 71/C5
Linden, N.J. 180/A3
Lindesnes (cape), Nor. 69/B3
Lindi, Tanz. 63/F5
Lindsay, Ont. 186/C3
Lindsborg, Kans. 147/B3
Lingayen (gulf), Phil. 108/C2
Linköping, Swed. 69/C3
Linz, Austria 82/C2
Lions (gulf), France 75/E6
Lipari (isls.), Italy 79/E5
Lipetsk, Russia 89/E4
Lippe (riv.), Ger. 70/C3
Lisbon (cap.), Port. 76/B3
Lisburn, N. Ire. 67/D3
Lisle, Ill. 178/A2
Lismore, Austr. 115/E3
Listowel, Ont. 186/B3
Litchfield, Conn. 136/A3
Litchfield, Minn. 153/B4
Lithuania 88/B3
Little America, Antarc. 118
Little Cayman (isl.), Cayman Is.
　50/B3
Little Current, Ont. 186/B2
Little Missouri (riv.), U.S. 164/C1
Little Rock (cap.), Ark. 131/B2
Littleton, Colo. 178/A4
Littleton, N.H. 158/B2
Liuzhou, China 104/D3
Livermore, Calif. 132/C1
Liverpool, Eng. 67/E4
Liverpool, N.S. 182/C4
Livingston, Mont. 156/C2
Livingston, N.J. 180/A2
Livingston, Scot. 66/C1
Livingstone, Zambia 63/E6
Livonia, Mich. 178/B4
Livorno (Leghorn), Italy 78/C3
Ljubljana (cap.), Slov. 84/A2
Llanos (plains), S. Amer. 56/B2
Lléida, Spain 77/G2
Lloydminster, Alta. 191/F2
Lloydminster, Sask. 188/A2
Llullaillaco (vol.), Chile 58/C5
Lobito, Angola 62/D6
Locarno, Switz. 81/D2
Lock Haven, Pa. 171/C3
Lockport, N.Y. 160/B1
Lod (Lydda), Isr. 99/B4
Lodi, Calif. 132/C2
Lodi, N.J. 180/B2
Łódź, Pol. 87/D3
Lofoten (isls.), Nor. 68/C1
Logan, Utah 174/B2
Logan (mt.), Yukon 129/B2
Logansport, Ind. 145/B2
Logroño, Spain 77/E1

Loire (riv.), France 74/C4
Lombard, Ill. 178/A2
Lombardy (reg.), Italy 78/B2
Lombok (isl.), Indon. 112/F7
Lomé (cap.), Togo 60/C4
Lompoc, Calif. 133/E2
London, Eng. (cap.), U.K. 67/F5
London, Ont. 186/B4
Londonderry, N. Ire. 66/C3
Londrina, Braz. 59/D5
Long (isl.), Bah. 50/C2
Long (isl.), N.Y. 160/B4
Long Beach, Calif. 179/C2
Long Beach (isl.), N.J. 159/C3
Long Beach, N.Y. 180/C2
Long Branch, N.J. 159/C2
Long Island (sound), U.S. 160/B4
Longmont, Colo. 134/A3
Long Point (bay), Ont. 186/C4
Longueuil, Que. 184/B1
Longview, Texas 173/F2
Longview, Wash. 175/F2
Lookout (cape), N.C. 163/F2
Lop Nur (Lop Nor) (dry lake),
  China 104/C1
Lopatka (cape), Russia 91/N3
Lorain, Ohio 166/A3
Lord Howe (isl.), Austr. 116/G9
Lorient, France 74/B4
Lorraine (prov.), France 74/G3
Lorrainville, Que. 184/A3
Los Alamos, N. Mex. 135/D3
Los Altos, Calif. 133/F1
Los Angeles, Calif. 133/E3
Los Gatos, Calif. 133/D1
Los Teques, Ven. 56/C2
Loughborough, Eng. 67/F4
Louisbourg, N.S. 183/F3
Louisiana (state), U.S. 150
Louisville, Ky. 149/E1
Lourdes, France 75/D6
Louvain (Leuven), Belg. 73/E6
Lovington, N. Mex. 135/E4
Lowell, Mass. 137/D1
Lower Red (lake), Minn. 153/B2
Lower Saxony (state), Ger. 70/C2
Lower Tunguska (riv.), Russia
  91/E2
Lowestoft, Eng. 67/G4
Loyalty (isls.), New Caledonia
  116/G3
Lualaba (riv.), Congo, Rep. of the
  63/E5
Luanda (cap.), Angola 62/D5
Luang Prabang, Laos 110/C3
Lubango, Angola 62/D6
Lubbock, Texas 172/C1
Lubec, Maine 151/C3
Lübeck, Ger. 70/D2
Lublin, Pol. 87/F3
Lubumbashi, Congo, Rep. of the
  63/E6
Lucca, Italy 78/C3
Lucerne (lake), Switz. 81/D2
Lucerne (Luzern), Switz. 81/D1
Lucknow, India 102/C2
Lüda (Dalian), China 105/E3
Lüderitz, Namibia 62/D7
Ludhiana, India 102/C1
Ludington, Mich. 152/A3
Ludwigshafen, Ger. 71/C4
Lufkin, Texas 173/F2
Lugano, Switz. 81/D2
Lugo, Spain 76/C1
Luhans'k, Ukraine 89/E5
Lumberton, N.C. 163/F2
Lund, Swed. 69/C3
Lundy (isl.), Eng. 67/D5
Lüneburger Heide (dist.), Ger.
  70/C2

Luoyang, China 105/E2
Luray, Va. 139/D3
Lusaka (cap.), Zambia 63/E6
Lusk, Wyo. 177/B1
Luton, Eng. 67/F5
Luts'k, Ukraine 89/B4
Luverne, Minn. 153/A4
Luxembourg 73/H8
Luxembourg (cap.), Lux. 73/H8
Luxor, Egypt 61/F3
Luzon (isl.), Phil. 108/C2
L'viv, Ukraine 89/B5
Lyallpur, Pak., see Faisalabad
Lydda, Isr. 99/B4
Lynchburg, Va. 139/D3
Lyndon B. Johnson Nat'l Hist.
  Site, Texas 173/D3
Lynn, Mass. 137/D1
Lynnwood, Wash. 175/B1
Lynwood, Calif. 179/B2
Lyons, France 75/F5

M

Ma'an, Jordan 99/E5
Maas (riv.), Neth. 72/F4
Maastricht, Neth. 73/G6
Macapá, Braz. 57/D2
Macau 105/E3
Macclesfield, Eng. 66/G2
Maceió, Braz. 57/F3
Machala, Ecuador 56/B3
Machias, Maine 151/C3
Machida, Japan 107/H2
Machilipatnam, India 102/D3
Mackay, Austr. 115/D3
Mackenzie (riv.), N.W.T. 42/C2
Mackenzie, Br. Col. 190/C2
Mackinac (isl.), Mich. 152/B2
Mackinaw City, Mich. 152/B2
Macomb, Ill. 144/A2
Macon, Ga. 142/B3
Ma'daba, Jordan 99/D4
Madagascar 6-7 63/G
Madang, Papua N.G. 112/B7
Madawaska (riv.), Ont. 187/D2
Madawaska, Maine 151/B1
Madeira (isl.), Port. 76/A2
Madeira (riv.), Braz. 56/C3
Madera, Calif. 133/D2
Madison, Ind. 145/C4
Madison, S. Dak. 165/E4
Madison (cap.), Wis. 176/B4
Madisonville, Ky. 148/C3
Madiun, Indon. 113/J2
Madras, India 102/D3
Madre de Dios (riv.), S. Amer.
  56/C4
Madrid (cap.), Spain 76/E2
Madura (isl.), Indon. 113/K2
Madurai, India 102/C4
Maebashi, Japan 106/E2
Maestra, Sierra (mts.), Cuba
  53/J4
Magadan, Russia 91/H3
Magdalena (riv.), Col. 56/B2
Magdeburg, Ger. 70/D2
Magelang, Indon. 113/J2
Magellan (str.), S. Amer. 58/C8
Maggiore (lake), Europe 81/D3
Magnitogorsk, Russia 90/D3
Magnolia, Ark. 131/C2
Magog, Que. 185/D4
Mahajanga, Madag. 63/G6
Mahilyow, Belarus 50/C4
Maidstone, Eng. 67/G5
Maiduguri, Nigeria 60/D3
Main (riv.), Ger. 71/C4

Maine (state), U.S. 151
Mainz, Ger. 71/C4
Maiquetía, Ven. 56/C1
Majorca (Mallorca) (isl.), Spain
  77/H3
Majuro (cap.), Marshall Is.
  116/H5
Makale, Eth. 61/F3
Makassar, Indon., see Ujung
  Pandang
Makassar (str.), Indon.
  112-113/F6
Makhachkala, Russia 89/G6
Makiyivka, Ukr. 89/E5
Malabo (cap.), Equat. Guin.
  60/C4
Malacca (str.), Asia 111/B7
Málaga, Spain 76/D4
Malakal, Sudan 61/F4
Malang, Indon. 113/K2
Malange, Angola 62/B5
Malatya, Turkey 97/H3
Malawi 63/F6
Malay (pen.), Asia 111/C6
Malaya (state), Malaysia 111/C7
Malaysia 111/C6, 112/D5
Malden, Mass. 137/F4
Maldives 93/F5
Male (cap.), Maldives 93/F5
Malheur (lake), Oreg. 169/C3
Mali 60/B2
Malibu, Calif. 179/B1
Malines (Mechelen), Belg. 73/E5
Malmédy, Belg. 73/H7
Malmö, Sweden 69/C3
Malone, N.Y. 161/E1
Malta 79/E7
Malvern, Ark. 131/B2
Malvinas (isls.), see Falkland
  (isls.)
Mamaroneck, N.Y. 180/C1
Mammoth Cave Nat'l Pk., Ky.
  148/C3
Mamoré (riv.), S. Amer. 56/C4
Man, Isle of 67/D3
Man, Iv. Coast 60/B4
Manado, Indon. 113/G5
Managua (cap.), Nic. 48/C2
Managua (lake), Nic. 48/C2
Manama (cap.), Bahrain 95/G4
Manassas, Va. 139/D3
Manaus, Braz. 56/D3
Mancha, La (reg.), Spain 77/E3
Manchester, Conn. 136/C2
Manchester, Eng. 67/E4
Manchester, N.H. 158/C4
Manchester Center, Vt. 158/A3
Mandalay, Burma 110/B2
Mandan, N. Dak. 164/C2
Mandeb, Bab el (str.) 94/E7
Mangalore, India 102/C3
Manhattan, Kans. 147/A3
Manhattan (borough), N.Y.
  180/B2
Manhattan Beach, Calif. 179/C1
Manila (cap.), Phil. 108/C3
Manisa, Turkey 96/B3
Manistee, Mich. 152/A3
Manistique, Mich. 152/A2
Manitoba (prov.), Can. 189
Manitoba (lake), Man. 189/E03
Manitou Spring, Colo. 134/B3
Manitoulin (isl.), Ont. 186/A2
Manitowoc, Wis. 176/C3
Maniwaki, Que. 184/B4
Manizales, Col. 56/B2
Mankato, Minn. 153/B4
Mannar (gulf), Asia 102/C4
Mannheim, Ger. 71/C4
Mansfield, Eng. 67/F4
Mansfield, Ohio 166/B3

Index

Mansfield, Pa. 171/D2
Mansfield (mt.), Vt. 158/A2
Manteo, N.C. 163/F1
Mantua, Italy 78/C2
Maple Creek, Sask. 188/A4
Maple Heights, Ohio 167/F4
Maple Ridge, Br. Col. 190/B1
Maplewood, Minn. 153/C1
Maplewood, N.J. 180/A2
Maputo (cap.), Moz. 63/F7
Mar del Plata, Arg. 59/D6
Maracaibo, Ven. 56/B1
Maracaibo (lake), Ven. 56/B2
Maracay, Ven. 56/C2
Maradi, Niger 60/C6
Marajó (isl.), Braz. 57/E3
Marañon (riv.), Peru 56/B3
Maraş, Turkey 97/G4
Marathon, Fla. 141/F3
Marburg, Ger. 71/C3
Marche (reg.), Italy 78/D3
Marco Island, Fla. 141/E5
Marcus (isls.), Japan 116/F3
Mardan, (Pak.) 102/C1
Margarita (isl.), Ven. 56/C1
Margate, Eng. 67/G5
Mariano, Cuba 50/A2, C1/52
Marianas, Northern 116/E4
Maribor, Slovenia 84/B2
Marie-Galante (isl.), Guad. 55/H
Mariel, Cuba 52/C1
Marietta, Ga. 142/B1
Marietta, Ohio 167/D4
Marinduque (isl.), Phil. 108/C4
Marinette, Wis. 176/C3
Marion, Ind. 145/C2
Marion, Iowa 146/B3
Marion, Ohio 166/C3
Marion (lake), S.C. 162/C3
Maritime Alps (mts.), Europe 75/G5
Mariupol', Ukraine 89/E5
Marka, Somalia 61/G4
Markham, Ont. 187/F3
Marlborough, Mass. 137/D2
Marmara (sea), Turkey 96/C2
Marne (riv.), France 74/F2
Maroni (riv.), S. Amer. 57/D2
Maroua, Cam. 60/D3
Marquesas (isls.), Fr. Poly. 117/N6
Marquette, Mich. 152/C1
Marrakech, Mor. 60/B1
Marseille, France 75/F6
Marshall, Texas 173/F1
Marshall Islands 116/G4
Marshalltown, Iowa 146/B3
Marshfield, Wis. 176/B3
Martha's Vineyard (isl.), Mass. 137/E2
Martin, Tenn. 148/B3
Martinique 50/G4, 54-55/J
Martinsburg, W. Va. 139/D2
Martinsville, Va. 138/C4
Mary (Merv), Turkmen. 90/D4
Marysville, Ohio 166/C2
Masan, S. Korea 106/C4
Masaya, Nic. 48/C3
Masbate (isl.), Phil. 108/D4
Mascouche, Que. 184/B1
Maseru (cap.), Lesotho 63/E8
Mashhad, Iran, see Meshed
Masira (isl.), Oman 95/H5
Masjed Soleiman, Iran 100/F5
Mask, Lough (lake), Ire. 67/B4
Mason City, Iowa 146/A3
Massachusetts (state), U.S. 136-137
Massawa, Eth. 61/F3

Massena, N.Y. 161/E1
Massillon, Ohio 166/D3
Masurian (lakes), Pol. 87/E2
Matadi, Congo, Rep. of the 62/D5
Matagorda (isl.), Texas 173/E3
Matamoros, Mex. 47/F3
Matane, Que. 185/E1
Matanzas, Cuba 52/D1
Matapan (cape), Greece 85/C4
Mathura, India 102/C2
Mato Grosso (plat.), Braz. 57/D4
Matrah, Oman 95/H5
Matsu (Mazu) (isl.), China 105/F3
Matsumoto, Japan 107/E3
Matsuyama, Japan 106/D4
Matterhorn (mt.), Switz. 80/C3
Mattoon, Ill. 144/C3
Maturín, Ven. 56/C2
Maui (isl.), Hawaii 129/C3
Maumee (riv.), Ohio 166/B1
Mauna Kea (mt.), Hawaii 129/C4
Mauna Loa (mt.), Hawaii 129/C4
Maurepas (lake), La. 150/C3
Mauritania 60/A3
Mauritius 35/M7
May (cape), N.J. 159/B4
Mayagüez, P. Rico 54/A1
Maykop, Russia 89/F6
Mayo, Yukon 42/C3
Mayotte 63/G6
Maysville, Ky. 149/E2
Mayville, N. Dak. 164/B4
Mazanillo, Cuba 53/J4
Mazar-i-Sharif, Afghan. 102/B1
Mazatenango, Guat. 48/B2
Mazatlán, Mex. 46/C3
Mazu (isl.), China 105/F3
Mbabane (cap.), Swaziland 63/F7
Mbandaka, Congo, Rep. of the 63/D5
Mbeya, Tanz. 63/F5
Mbuji-Mayi, Congo, Rep. of the 63/E5
McAlester, Okla. 168/B4
McAllen, Texas 173/D4
McComb, Miss. 154/B4
McConaughy (lake), Nebr. 157/B2
McCook, Nebr. 157/C2
McDonald (isls.), Austr. 35/M8
McKeesport, Pa. 170/B2
McKinley (mt.), Alaska 129/B2
McKinney, Texas 173/E1
McLean, Va. 139/D1
M'Clintock (chan.), N.W.T. 42/F1
McMinnville, Oreg. 169/A2
McMinnville, Tenn. 149/D4
McPherson, Kans. 147/B3
Mead (lake), U.S. 133/D4
Meade, Kans. 147/A3
Meadow Lake, Sask. 188/A2
Meadville, Pa. 170/A2
Mecca, Saudi Arabia 94/E5
Mecklenburg (state), Ger. 70/D-E2
Medan, Indon. 112/B5
Medellín, Col. 56/C2
Medford, Mass. 137/F4
Medford, Oreg. 169/A2
Medicine Hat, Alta. 191/F4
Medina, Saudi Arabia 94/E5
Mediterranean (sea) 64-65/D-H5
Meerut, India 102/C2
Megiddo, Isr. 98/C2
Meknès, Mor. 60/B1
Mekong (riv.), Asia 111/D4
Melaka (Malacca), Malaya 111/C5
Melanesia (reg.), Pacific 116/E-H5-8
Melbourne, Austr. 115/D4
Melbourne, Fla. 140/C4
Melfort, Sask. 188/C2

Melilla, Spain 60/B1
Melitopol, Ukraine 89/D5
Melun, France 74/E3
Melville (isl.), Austr. 114/C2
Melville (isl.), N.W.T. 42/E1
Melville (pen.), N.W.T. 43/H2
Melville, Sask. 188/C3
Memphis, Tenn. 148/A1
Memphremagog (lake), N. Amer. 158/B1
Menderes (riv.), Turkey 96/C4
Mendocino (cape), Calif. 132/B4
Mendoza, Arg. 58/C6
Menlo Park, Calif. 133/F1
Menominee, Mich. 152/A2
Menomonee Falls, Wis. 176/A1
Menomonie, Wis. 176/A3
Mentor, Ohio 166/A4
Mequon, Wis. 176/B5
Merced, Calif. 133/D2
Meredith (lake), Texas 172/A1
Mergui (arch.), Burma 111/B5
Mérida, Mex. 47/G4
Mérida, Spain 76/C3
Mérida, Ven. 56/B2
Meriden, Conn. 136/B3
Meridian, Miss. 154/C3
Merowe, Sudan 94/C6
Merriman, Nebr. 157/A2
Merritt, Br. Col. 190/C4
Merritt Island, Fla. 140/C4
Mersá Matrûh, Egypt 61/E1
Mersey (riv.), Eng. 66/F2
Mersin, Turkey 96/F4
Merthyr Tydfil, Wales 67/E5
Mesa, Ariz. 130/B1
Mesabi (range), Minn. 153/C2
Mesa Verde Nat'l Pk., Colo. 134/C1
Meshed, Iran 101/L2
Mesopotamia (reg.), Iraq 100/B3-E-5
Mesquite, Texas 172/C4
Messina, Italy 79/E5
Meta (riv.), S. Amer. 56/B2
Metairie, La. 150/A4
Metz, France 74/G3
Meuse (riv.), Europe 74/F2
Mexicali, Mex. 46/A1
Mexico 46-47
Mexico, Maine 151/A3
Mexico, Mo. 155/A3
Mexico (gulf), N. Amer. 41/JK7
Mexico City (cap.), Mex. 47/E4
Miami Beach, Fla. 141/D1
Miami, Fla. 141/D1
Miami, Okla. 168/A4
Miass, Russia 88/K4
Michigan (lake), U.S. 45/J2
Michigan (state), U.S. 152
Michigan City, Ind. 145/B1
Michurinsk, Russia 89/F4
Micronesia, Fed. States of 116/F5
Middelburg, Neth. 73/B5
Middlebury, Vt. 158/A2
Middlesboro, Ky. 149/E4
Middlesbrough, Eng. 67/F3
Middletown, Conn. 136/B3
Middletown, N.Y. 161/B4
Middletown, Ohio 167/D1
Midland, Mich. 152/B3
Midland, Ont. 186/C2
Midland, Texas 172/C2
Midway Islands 116/H3
Midwest City, Okla. 168/B3
Mikonos (isl.), Greece 85/D4
Milan, Italy 78/B2
Milan, Tenn. 148/B4
Milbank, S. Dak. 165/D4
Miles City, Mont. 156/B4

Milford, Conn. 136/B3
Milford, Del. 139/F2
Milford, Mass. 137/D2
Milford Haven, Wales 67/D5
Milk (riv.), N. Amer. 156/A3, 191/F4
Milledgeville, Ga. 142/B3
Mille Lacs (lake), Minn. 153/B3
Millington, Tenn. 148/A4
Millinocket, Maine 151/B2
Millville, N.J. 139/F2
Milpitas, Calif. 133/F2
Milton, Ont. 187/E4
Milton-Freewater, Oreg. 169/A3
Milwaukee, Wis. 176/B1
Milwaukie, Oreg. 180/A4
Minas (basin), N.S. 183/D3
Mindanao (isl.), Phil. 109/DE7
Minden, La. 150/A1
Minden, Nebr. 157/C3
Mindoro (isl.), Phil. 108/C4
Mineola, N.Y. 180/C2
Mineral Wells, Texas 173/D1
Minneapolis, Minn. 153/A3
Minnesota (riv.), Minn. 153/B4
Minnesota (state), U.S. 153
Minnetonka, Minn. 153/B3
Miño (riv.), Spain 76/C1
Minorca (Menorca) (isl.), Spain 77/H2
Minot, N. Dak. 164/B2
Minsk (cap.), Belarus 89/C4
Minya, Egypt, see El Minya
Miramar, Fla. 141/D1
Miramichi (bay), N. Br. 182/C3
Mirim (lag.), Braz. 59/D6
Mishawaka, Ind. 145/B1
Miskolc, Hung. 83/F2
Mississauga, Ont. 187/F4
Mississippi (riv.), U.S. 45/H4
Mississippi (state), U.S. 154
Missoula, Mont. 156/B1
Missouri (riv.), U.S. 45/H3
Missouri (state), U.S. 155
Missouri City, Texas 173/E4
Misti, El (vol.), Peru 56/D4
Misty Fjords Nat'l Mon., Alaska 129/C2
Misurata, Libya 60/B1
Mitchell, Nebr. 157/B1
Mitchell, S. Dak. 165/D4
Mitla (ruin), Mex. 47/F5
Mito, Japan 107/F3
Miyazaki, Japan 106/C5
Moab, Utah 174/C3
Moberly, Mo. 155/A2
Mobile, Ala. 128/A4
Mobridge, S. Dak. 165/D2
Mocha, Yemen 94/E7
Modena, Italy 78/C2
Modesto, Calif. 132/C2
Mogadishu (cap.), Somalia 61/G4
Mojave, Calif. 133/A3
Mokp'o, S. Korea 106/B4
Moldau (Vltava) (riv.), Czech Rep. 82/C2
Moldova 89/C5
Moline, Ill. 144/A1
Molise (reg.), Italy 78/E4
Mollendo, Peru 56/B4
Molokai (isl.), Hawaii 129/G3
Moluccas (isls.), Indon. 113/H6
Mombasa, Kenya 63/G5
Mona (passage), W. Indies 51/E3
Monaco 75/G6
Monahans, Texas 172/B2
Mönchengladbach, Ger. 71/B3
Monclova, Mex. 46/E2
Moncton, N. Br. 182/C2
Mongolia 104-105/C-E1

Mono (lake), Calif. 132/C3
Monongahela (riv.), U.S. 170/A4
Monroe (lake), Ind. 145/B3
Monroe, La. 150/A2
Monroe, Mich. 152/C4
Monroeville, Pa. 170/B1
Monrovia (cap.), Liberia 60/A4
Mons, Belg. 72/D7
Mont-Joli, Que. 185/D1
Mont-Laurier, Que. 184/C3
Mont-Royal, Que. 184/A1
Montana (state), U.S. 156
Montauk (pt.), N.Y. 160/C4
Montbéliard, France 74/G4
Montclair, N.J. 180/A2
Montebello, Calif. 179/B2
Montego Bay, Jam. 53/V9
Montenegro (rep.), Yugo. 84/B3
Monterey, Calif. 133/D1
Monterey Park, Calif. 179/B2
Monteria, Col. 56/B2
Monterrey, Mex. 47/E3
Montevideo (cap.), Urug. 59/D6
Montezuma Castle Nat'l Mon., Ariz. 130/D3
Montgomery (cap.), Ala. 128/B3
Monticello, N.Y. 161/E4
Montmagny, Que. 185/E3
Montpelier, Idaho 143/C4
Montpelier (cap.), Vt. 158/A2
Montpellier, France 75/E6
Montréal, Que. 185/D4
Montréal-Nord, Que. 184/A1
Montreux, Switz. 80/B2
Montserrat 51/G3
Monza, Italy 78/B2
Moorcroft, Wyo. 177/A2
Moorea (isl.), Fr. Poly. 117/L7
Moore's Creek Nat'l Battlfld., N.C. 163/E2
Moorhead, Minn. 153/A3
Moosehead (lake), Maine 151/B2
Moose Jaw, Sask. 188/B4
Moosomin, Sask. 189/D3
Mopti, Mali 60/B3
Moradabad, India 102/C2
Moratuwa, Sri Lanka 102/C7
Morava (riv.), Czech Rep. 83/D2
Morava (riv.), Yugo. 84/C3
Moray (firth), Scot. 66/E2
Morecambe (bay), Eng. 67/E4
Morehead, Ky. 149/E2
Morehead City, N.C. 163/F3
Morelia, Mex. 46/E4
Morgan City, La. 150/C2
Morgantown, W. Va. 138/C2
Morioka, Japan 107/F3
Moro (gulf), Phil. 109/D7
Moro Bay, Calif. 133/E2
Morocco 60/B1
Morogoro, Tanz. 63/F5
Moroni (cap.), Comoros 63/G6
Morotai (isl.), Indon. 113/H5
Morrison, Colo. 178/A4
Morristown, N.J. 159/E3
Morristown, Tenn. 149/E3
Moscow, Idaho 143/A2
Moscow (cap.), Russia 88/F3
Moses Lake, Wash. 175/B4
Mosel (Moselle) (riv.), Europe 71/B3
Mosi Oa Tunya (Victoria) (falls), Africa 63/E6
Mosquito (gulf), Pan. 49/D3
Mosquito Coast (reg.), Nic. 49/D2
Moss Point, Miss. 154/C4
Mosul, Iraq 100/C2
Motherwell and Wishaw, Scot. 66/B1
Moulmein, Burma 110/B3
Moultrie, Ga. 142/B4

Moultrie (lake), S.C. 162/C3
Moundou, Chad 60/D4
Moundsville, W. Va. 138/C2
Mountain Home, Idaho 143/A4
Mountain View, Calif. 133/F1
Mt. Clemens, Mich. 178/D2
Mountlake Terr., Wash. 175/B1
Mt. Lebanon, Pa. 170/A1
Mt. Pearl, Newf. 183/F1
Mt. Pleasant, Iowa 146/C3
Mt. Pleasant, Mich. 152/B3
Mt. Pleasant, S.C. 163/D4
Mount Rainier Nat'l Pk., Wash. 175/B2
Mount Rushmore Nat'l Mem., S. Dak. 165/E1
Mount St. Helens Nat'l Volcanic Mon., Wash. 175/C2
Mt. Vernon, Ill. 144/B4
Mt. Vernon, N.Y. 180/C1
Mt. Vernon, Ohio 166/C3
Mt. Vernon, Wash. 175/A2
Mouscron, Belg. 73/D7
Mozambique 63/F6-7
Mozambique (chan.), Africa 63/G6-7
Mudanjiang, China 105/G1
Mufulira, Zambia 63/E6
Muir Woods Nat'l Mon., Calif. 133/E1
Mukalla, Yemen 94/F7
Mukden, China, see Shenyang
Mulhacén (mt.), Spain 77/E4
Mulhouse, France 74/G4
Mull (isl.), Scot. 66/C2
Multan, Pak. 102/C1
Muncie, Ind. 145/C2
Mundelein, Ill. 178/A1
Münden, Ger. 70/C3
Munich (München), Ger. 71/D4
Münster, Ger. 70/B3
Muonio (riv.), Europe 68/D1
Mur (Mura) (riv.), Europe 84/A2
Murcia, Spain 77/F4
Mures (riv.), Rom. 84/C2
Murfreesboro, Tenn. 148/C4
Murmansk, Russia 88/D1
Murom, Russia 89/F3
Murray (riv.), Austr. 115/D4
Murray, Ky. 148/B3
Murray (lake), S.C. 162/C3
Murray, Utah 174/C1
Mururoa (isl.), Fr. Poly. 117/M8
Muscat (cap.), Oman 95/H5
Muscatine, Iowa 146/C3
Musgrave (ranges), Austr. 114/C3
Muskego, Wis. 176/A1
Muskegon, Mich. 152/A4
Muskingum (riv.), Ohio 167/D3
Muskogee, Okla. 168/B4
Muskoka (lake), Ont. 186/C2
Mutare, Zimb. 63/F6
Mwanza, Tanz. 63/F5
Mweru (lake), Africa 63/E5
Myingyan, Burma 110/A2
Myitkyina, Burma 110/B1
Mykolayiv, Ukraine 89/D5
Myrtle Beach, S.C. 163/D3
Mysore, India 102/C3
Mystic, Conn. 136/C3
Mytilíni, Greece 85/D4

N

Naberezhnye Chelny, Russia 88/H3
Nablus, West Bank 98/C3
Nacala, Moz. 63/G6
Nacogdoches, Texas 173/F2
Naga, Phil. 108/D4

Index

Nagano, Japan 107/E3
Nagaoka, Japan 107/E3
Nagasaki, Japan 107/E4
Nagercoil, India 102/C4
Nagoya, Japan 106/E4
Nagpur, India 102/C4
Nags Head, N.C. 163/F1
Naha, Japan 107/G4
Nahanni Nat'l Pk., N.W.T. 129/C3
Nahariyya, Isr. 98/C1
Nairobi (cap.), Kenya 63/F5
Nakhodka, Russia 91/G3
Nakhon Ratchasima, Thai. 110/C4
Naktong (riv.), S. Korea 106/C4
Nakuru, Kenya 63/F5
Nalchik, Russia 89/F6
Namangan, Uzbek. 90/D3
Namib (des.), Namibia 62/D6-7
Namibe, Angola 62/D6
Namibia 62/D6
Nampa, Idaho 143/A3
Namp'o, N. Korea 106/B3
Nampo-Shoto (isls.), Japan 107/G2
Nampula, Moz. 63/F6
Namur, Belg. 73/E7
Nanaimo, Br. Col. 190/B4
Nanchang, China 105/E3
Nanchong, China 104/D2
Nancy, France 74/G3
Nanjing (Nanking), China 105/E2
Nanning, China 104/D3
Nansei Shoto (isls.), Japan 107/G4
Nantes, France 74/C4
Nanticoke, Ont. 186/C4
Nantucket (isl.), Mass. 137/F3
Naolehu, Hawaii 129/C4
Napa, Calif. 132/C1
Naperville, Ill. 178/A2
Napier, N.Z. 115/F4
Naples, Fla. 141/E3
Naples, Italy 79/D4
Napo (riv.), S. Amer. 56/B3
Nara, Japan 107/F4
Narew (riv.), Pol. 87/E2
Narmada (riv.), India 102/C2
Narvik, Nor. 68/C1
Nashua, N.H. 158/C4
Nashville (cap.), Tenn. 148/B1
Nasik, India 102/C3
Nassau (cap.), Bah. 50/C1
Nasser (lake), Egypt 94/C4
Natal, Braz. 57/F3
Natal (prov.), S. Africa 63/F7
Natchez, Miss. 154/A3
Natchitoches, La. 150/A1
Natick, Mass. 137/D2
N.A.S.A. Space Center, Texas 173/F4
National City, Calif. 180/C4
Natuna (isls.), Indon. 112/D5
Nauru 116/G6
Navajo Nat'l Mon., Ariz. 130/C2
Navarin (cape), Russia 91/K2
Navarre (reg.), Spain 77/F1
Navassa (isl.), U.S. 50/C3
Naxçivan, Azer. 89/F7
Náxos (isl.), Greece 85/D4
Nazareth, Isr. 98/C2
N'Djamena (cap.), Chad 60/D3
Ndola, Zambia 63/E6
Neagh (lake), N. Ire. 67/C3
Nebitdag, Turkmen. 90/C4
Nebo (mt.), Jordan 99/D3
Nebraska (state), U.S. 157
Nebraska City, Nebr. 157/C4
Neckar (riv.), Ger. 71/C4
Needles, Calif. 133/E4

Neenah, Wis. 176/C3
Neepawa, Man. 189/E4
Nefud (des.), Saudi Arabia 94/E4
Negev (reg.), Isr. 99/D5
Negro (riv.), Arg. 58/C6
Negro (riv.), Braz. 56/C3
Negros (isl.), Phil. 109/D6
Nei Monggol Zizhiqu (aut. reg.), China 105/E1
Neisse (riv.), Europe 71/F3
Nejd (reg.), Saudi Arabia 94/E4-5
Neligh, Nebr. 157/B3
Nelson, Br. Col. 191/D4
Nelson (riv.), Man. 42/G4
Nelson, N.Z. 115/F4
Neosho, Mo. 155/C2
Nepal 102/D2
Ness, Loch (lake), Scot. 66/D2
Netanya, Isr. 98/B3
Netherlands 72–73
Netherlands Antilles 51/E4, F3
Neuchâtel, Switz. 80/B2
Neuquén, Arg. 58/C6
Neuse (riv.), N.C. 163/F2
Neusiedler See (lake), Austria 82/D3
Nevada (state), U.S. 132-133
Nevada, Sierra (mts.), Spain 77/E4
Nevada, Sierra (mts.), U.S. 44/C3
Nevis (isl.), St. Kitts & Nevis 51/F3, 55/W
New Albany, Ind. 145/C4
Newark, Calif. 133/F1
Newark, N.J. 180/A2
Newark, Ohio 166/C3
New Bedford, Mass. 137/E3
New Berlin, Wis. 176/A1
New Bern, N.C. 163/F2
New Braunfels, Texas 173/D3
New Britain, Conn. 136/B3
New Britain (isl.), Papua N.G. 116/F4
New Brunswick (prov.), Can. 182
New Brunswick, N.J. 159/B2
Newburgh, N.Y. 161/E4
Newburyport, Mass. 137/E1
New Caledonia 116/G8
New Canaan, Conn. 136/A3
Newcastle, Austr. 115/E4
New Castle, Ind. 145/C3
Newcastle, N. Br. 182/C3
Newcastle, Ont. 187/D3
New Castle, Pa. 170/A3
Newcastle upon Tyne, Eng. 66/E3
New Delhi (cap.), India 102/C2
Newfoundland (isl.), Can. 183/F1
Newfoundland (prov.), Can. 43/L5
New Glasgow, N.S. 183/E3
New Guinea (isl.), Pacific 116/D6
New Hampshire (state), U.S. 158
New Harmony, Ind. 145/A4
New Haven, Conn. 136/B3
New Hope, Minn. 153/B1
New Iberia, La. 150/C2
New Ireland (isl.), Papua N.G. 116/F4
New Jersey (state), U.S. 159
New Liskeard, Ont. 186/C1
New London, Conn. 136/C3
New Madrid, Mo. 155/C4
Newmarket, Ont. 187/F3
New Mexico (state), U.S. 135
New Milford, Conn. 136/A3
New Milford, Pa. 171/E2
New Orleans, La. 150/A4
New Philadelphia, Ohio 166/C4
New Plymouth, N.Z. 115/F4

Newport, Ky. 149/D1
Newport, N.H. 158/B3
Newport, Oreg. 169/B1
Newport, R.I. 137/D3
Newport, Vt. 158/B1
Newport, Wales 67/E5
Newport Bch., Calif. 133/F3
Newport News, Va. 138/M4
New Port Richey, Fla. 140/D4
New Providence (isl.), Bah. 50/C1
New Rochelle, N.Y. 180/C1
Newry, N. Ire. 67/C3
New Siberian (isls.), Russia 91/H2
New Smyrna Bch., Fla. 140/B4
New South Wales (state), Austr. 115/D4
Newton, Iowa 146/B3
Newton, Kans. 147/B3
Newton, Mass. 137/F4
New Ulm, Minn. 153/B4
New Westminster, Br. Col. 190/A1
New York (state), U.S. 160-161
New York City, N.Y. 180/C2
New Zealand 115/F4
Nez Perce Nat'l Hist. Pk., Idaho 143/A2
Nha Trang, Viet. 111/E4
Niagara (riv.), N. Amer. 160/A1
Niagara Falls, N.Y. 160/B3
Niagara Falls, Ont. 187/F4
Niagara-on-the-Lake, Ont. 187/F4
Niamey (cap.), Niger 60/C3
Nias (isl.), Indon. 112/B5
Nicaragua 48/C2
Nicaragua (lake), Nic. 48/C3
Nice, France 75/G6
Nicobar (isls.), India 103/E4
Nicosia (cap.), Cyprus 96/E5
Nicoya (gulf), C. Rica 48/C3
Niger 60/C3
Niger (riv.), Africa 60/C4
Nigeria 60/C4
Niigata, Japan 107/E3
Niihau (isl.), Hawaii 129/A3
Nijmegen, Neth. 72/G4
Nile (riv.), Africa 61/F2
Niles, Ohio 166/B4
Nîmes, France 75/F5
Nineveh (ruins), Iraq 100/C2
Ningbo (Ningpo), China 105/F3
Ningxia (Ningsia) Huizu (aut. reg.), China 104/D2
Niobrara, Nebr. 157/A3
Niobrara (riv.), Nebr. 157/A3
Nipawin, Sask. 188/C2
Nipigon (lake), Ont. 187/D1
Nipissing (lake), Ont. 186/C2
Niš (Nish), Yugo. 84/C3
Nishinomiya, Japan 107/E4
Niterói Braz. 59/E5
Nitra, Slovakia 83/E2
Niue 117/K7
Nizhnevartovsk, Russia 90/D2
Nizhniy Novgorod (Gor'kiy), Russia 88/F3
Nizhniy Tagil, Russia 90/D3
Njazidja (isl.), Comoros 63/G6
Nkongsamba, Cam. 60/D4
Noblesville, Ind. 145/B2
Nogales, Ariz. 130/B4
Nome, Alaska 129/A1
Nootka (isl.), Br. Col. 190/A4
Noranda, Que. 184/A2
Nord Ostsee (canal), Ger. 70/C1
Norfolk, Nebr. 157/A3
Norfolk, Va. 138/A1
Norfolk I. (terr.), Austr. 116/G8
Noril'sk, Russia 91/E2
Normal, Ill. 144/B2

Norman, Okla. 168/B3
Normandy (prov.), France 74/C3
Norman Wells, N.W.T. 42/D2
Norris (lake), Tenn. 149/E3
Norristown (Pa. 171/D1
Norrköping, Swed. 69/C3
North (sea), Europe 64/E3
North (isl.), N.Z. 115/F4
North (cape), Nor. 68/E1
N. Adams, Mass. 136/M3
North America 40-41
Northampton, Eng. 67/F4
Northampton, Mass. 136/B2
North Atlantic Ocean 35/H4
N. Battleford, Sask. 188/A2
North Bay, Ont. 186/C2
North Bend, Oreg. 169/B1
North Carolina (state), U.S.
162-163
North Cascades Nat'l Pk., Wash.
175/A3
N. Chicago, Ill. 178/B1
N. Conway, N.H. 158/C2
North Dakota (state), U.S. 164
Northern Ireland, U.K. 66/C3
Northern Marianas (isls.), U.S.
116/E4
Northern Territory, Austr. 114/C3
Northern Yukon Nat'l Pk., Yukon
129/N1
Northfield, Minn. 153/B4
N. Frisian (isls.), Eur. 70/C1
Northglenn, Colo. 178/A4
North Haven, Conn. 136/B3
North Korea 106/C3
N. Las Vegas, Nev. 133/D4
N. Little Rock, Ark. 131/B3
N. Miami Bch., Fla. 141/D1
N. Olmsted, Ohio 167/F3
North Platte, Nebr. 157/B2
North Platte (riv.), U.S. 44/F2
North Rhine-Westphalia (state),
Ger. 70-71/B3
North Saskatchewan (riv.), Can.
188/B2
N. Sydney, N.S. 183/F2
Northumberland (str.), Can.
183/F2
N. Vancouver, Br. Col. 190/A1
North West (cape), Austr. 114/A3
Northwest Territories, Can.
42-43/E-J2
Norwalk, Calif. 179/B2
Norwalk, Conn. 136/A4
Norwalk, Ohio 166/B3
Norway 68-69
Norwegian (sea), Europe 35/JK5
Norwich, Conn. 136/C3
Norwich, Eng. 67/G4
Norwood, Mass. 137/D2
Norwood, Ohio 167/F1
Noto (pen.), Japan 106/E3
Nottawasaga (bay), Ont. 186/C2
Nottingham, Eng. 67/F4
Nouadhibou, Maur. 60/A2
Nouakchott (cap.), Mauritania
60/A3
Nouméa (cap.), New Caledonia
116/G8
Nova Iguaçu, Braz. 59/E5
Novara, Italy 78/B2
Nova Scotia (prov.), Can. 182-183
Novato, Calif. 133/D1
Novaya Zemlya (isls.), Russia
90/C2
Novgorod, Russia 88/D3
Novi Sad, Yugo. 84/C2
Novocherkassk, Russia 89/F5
Novokuznetsk, Russia 90/D3
Novomoskovsk, Russia 89/E4
Novorossiysk, Russia 89/E6

Novosibirsk, Russia 90/D3
Novyy Urengoy, Russia 90/D2
Nubian (des.), Sudan 61/F2
Nueces (riv.), Texas 173/D3
Nuevo Laredo, Mex. 47/E2
Nuku'alofa (cap.), Tonga 117/J8
Nukus, Uzbek. 90/C3
Numazu, Japan 107/E4
Nuneaton, Eng. 67/F4
Nuremberg (Nürnberg), Ger.
71/D4
Nutley, N.J. 180/A2
Nuuk (cap.), Greenl. 40/N3
Nyala, Sudan 61/E3
Nyasa (lake), Africa 63/F6
Nyasaland, see Malawi
Nyíregyháza, Hung. 83/F3

O

Oahe (lake), U.S. 165/D2
Oahu (isl.), Hawaii 129/B4
Oak Harbor, Wash. 175/A2
Oakland, Calif. 133/E1
Oakland Park, Fla. 141/D3
Oak Lawn, Ill. 178/B2
Oakley, Kans. 147/B1
Oak Park, Ill. 178/B2
Oak Ridge, Tenn. 149/E3
Oakville, Ont. 187/E4
Oaxaca de Juárez, Mex. 47/F5
Ob' (riv.), Russia 90/D2
Oberammergau, Ger. 71/D5
Oberlin, Ohio 166/B3
Oberstdorf, Ger. 71/D5
Ocala, Fla. 140/B3
Ocean (Banaba) (isl.), Kiribati
116/G6
Ocean City, Md. 139/F3
Ocean City, N.J. 159/B4
Oceania 116-117
Oceanside, Calif. 180/B3
Ocean Springs, Miss. 154/C4
Ocho Rios, Jam. 53/V9
Ocracoke, N.C. 163/F2
Odense, Den. 69/B3
Oder (riv.), Europe 70/F2
Odesa, Ukraine 89/D5
Odessa, Texas 172/C2
Offenbach, Ger. 71/C3
Ogaden (reg.), Eth. 61/G4
Ogbomosho, Nigeria 60/C4
Ogden, Utah 174/B2
Ogden Dunes, Ind. 178/C3
Ogdensburg, N.Y. 161/D1
Ogunquit, Maine 151/A4
Ohio (riv.), U.S. 45/J3
Ohio (state), U.S. 166-167
Ohrid (lake), Europe 85/C3
Oil City, Pa. 170/A3
Oise (riv.), France 74/E3
Oita, Japan 106/D4
Ojos del Salado (mt.), S. Amer.
58/C5
Oka (riv.), Russia 89/E4
Okayama, Japan 106/D4
Okazaki, Japan 106/E4
Okeechobee (lake), Fla. 141/D4
Okefenokee (swamp), U.S.
142/B4
Okhotsk (sea), Russia 91/H3
Oki (isls.), Japan 106/D3
Okinawa (isl.), Japan 107/G4
Oklahoma (state), U.S. 168
Oklahoma City (cap.), Okla.
168/B3
Okmulgee, Okla. 168/B4
Okotoks, Alta. 191/B4
Oktyabr'skiy, Russia 89/H4

Öland (isl.), Swed. 69/C3
Olathe, Kans. 147/B4
Oldenburg, Ger. 70/C2
Oldham, Eng. 66/G2
Old Orchard Bch., Maine 151/A4
Olds, Alta. 191/E3
Old Town, Maine 151/B3
Old Wives (lake), Sask. 188/B4
Olean, N.Y. 160/B3
Olinda, Braz. 57/F3
Olomouc, Czech Rep. 82/D2
Olongapo, Phil. 108/C3
Olsztyn, Pol. 87/E2
Olten, Switz. 80/C1
Olympia (cap.), Wash. 175/B2
Olympic Nat'l Pk., Wash. 175/B2
Olympus (mt.), Greece 84/C3
Omagh, N. Ire. 67/C3
Omaha, Nebr. 157/B4
Oman 95/H6
Oman (gulf), Asia 95/H5
Omdurman, Sudan 61/F3
Omiya, Japan 107/E4
Omsk, Russia 90/D3
Omuta, Japan 106/D4
Onega (lake), Russia 88/E2
One Hundred Mile House, Br. Col.
190/C3
Oneida (lake), N.Y. 161/D3
O'Neill, Nebr. 157/A3
Oneonta, N.Y. 161/E3
Onitsha, Nigeria 60/C4
Ontario, Calif. 179/D3
Ontario (prov.), Can. 186-187
Ontario (lake), N. Amer. 45/L2
Ontario, Oreg. 169/B4
Oostende (Ostend), Belg. 73/A5
Opelika, Ala. 128/C2
Opelousas, La. 150/B2
Opole, Pol. 86/C3
Oporto, Port. 76/B2
Opportunity, Wash. 175/B2
Oradea, Rom. 84/C2
Oral, Kazak. 90/C3
Oran, Alg. 60/B1
Orange (riv.), Africa 63/D7
Orange, Austr. 115/D4
Orange, Calif. 179/C3
Orange, Texas 173/F3
Orangeburg, S.C. 162/C3
Orange Free State (prov.), S.
Africa 63/E7
Orangeville, Ont. 186/C3
Orange Walk Town, Belize 48/B1
Oranjestad (cap.), Aruba 55/O
Örebro, Swed. 69/C3
Oregon (state), U.S. 169
Oregon Caves Nat'l Mon., Oreg.
169/C2
Oregon City, Oreg. 169/A2
Orel, Russia 89/E4
Orem, Utah 174/B2
Orenburg, Russia 89/J4
Orense, Spain 76/C1
Organ Pipe Cactus Nat'l Mon.,
Ariz. 130/B4
Orillia, Ont. 186/C3
Orinoco (riv.), S. Amer. 56/C2
Orkney (isls.), Scot. 66/E1
Orlando, Fla. 140/B3
Orléans, France 74/D4
Ormoc, Phil. 109/E5
Ormond Beach, Fla. 140/B3
Oromocto, N. Br. 182/B3
Orono, Maine 151/B3
Orontes (riv.), Syria 97/G5
Orsha, Belarus 89/D4
Orsk, Russia 89/J4
Orumiyeh, Iran, see Urmia
Oruro, Bol. 56/C4
Osaka, Japan 106/D4

Index

Osh, Kyrgyz. 90/B3
Oshawa, Ont. 187/F3
Oshkosh, Wis. 176/C3
Oshogbo, Nigeria 60/C4
Osijek, Croatia 84/B2
Öskemen, Kazak. 90/D3
Oslo (cap.), Nor. 69/B2
Osmaniye, Turkey 97/G4
Osnabrück, Ger. 70/C2
Ostend, Belg. 73/A5
Ostrava, Czech Rep. 83/D2
Ostrołęka, Pol. 87/E2
Oswego, N.Y. 161/D2
Oświęcim, Pol. 86/D3
Otaru, Japan 107/F2
Otranto (str.), Europe 85/B4
Otsego (lake), N.Y. 161/E3
Otsu, Japan 107/F1
Ottawa (riv.), Can. 184/A4
Ottawa, Ont. (cap.), Canada 186/A1
Ottumwa, Iowa 146/C3
Ouagadougou (cap.), Burkina Faso 60/B3
Ouargla, Alg. 60/C1
Oujda, Mor. 60/B1
Oulu, Fin. 68/D2
Our (riv.), Europe 73/H7
Ouse (riv.), Eng. 67/G4
Outremont, Que. 184/B1
Oviedo, Spain 76/C1
Owatonna, Minn. 153/B4
Owensboro, Ky. 148/C2
Owen Sound, Ont. 186/B3
Owyhee (riv.), Oreg. 169/B4
Oxford, Eng. 67/F5
Oxford, Miss. 154/B1
Oxnard, Calif. 133/E3
Oyapock (riv.), S. Amer. 57/D2
Ozark, Ala. 128/C3
Ozarks, Lake of the (lake), Mo. 155/B2

P

Paarl, S. Africa 63/D8
Pacifica, Calif. 133/F1
Pacific Ocean 116-117
Pacific Rim Nat'l Pk., Br. Col. 190/A4
Padang, Indon. 112/B6
Paderborn, Ger. 71/C3
Padua (Padova), Italy 78/C2
Paducah, Ky. 148/B3
Pago Pago (cap.), Amer. Samoa 117/J7
Pahala, Hawaii 129/C4
Painesville, Ohio 166/A4
Paisley, Scot. 66/C3
Pakistan 102/B-C1-2
Pakse, Laos 110/D4
Palana, Russia 91/J3
Palatine, Ill. 178/A1
Palatka, Fla. 140/D3
Palau 116/C2
Palawan (isl.), Phil. 109/B6
Palembang, Indon. 112/C6
Palencia, Spain 76/D1
Palermo, Italy 79/C5
Palestine, Texas 173/E2
Palikir (cap.), Micronesia 116/F5
Palma de Mallorca, Spain 77/H3
Palmas (cape), Liberia 60/B4
Palm Bay, Fla. 140/C4
Palm Beach, Fla. 141/D4
Palmdale, Calif. 133/E3
Palmer Land, Antarc. 118
Palmerston North, N.Z. 115/F4
Palmira, Col. 56/B2

Palm Springs, Calif. 133/F3
Palmyra, Syria, see Tadmor
Palmyra Atoll (isl.), U.S. 117/K5
Palo Alto, Calif. 133/F1
Pamir (plat.), Asia 102/C1
Pamlico (sound), N.C. 163/F3
Pampa, Texas 172/B1
Pampas (plain), Arg. 58/C8
Pamplona, Spain 77/F1
Panama 49/D3
Panama (cap.), Pan. 49/E3
Panama (canal), Pan. 49/E3
Panama City, Fla. 141/F2
Panay (isl.), Phil. 109/D5
Panda, Congo, Rep. of the 63/E6
P'anmunjŏm, Korea 106/B3
Pantelleria (isl.), Italy 79/C6
Papua New Guinea 116/E6
Pará (riv.), Braz. 57/D3
Paracel (isls.), China 112/E2
Paradise Valley, Ariz. 130/B2
Paraguay 58-59/D5
Paraguay (riv.), S. Amer. 58/D5
Paramaribo (cap.), Suriname 57/D2
Paramus, N.J. 180/B1
Paraná, Arg. 58/C6
Paraná (riv.), S. Amer. 58/D5
Pardubice, Czech Rep. 82/C1
Paria (gulf) 51/F5
Paris (cap.), France 74/B2
Paris, Ky. 149/E2
Paris, Tenn. 148/B3
Paris, Texas 173/E1
Parkersburg, W. Va. 138/B2
Park Forest, Ill. 178/B3
Parkland, Wash. 175/B3
Park Ridge, Ill. 178/B2
Parkville, Md. 139/F1
Parma, Italy 78/C2
Parma, Ohio 167/F4
Parnaíba (riv.), Braz. 57/E3
Parnassus (mt.), Greece 85/C4
Páros (isl.), Greece 85/D4
Parry (chan.), N.W.T. 42/F-G1
Parry Sound, Ont. 186/C2
Parsons, Kans. 147/C4
Pasadena, Calif. 133/F1
Pasadena, Texas 173/F4
Pascagoula, Miss. 154/C4
Pasco, Wash. 175/C4
Passaic, N.J. 180/A2
Pastaza (riv.), S. Amer. 56/B3
Pasto, Col. 56/B2
Patagonia (reg.), Arg. 58/C7
Patapsco (riv.), Md. 139/F2
Paterson, N.J. 180/A1
Patiala, India 102/C1
Pátmos (isl.), Greece 85/D4
Patna, India 102/D2
Patoka (lake), Ind. 145/B4
Patos (lag.), Braz. 59/E6
Pátrai, Greece 85/C4
Pavia, Italy 78/B2
Pavlodar, Kazak. 90/D3
Pawtucket, R.I. 137/D2
Paysandú, Urug. 59/D6
Peace (riv.), Can. 42/E4
Peace River, Alta. 191/D1
Pearl (harb.), Hawaii 129/A4
Pearl City, Hawaii 129/A4
Peary Land, Greenl. 40/C1
Pechora (riv.), Rus. 88/H1
Pecos, Texas 172/B2
Pecos (riv.), Texas 172/C3
Pecos Nat'l Hist. Pk., N. Mex. 135/D3

Pecs, Hung. 83/E3
Pédro Juan Caballero, Par. 59/D5
Pee Dee (riv.), S.C. 163/D3
Peekskill, N.Y. 161/F3
Pegu, Burma 110/B3
Peipus (lake), Eur. 88/C3
Pekalongan, Indon. 113/J2
Pekin, Ill. 144/B2
Peking (Beijing) (cap.), China 105/E1
Pelée (vol.), Martinique 51/G4, 54/J
Pelée (isl.), Ont. 186/A4
Pelotas, Braz. 59/D6
Pemba, Moz. 63/F6
Pemba (isl.), Tanz. 63/G5
Pembroke, Ont. 187/D2
Pembroke Pines, Fla. 141/D1
Pendleton, Oreg. 169/A3
Pend Oreille (lake), Idaho 143/A
Pennine Alps (mts.), Europe 80/C3
Pennsylvania (state), U.S. 170-171
Penobscot (riv.), Maine 151/B2
Pensacola, Fla. 141/E1
Penticton, Br. Col. 190/C4
Pentland (firth), Scot. 66/E1
Penza, Russia 89/F4
Peoria, Ariz. 130/A1
Peoria, Ill. 144/B2
Percé, Que. 185/F1
Pereira, Col. 56/B2
Perigueux, France 75/D5
Perim (isl.), Yemen 94/E7
Perlas (arch.), Pan. 49/E3
Pérm', Russia 88/J3
Pernambuco, Braz., see Recife
Pernik, Bulg. 84/C3
Perpignan, France 75/E6
Perry's Victory and Int'l Peace Mem., Ohio 166/A2
Perryton, Texas 172/B1
Persian (gulf), Asia 94-95/F-G4
Perth, Austr. 114/A4
Perth, Ont. 187/E2
Perth, Scot. 66/E2
Perth Amboy, N.J. 180/B3
Perth-Andover, N. Br. 182/B2
Peru 56/B3-4
Peru, Ind. 145/B2
Perugia, Italy 78/D3
Pescara, Italy 78/E3
Peshawar, Pak. 102/C1
Petah Tiqwa, Isr. 99/B3
Petaluma, Calif. 132/C1
Peter I (isl.), Nor. 118
Peterborough, Eng. 67/F4
Peterborough, Ont. 187/D3
Petersburg, Va. 139/E4
Petitcodiac, N. Br. 182/C3
Petoskey, Mich. 152/B2
Petra (ruins), Jordan 99/D5
Petrified Forest Nat'l Pk., Ariz. 130/C3
Petropavl, Kazak. 90/D3
Petropavlovsk-Kamchatskiy, Russia 91/J3
Petrozavodsk, Russia 88/D2
Pforzheim, Ger. 71/C4
Pharr, Texas 173/D4
Phenix City, Ala. 128/C3
Philadelphia, Miss. 154/C4
Philadelphia, Pa. 171/E1
Philippines 108-109
Phillipsburg, N.J. 159/A2
Phitsanulok, Thai. 110/C3
Phnom Penh (cap.), Camb. 111/D3
Phoenix (cap.), Ariz. 130/A1
Phoenix (isls.), Kiribati 117/J6

Piacenza, Italy 78/B2
Piatra Neamţ, Rom. 84/D2
Piave (riv.), Italy 78/D2
Picayune, Miss. 154/B4
Pickering, Ont. 187/F3
Pico Rivera, Calif. 179/B2
Picton, Ont. 187/D3
Pictou, N.S. 183/E3
Piedmont (reg.), Italy 78/AB2
Pierre (cap.), S. Dak. 165/E2
Pietermaritzburg, S. Africa 63/F7
Pigs, Bay of (bay), see Cochinos (bay)
Pikesville, Md. 139/E1
Pikeville, Ky. 149/F3
Pilar, Par. 58/D5
Pilcomayo (riv.), S. Amer. 58/C5
Pilsen, Czech Rep., see Plzeň
Pinang, Malaysia, see George Town
Pinar del Rio, Cuba 52/B2
Pindus (mts.), Greece 85/C4
Pine Bluff, Ark. 131/B2
Pinellas Park, Fla. 140/C4
Pine Ridge, S. Dak. 165/F1
Pines (Juventud) (isl.), Cuba 50/A2
Pinnacles Nat'l Mon., Calif. 133/D1
Pinsk, Belarus 89/D4
Pipe Springs Nat'l Mon., Ariz. 130/B2
Pipestone Nat'l Mon., Minn. 153/A4
Piqua, Ohio 166/C1
Piraiévs, Greece 85/C4
Pisa, Italy 78/C3
Pisco, Peru 56/B4
Pitcairn (isl.), Pacific 117/O8
Piteşti, Rom. 84/D2
Pittsburg, Calif. 132/C1
Pittsburg, Kans. 147/C3
Pittsburgh, Pa. 170/A1
Pittsfield, Mass. 136/A1
Piura, Peru 56/A3
Plainfield, N.J. 159/B2
Plainview, Texas 172/C1
Plano, Texas 173/F3
Plantation, Fla. 141/F6
Plant City, Fla. 140/C3
Plata, Rio de la (est.), S. Amer. 59/D6
Platte (riv.), Nebr. 157/C2
Platteville, Wis. 176/B4
Plattsburgh, N.Y. 161/F1
Pleasant Hill, Calif. 133/E1
Pleiku, Viet. 111/E4
Plessisville, Que. 185/E4
Pleven, Bulg. 84/D3
Płock, Pol. 87/D2
Ploieşti, Rom. 84/D2
Plovdiv, Bulg. 84/D3
Plum, Pa. 170/B1
Plymouth, Eng. 67/E5
Plymouth, Mass. 137/E2
Plymouth, N.H. 158/B3
Plzeň, Czech Rep. 82/B2
Po (riv.), Italy 78/C2
Pocatello, Idaho 143/C4
Pocomoke City, Md. 139/F3
Podgorica, Yugo 84/B3
P'ohang, S. Korea 106/C3
Pohnpei (Ponape) (isl.), Micronesia 116/F5
Point Pelée Nat'l Pk., Ont. 186/A4
Point Pleasant, N.J. 159/B4
Point Reyes Nat'l Seashore, Calif. 132/C1
Pointe-aux-Trembles, Que. 184/B1
Pointe-Noire, Congo, Rep. of the 62/B5

Poitiers, France 75/D4
Poland 86-87
Poltava, Ukraine 89/D5
Polynesia (reg.), Pacific 117/J-M4-8
Pomona, Calif. 179/B3
Pompano Bch., Fla. 141/E4
Ponca City, Okla. 168/A3
Ponce, P. Rico 51/E3, 54/E1
Pondicherry, India 102/D3
Ponoka, Alta. 191/E3
Pontchartrain (lake), La. 150/A4
Pontiac, Mich. 178/C3
Pontianak, Indon. 112/D5
Pontic (mts.), Turkey 97/H2
Pontine (isls.), Italy 79/C4
Poole, Eng. 67/E5
Poona, India 102/C3
Poopó (lake), Bol. 56/C4
Popayán, Col. 56/B2
Poplar Bluff, Mo. 155/C3
Popocatépetl (mt.), Mex. 47/F2
Porcupine (riv.), N. Amer. 42/B2
Pori, Fin. 69/D2
Porsanger (fjord), Nor. 68/E1
Portage la Prairie, Man. 189/E4
Port Alberni, Br. Col. 190/B4
Portales, N. Mex. 135/E4
Port Angeles, Wash. 175/A2
Port Arthur, Texas 173/F3
Port-au-Prince (cap.), Haiti 50/D3, P7/52
Port Charlotte, Fla. 141/D3
Port Chester, N.Y. 180/C1
Port Clinton, Ohio 166/A2
Port Colborne, Ont. 187/F4
Port Coquitlam, Br. Col. 190/B1
Port Elgin, Ont. 186/B3
Port Elizabeth, S. Africa 63/E8
Port-Gentil, Gabon 62/C5
Port Harcourt, Nigeria 60/C5
Port Hardy, Br. Col. 183/A3
Port Hastings, N.S. 183/E3
Port Hawkesbury, N.S. 183/E3
Port Huron, Mich. 152/C4
Portland, Maine 151/A4
Portland, Oreg. 169/A2
Port Lavaca, Texas 173/E3
Port Moresby, Papua N.G. 112/B7
Portneuf Res., Que. 185/D3
Porto (Oporto), Port. 76/B2
Porto Alegre, Braz. 59/D6
Port-of-Spain (cap.), Trin. & Tob. 51/G5, 55/T
Porto-Novo (cap.), Benin 60/C4
Port Orange, Fla. 140/D3
Port Orford, Oreg. 169/C1
Porto Velho, Braz. 56/C3
Portoviejo, Ecuador 56/A3
Port Said, Egypt 61/F1
Port St. Joe, Fla. 141/F2
Portsmouth, Eng. 67/F5
Portsmouth, N.H. 158/C4
Portsmouth, Ohio 167/E2
Portsmouth, Va. 138/A1
Portugal 76
Port-Vila (cap.), Vanuatu 116/G7
Posadas, Arg. 59/D5
Potholes (res.), Wash. 175/B3
Potomac (riv.), U.S. 139/D2
Potosí, Bol. 56/C4
Potsdam, Ger. 70/E2
Potsdam, N.Y. 161/E1
Pottstown, Pa. 171/E4
Pottsville, Pa. 171/E3
Poughkeepsie, N.Y. 161/F4
Powell (lake), U.S. 174/B4
Powell River, Br. Col. 190/B4

Poyang Hu (lake), China 105/E3
Poznań, Pol. 86/C2
Prague (Praha) (cap.), Czech Rep. 82/C1
Prairie Dog Town Fork (riv.), Texas 172/A1, C1
Prairie du Chien, Wis. 176/A4
Prato, Italy 78/C3
Prattville, Ala. 128/B3
Prescott, Ariz. 130/B3
Prescott, Ont. 187/E2
Presidio, Texas 172/B3
Prešov, Slvk. 83/F2
Prespa (lake), Europe 85/C3
Presque Isle, Maine 151/C2
Preston, Eng. 67/E4
Preston, Idaho 143/C4
Prestwick, Scot. 66/D3
Pretoria (cap.), S. Africa 63/E7
Price, Utah 174/B3
Prichard, Ala. 128/A4
Prince Albert, Sask. 188/B2
Prince Albert Nat'l Pk., Sask. 188/B1
Prince Charles (isl.), N.W.T. 43/J2
Prince Edward (isls.), S. Africa 35/L8
Prince Edward Island (prov.), Can. 183/D2
Prince Edward I. Nat'l Pk., P.E.I. 183/D2
Prince George, Br. Col. 190/C2
Prince of Wales (isl.), N.W.T. 42/G1
Prince Patrick (isl.), N.W.T. 34/C2
Prince Rupert, Br. Col. 42/C5
Princeton, Br. Col. 190/C4
Princeton, N.J. 159/B2
Prineville, Oreg. 169/B3
Priština, Yugo. 84/C3
Probolinggo, Indon. 113/K2
Prokop'yevsk, Russia 90/E3
Provence (prov.), France 75/F6
Providence (cap.), R.I. 137/D2
Providencia (isl.), Col. 50/B4
Provincetown, Mass. 137/F2
Provo, Utah 174/B2
Prudhoe Land, Greenl. 40/M2
Prut (riv.), Europe 84/E2
Pryor, Okla. 168/A4
Przemyśl, Pol. 87/F4
Pskov, Russia 88/C3
Puebla de Zaragoza, Mex. 47/G2
Pueblo, Colo. 134/B3
Puerto Armuelles, Pan. 49/D3
Puerto Barrios, Guat. 48/C2
Puerto Cabello, Ven. 56/C1
Puerto Cortés, Hond. 48/C2
Puerto La Crúz, Ven. 56/C1
Puerto Montt, Chile 58/B7
Puerto Plata, Dom. Rep. 52/R6
Puerto Rico 51/E3, 54/D2
Puerto Vallarta, Mex. 46/D4
Puget (sound), Wash. 175/B1
Pukaskwa Nat'l Pk., Ont. 187/E1
Pulaski, Va. 138/C4
Pullman, Wash. 175/C4
Pune, see Poona
Puno, Peru 56/B4
Punta Arenas, Chile 58/B8
Puntarenas, C. Rica 48/C3
Punta Gorda, Fla. 141/D3
Punxsutawney, Pa. 170/B3
Puri, India 102/D3
Purus (riv.), S. Amer. 56/C3
Pusan, S. Korea 106/C4
Pushkin, Russia 88/D3
Putumayo (riv.), S. Amer. 56/B3
Puuhonua O Honaunau Nat'l Hist. Pk., Hawaii 129/C4
Puy-de-Dôme (mt.), France 75/E5

Index

Puyallup, Wash. 175/C1
Pymatuning (lake), U.S. 166/A4, 170/A2
P'yŏngyang (cap.), N. Korea 106/B2
Pyrenees (mts.), Europe 64/D-E4
Pyu, Burma 110/B3

Q

Qandahar, Afghan. 102/B1
Qaraghandy, Kazak. 90/D3
Qarshi, Uzbek. 90/D4
Qatar 95/E2
Qatara (depr.), Egypt 94/B4
Qaqortoq, Greenl. 40/P3
Qazvin, Iran 100/G2
Qeshm (isl.), Iran 101/J7
Qilian Shan (range), China 104/C2
Qingdao, China 105/F2
Qinghai (prov.), China 104/C2
Qinghai Hu (lake), China 104/C2
Qiqihar, China 105/F1
Qiryat Shemona, Isr. 98/C1
Qiryat Yam, Isr. 98/C2
Qizilkum (des.), Asia 90/D3
Qom, Iran 100/G3
Qostanay, Kazak. 90/B3
Quabbin (res.), Mass. 136/C2
Quang Tri, Viet. 110/D3
Quantico, Va. 139/E3
Qu'Appelle (riv.), Sask. 188/C4
Québec (cap.), Que. 185/F2
Québec (prov.), Can. 184-185
Queen Charlotte (isls.), Br. Col. 42/C5
Queens (borough), N.Y. 180/C2
Queensland (state), Austr. 115/D3
Queenstown, S. Africa 63/E8
Quelimane, Moz. 63/F6
Quemoy, China, see Jinmen
Quesnel, Br. Col. 190/B2
Quetta, Pak. 102/B1
Quezaltenango, Guat. 48/B2
Quezon City, Phil. 108/E3
Qui Nhon, Viet. 111/E4
Quill (lakes), Sask. 188/C3
Quincy, Ill. 144/A3
Quincy, Mass. 137/F4
Quito (cap.), Ecua. 56/C1
Qum (riv.), Iran 100/G3
Qumran, West Bank, see Khirbet Qumran
Qyzylorda, Kazak. 90/D3

R

Rabat (cap.), Mor. 60/B1
Race (cape), Newf. 43/L6
Racine, Wis. 176/C4
Radcliff, Ky. 149/D2
Radford, Va. 138/C4
Radom, Pol. 87/E3
Rainbow Bridge Nat'l Mon., Utah 174/C4
Rainier (mt.), Wash. 175/B3
Rainy (lake), N. Amer. 153/B2
Raipur, India 102/D3
Rajahmundry, India 102/D3
Rajkot, India 102/C3
Rakata (isl.), Indon. 112/C7
Raleigh (cap.), N.C. 163/D2
Ramadi, Iraq 100/D4
Ramallah, West Bank 99/C4
Ramat Gan, Isr. 99/B3
Ramla, Isr. 99/B4

Ramree (isl.), Burma 110/A3
Rancagua, Chile 58/B6
Ranchi, India 102/D2
Rancho Cucamonga, Calif. 179/B3
Randers, Den. 69/B3
Rangoon (cap.), Burma 110/B3
Rantoul, Ill. 144/C2
Rapa (isl.), Fr. Poly. 117/M8
Rapa Nui (Easter) (isl.), Chile 117/P8
Rapid City, S. Dak. 165/F1
Rappahannock (riv.), Va. 139/E3
Raqqa, Syria, see El Rashid
Rarotonga (isl.), Cook Is. 117/K8
Ras Aser (cape), Somalia 61/H3
Ras Dashan (mt.), Eth. 61/F3
Rasht, Iran 100/F2
Raton, N. Mex. 134/C3
Ravenna, Italy 78/D2
Ravensburg, Ger. 71/C5
Rawalpindi, Pak. 102/C1
Rawlins, Wyo. 177/C2
Rawson, Arg. 58/C7
Raytown, Mo. 155/C1
Reading, Eng. 67/F4
Reading, Pa. 171/E4
Recife, Braz. 57/F5
Recklinghausen, Ger. 70/B3
Red (sea) 94/D5-6
Red (riv.), Asia 110/C2
Red (riv.), U.S. 45/H4
Red Bank, N.J. 159/C2
Red Bank, Tenn. 149/D4
Red Cloud, Nebr. 157/C3
Red Deer, Alta. 191/E3
Red Deer (riv.), Alta. 191/E4
Redding, Calif. 132/B1
Redfield, S. Dak. 165/G1
Redlands, Calif. 133/F1
Redmond, Oreg. 169/B3
Redmond, Wash. 175/B1
Redondo Bch., Calif. 179/C1
Red River of the North (riv.), N. Amer. 153/A3, 164/A4, 189/F4
Red Wing, Minn. 153/C2
Redwood City, Calif. 133/F1
Redwood Nat'l Pk., Calif. 132/A1
Ree, Lough (lake), Ire. 67/C4
Reedsport, Oreg. 169/A3
Regensburg, Ger. 71/D4
Reggio di Calabria, Italy 79/E5
Reggio nell'Emilia, Italy 78/C2
Regina (cap.), Sask. 188/C4
Rehoboth Bch., Del. 139/F3
Rehovot, Isr. 99/B4
Reims, France 74/F3
Reina Adelaida (arch.), Chile 58/B8
Reifehber (lake), Can. 42/F4
Reisterstown, Md. 139/F2
Rennes, France 74/C3
Reno, Nev. 132/B2
Renton, Wash. 175/C1
Repentigny, Que. 184/B1
Republican (riv.), U.S. 147/A1
Resistencia, Arg. 58/C5
Reşiţa, Rom. 84/C2
Resolution (isl.), N.W.T. 43/K3
Restigouche (riv.), N. Br. 182/B1
Réunion 35/L7
Reus, Spain 77/G2
Reutlingen, Ger. 71/C4
Revelstoke, Br. Col. 191/D4
Revillagigedo (isls.), Mex. 46/B4
Rexburg, Idaho 143/C3
Reykjavík (cap.), Iceland 64/B2
Reynosa, Mex. 47/F3
Rhaetian Alps (mts.), Europe 81/E2

Rhine (riv.), Europe 64/E4
Rhinelander, Wis. 176/B3
Rhode Island (state), U.S. 137/D3
Rhodes, Greece 85/E4
Rhodope (mts.), Europe 85/D3
Rhondda, Wales 67/E5
Rhône (riv.), Europe 75/F5
Riau (arch.), Indon. 112/C5
Ribeirão Preto, Braz. 59/E5
Richardson, Texas 172/C4
Richfield, Minn. 153/B1
Richfield, Utah 174/B3
Richibucto, N. Br. 182/C2
Richland, Wash. 175/C4
Richmond, Br. Col. 190/A1
Richmond, Calif. 133/E1
Richmond, Ind. 145/C3
Richmond, Ky. 149/D2
Richmond (cap.), Va. 139/E3
Richmond Hill, Ont. 187/B3
Riding Mtn. Nat'l Pk., Man. 189/D3
Riga (cap.), Latvia 88/B3
Rigi (mt.), Switz. 81/D1
Rijeka, Croatia 84/A2
Rimini, Italy 78/D2
Rimouski, Que. 185/F2
Riobamba, Ecua. 56/B3
Rio Branco, Braz. 56/C3
Rio de Janeiro, Braz. 59/E5
Rio Gallegos, Arg. 58/C8
Rio Grande (riv.), N. Amer. 44/F46/D1
Rio Grande, Braz. 59/D8
Riohacha, Col. 56/B1
Ripon, Wis. 176/C3
Rishon Le Ziyyon, Isr. 99/B4
Riverside, Calif. 179/B4
Riverton, Wyo. 177/B3
Riverview, N. Br. 182/C3
Riviera (region), Europe 75/G6
Riviera Beach, Fla. 141/F5
Rivière-du-Loup, Que. 185/D1
Rivne, Ukraine 89/C4
Riyadh (cap.), Saudi Arabia 94/F5
Road Town (cap.), V.I. (Br.) 54/F
Roanne, France 75/F4
Roanoke (riv.), U.S. 139/D4, 163/E1
Roanoke, Va. 138/C4
Roanoke Rapids, N.C. 163/E1
Roatán, Hond. 48/C1
Rochdale, Eng. 66/G2
Rochester, Minn. 153/C2
Rochester, N.H. 158/C3
Rochester, N.Y. 160/C3
Rockford, Ill. 144/B1
Rockhampton, Austr. 115/E3
Rock Hill, S.C. 162/C2
Rock Island, Ill. 144/A1
Rockland, Maine 151/B4
Rock Springs, Wyo. 177/C3
Rockville, Md. 139/E2
Rocky (mts.), N. Amer. 40-41/F-G4-6
Rocky Mount, N.C. 163/E1
Rocky Mountain House, Alta. 191/E3
Rocky Mountain Nat'l Pk., Colo. 134/A2
Roeselare (Roulers), Belg. 73/A6
Rogers, Ark. 131/A1
Rogue (riv.), Oreg. 169/C2
Rolla, Mo. 155/B3
Romania 84/C2
Rome, Ga. 142/A2
Rome (cap.), Italy 78/D3
Rome, N.Y. 161/D3
Ronda, Spain 76/D4
Roosevelt (isl.), Antarc. 118

Roosevelt (riv.), Braz. 56/C3
Roosevelt Campobello Int'l Pk., N. Amer. 151/C4
Roraima (mt.), S. Amer. 56/C2
Rosa (mt.), Europe 78/A2
Rosario, Árg. 58/C6
Roseau (cap.), Dominica 51/G4, 55/K
Roseburg, Oreg. 169/C2
Rosenburg, Texas 173/E3
Rosetown, Sask. 188/A3
Roseville, Minn. 153/C1
Ross (sea), Antarc. 118
Rostock, Ger. 70/E1
Rostov-na-Donu, Rus. 89/F5
Roswell, Ga. 142/A2
Roswell, N. Mex. 135/E4
Rothenberg, Ger. 71/D4
Rotherham, Eng. 67/F4
Rotterdam, Neth. 72/D4
Rotuma (isl.), Fiji 116/H7
Roubaix, France 74/E2
Rouen, France 74/D3
Roundup, Mont. 156/M5
Rouyn, Que. 184/A2
Rovuma (riv.), Africa 63/F6
Roxas, Phil. 109/D5
Royal Oak, Mich. 178/C4
Rub' al Kahli (des.), Asia 94-95/F5
Rubtsovsk, Russia 90/E3
Ruda Slaska, Pol. 86/A4
Rudolf (lake), Africa, see Turkana
Rufiji (riv.), Tanz. 63/F5
Rugby, N. Dak. 164/B3
Rügen (isl.), Ger. 70/E1
Ruhr (riv.), Ger. 70/C3
Rukwa (lake), Tanz. 63/F5
Rum (Rhum) (isl.), Scot. 66/C2
Rumford, Maine 151/A3
Rururtu (isl.), Fr. Poly. 117/L8
Ruse, Bulg. 84/D3
Russell Cave Nat'l Mon., Ala. 128/C1
Russellville, Ark. 131/B2
Russellville, Ky. 148/C3
Russia 90/B3
Ruston, La. 150/A2
Rutland, Vt. 158/A3
Rwanda 63/F5
Ryazan', Russia 89/E4
Rybinsk, Russia 88/E3
Rybnik, Pol. 86/D3
Ryukyu (isls.), Japan 107/F-G3-4
Rzeszow, Pol. 87/F3
Rzhev, Russia 88/D3

S

Saale (riv.), Ger. 70/D3
Saar, Europe 71/B4
Saarbrücken, Ger. 71/B4
Saaremaa (isl.), Est. 88/B3
Saarland (state), Ger. 71/B4
Saba (isl.), Neth. Ant. 51/H3
Sabadell, Spain 77/H2
Sabah (state), Malaysia 112/F4
Sabine (riv.), U.S. 150/B1, 173/F2
Sable (cape), Fla. 141/F3
Sable (cape), N.S. 43/K7
Sable (isl.), N.S. 43/L7
Sacajawea (lake), Wash. 175/C4
Sackets Harbor, N.Y. 161/D2
Sackville, N.S. 183/D3
Saco, Maine 151/A4
Sacramento (cap.), Calif. 132/C2
Sacramento (riv.), Calif. 132/B1
Sacramento (mts.), N. Mex. 135/E2

Sado (isl.), Japan 107/E3
Safad, Isr., see Zefat
Safi, Mor. 60/D1
Saga, Japan 106/C4
Saginaw, Mich. 152/C3
Saguaro Nat'l Park, Ariz. 130/B4
Sahara (des.), Africa 60-61/B-E3
Saharanpur, India 102/C2
Saigon, Viet., see Ho Chi Minh City
St. Albans, Eng. 67/F5
St. Albans, Vt. 158/A2
St. Albans, W. Va. 138/B3
St. Albert, Alta. 191/F4
St. Andrews, Scot. 66/E2
St. Anthony, Newf. 183/F1
St. Augustine, Fla. 140/A3
St. Bernard (pass), Eur. 80/C3
St-Brieuc, France 74/B3
St. Catharines, Ont. 187/F4
St. Charles, Mo. 155/A4
Saint Christopher, see Saint Kitts
St. Clair (lake), N. Amer. 152/C4, 186/A4
St. Clair Shores, Mich. 178/C4
St. Cloud, Minn. 153/B3
St. Croix (isl.), U.S. 153/C3, 176/A2
Saint Croix (isl.), V.I. (U.S.) 51/H2, 54/G
St-Denis, France 74/B1
Ste. Anne, Man. 189/F4
Ste-Foy, Que. 185/E3
Sainte-Marie (cape), Madag., see Vohimena
Ste-Thérèse, Que 184/A1
St-Étienne, France 75/F5
St-Eustache, Que. 184/A1
St. Eustatius (isl.), Neth. Ant. 51/F3
St-Félicien, Que. 185/D2
St. George, Utah 174/A4
Saint George's (chan.), Eur. 67/C5
St. George's (cap.), Grenada 51/F5, 55/R
Saint Georges (bay), N.S. 183/E3
Saint Gotthard (tunnel), Switz. 81/D2
Saint Helena (isl.), U.K. 35/J6
St. Helens, Eng. 66/G2
Saint Helens (vol.), Wash. 175/C2
St-Hubert, Que. 184/B1
St-Hyacinthe, Que. 185/D4
St. Ignace, Mich. 152/B2
St. Ignatius, Mont. 156/B1
St-Jean, Que. 185/D4
Saint-Jean (lake), Que. 185/D2
St-Jérôme, Que. 184/A1
St. John, N. Br. 182/C3
Saint John (riv.), N. Bruns. 182/A2
Saint John (isl.), V.I. (U.S.) 54/F
St. Johns (cap.), Antigua & Barbuda 51/G3, 55/V
Saint Johns (riv.), Fla. 140/A3
St. John's (cap.), Newf. 183/F1
St. Johnsbury, Vt. 158/B2
St. Joseph, Mo. 155/A2
Saint Joseph (isl.), Ont. 186/A1
Saint Kitts (isl.), St. Kitts & Nevis 51/F3, 55/W
Saint Kitts and Nevis 51/F3
St-Laurent, Que. 184/A1
Saint Lawrence (isl.), Alaska 40/A3
Saint Lawrence (gulf), Can. 43/K6
Saint Lawrence (riv.), N. Amer. 185/F2
Saint Lawrence Is. Nat'l Pk., Ont. 187/D2

St-Lô, France 74/C3
St. Louis, Mo. 155/A4
St-Louis, Sen. 60/A3
St. Louis Park, Minn. 153/B1
Saint Lucia 51/G4
Saint-Malo (gulf), France 74/B3
Saint Martin (isl.), Fr., Neth. Ant. 51/F3
St. Marys, Ohio 166/C1
St. Matthews, Ky. 149/F1
St. Moritz, Switz. 81/E2
St-Nazaire, France 74/B4
St. Paul (cap.), Minn. 153/C1
Saint Paul (isl.), Fr. 35/M7
St. Petersburg, Fla. 140/C1
St. Petersburg (Leningrad), Russia 88/D3
St-Pierre, Mart. 54/J
Saint Pierre & Miquelon 43/L6
St-Siméon, Que. 185/E3
St. Stephen, N. Br. 182/B3
St. Thomas, Ont. 186/B4
Saint Thomas (isl.), V.I. (U.S.) 51/H3, 54/F
St-Tropez, France 75/G6
Saint Vincent (cape), Port. 76/B4
Saint Vincent & the Grenadines 51/G4, 55/P
Saipan (cap.), N. Marianas 116/E4
Saitama, Japan 107/E5
Sakakawea (lake), N. Dak. 164/B1
Sakarya (riv.), Turkey 96/D2
Sakhalin (isl.), Russia 91/H3
Sakishima (isls.), Japan 107/F3
Salaberry-de-Valleyfield, Que. 184/C4
Salado (riv.), Arg. 58/C6
Salala, Oman 95/G6
Salamanca, N.Y. 160/B3
Salamanca, Spain 76/D2
Sala y Gómez (isl.), Chile 117/Q8
Salekhard, Russia 90/D2
Salem, India 102/C3
Salem, Mass. 137/E1
Salem, N.J. 159/A3
Salem (cap.), Oreg. 169/A2
Salem, Va. 138/C4
Salerno, Italy 79/E4
Salford, Eng. 66/G2
Salgitter, Ger. 70/D2
Salida, Colo. 134/B3
Salina, Kans. 147/B3
Salinas, Calif 133/D1
Salinas Pueblo Missions Nat'l Mon., N. Mex. 135/E2
Salisbury, Eng. 67/F5
Salisbury, Md. 139/F3
Salisbury, N.C. 162/C2
Salisbury, Zimb., see Harare
Salmon, Idaho 143/B3
Salmon (riv.), Idaho 143/A3
Salmon Arm, Br. Col. 190/C3
Salonika, Greece, see Thessaloníki
Sal'sk, Russia 89/F5
Salt, Jordan, see Es Salt
Saltillo, Mex. 46/E3
Salt Lake City (cap.), Utah 174/C1
Salto, Urug. 58/D6
Salton Sea (lake), Calif. 133/F4
Saluda (riv.), S.C. 162/B2
Salvador, Braz. 57/N5
Salween (riv.), Asia 110/B2
Salzach (riv.), Europe 82/C3
Salzburg, Austria 82/B3
Samar (isl.), Phil. 108/D5
Samara, Russia 89/H4
Samaria (reg.), West Bank 98/C3

Index

Samarinda, Indon. 112/F6
Samarqand, Uzbek. 90/B4
Samarra, Iraq 100/C3
Samoa 117/J7
Sámos (isl.), Greece 85/D4
Samothráki (isl.), Greece 85/D3
Sam Rayburn (res.), Texas 173/F2
Samsun, Turkey 97/G2
San (riv.), Pol. 87/F3
San'a (cap.), Yemen 94/E6
San Andrés (isl.), Col. 5/B4
San Angelo, Texas 172/C2
San Antonio, Texas 173/D3
San Bernardino, Calif. 179/B4
San Bernardino (mts.), Calif. 179/A4
San Bernardino (str.), Phil. 108/E4
San Blas (gulf), Pan. 49/E3
San Bruno, Calif. 133/F1
San Carlos, Phil. 109/D5
San Carlos de Bariloche, Arg. 58/B7
San Clemente, Calif. 133/F3
San Clemente (isl.), Calif. 133/F3
San Cristóbal, Dom. Rep. 52/R7
San Cristóbal, Ven. 56/C3
Sancti Spíritus, Cuba 52/F3
Sand (hills), Nebr. 157/A1
Sandakan, Malaysia 113/F4
San Diego, Calif. 180/C4
Sandpoint, Idaho 143/A1
Sand Springs, Okla. 168/D3
Sandusky, Ohio 166/A3
Sandy, Utah 174/B2
Sandy Hook (spit), N.J. 159/C2
Sanford, Fla. 140/B3
Sanford, Maine 151/A4
Sanford, N.C. 163/D2
San Fernando, Calif. 179/A1
San Fernando, Trin. & Tob. 55/T
San Francisco, Calif. 133/E1
San Francisco (bay), Calif. 133/E1
San Gabriel, Calif. 179/B2
San Gabriel (mts.), Calif. 179/A2
Sanibel (isl.), Fla. 141/E4
San Jacinto Mon., Texas 173/F4
San Joaquin (riv.), Calif. 133/D2
San Jorge (gulf), Arg. 58/C7
San Jose, Calif. 133/F2
San José (cap.), C. Rica 49/D3
San Juan, Arg. 58/C6
San Juan (riv.), Cent. Amer. 48/C3
San Juan (cap.), P. Rico 51/G1, 54/C1
San Juan Capistrano, Calif. 133/F3
San Juan del Norte, Nic. 49/D3
San Juan del Sur, Nic. 48/C3
Sankt Gallen, Switz. 81/E1
Sankt Pölten, Austria 82/C2
San Leandro, Calif. 133/E1
San Lucas (cape), Mex. 46/B3
San Luis, Arg. 58/C6
San Luis Obispo, Calif. 133/E2
San Luis Potosí, Mex. 46/E3
San Marcos, Texas 173/D3
San Marino 78/D3
San Mateo, Calif. 133/F1
San Matías (gulf), Arg. 58/C7
San Miguel, El Sal. 48/C2
San Miguel de Tucumán, Arg. 58/C5
San Pedro, Calif. 179/C4
San Pedro de Macorís, Dom. Rep. 53/S7
San Pedro Sula, Hond. 48/B2
Sandpoint, Idaho 143/A1

San Rafael, Calif. 133/E1
San Remo, Italy 78/A3
San Salvador (isl.), Bah. 50/C1
San Salvador (cap.), El Sal. 48/B2
San Sebastián, Spain 77/E1
San Simeon, Calif. 133/D2
Santa Ana, Calif. 179/C3
Santa Ana, El Sal. 48/B2
Santa Barbara, Calif. 133/E2
Santa Catalina (isl.), Calif. 133/F3
Santa Clara, Calif. 133/F1
Santa Clara, Cuba 52/E2
Santa Cruz, Bol. 56/C4
Santa Cruz, Calif. 133/D1
Santa Cruz (isls.), Sol. Is. 116/G6
Santa Cruz de Tenerife, Spain 76/B4
Santa Fe, Arg. 58/C6
Santa Fe (cap.), N. Mex. 135/D3
Santa Inés (isl.), Chile 58/B8
Santa Maria, Braz. 59/D5
Santa Maria, Calif. 133/E2
Santa Marta, Col. 56/C1
Santa Monica, Calif. 179/B1
Santander, Spain 76/D1
Santanilla (isls.), Hond. 48/C1
Santa Rosa, Arg. 58/C6
Santa Rosa, Calif. 132/C1
Santee (riv.), S.C. 163/D3
Santiago (cap.), Chile 58/B6
Santiago, Dom. Rep. 50/D3, 52/R6
Santiago, Panama 49/D7
Santiago de Compostela, Spain 76/B1
Santiago de Cuba, Cuba 53/J5
Santiago del Estero, Arg. 58/C5
Säntis (mt.), Switz. 81/E1
Santo Domingo (cap.), Dom. Rep. 52/S7
Santos, Braz. 59/E5
São Francisco (riv.), Braz. 57/E4
São Luís, Braz. 57/E3
Saône (riv.), France 75/F4
São Paulo, Braz. 59/E5
São Roque (cape), Braz. 57/F3
São Tomé e Príncipe 62/C4
São Vincent (cape), Port. 76/B4
Sapporo, Japan 107/F2
Sapulpa, Okla. 168/D3
Saragossa, Spain 77/F2
Sarajevo (cap.), Bos. & Herc. 84/B2
Saranac Lake, N.Y. 161/E2
Saransk, Russia 89/F4
Sarapul, Russia 88/H3
Sarasota, Fla. 141/D3
Saratoga Sprs., N.Y. 161/E3
Saratov, Russia 89/G4
Sarawak (state), Malaysia 112/E5
Sardinia (isl.), Italy 79/B4-5
Sardis (lake), Miss. 154/B1
Sargodha, Pak. 102/C1
Sarh, Chad 60/D4
Sari, Iran 101/H2
Sarnia, Ont. 186/A4
Sasebo, Japan 106/C4
Saskatchewan (riv.), Can. 188/B3
Saskatchewan (prov.), Can. 188-189
Saskatoon, Sask. 188/B3
Sassari, Italy 79/B4
Satu Mare, Rom. 84/C2
Saudi Arabia 94/E4-F4-5
Sauk Center, Minn. 153/B3
Sault Ste. Marie, Mich. 152/B2
Sault Ste. Marie, Ont. 187/F1
Sausalito, Calif. 133/E1
Sava (riv.), Eur. 84/B2
Savannah, Ga. 142/C3
Savannah (riv.), U.S. 126/K4

Savannakhet, Laos 110/D3
Save (riv.), Moz. 63/F7
Savu (sea), Indon. 113/G7
Sawtooth Nat'l Rec. Area, Idaho 143/B3
Sawu (isl.), Indon. 113/G7
Saxony (state), Ger. 71/E3
Sayre, Pa. 171/D2
Scapa Flow (chan.), Scot. 66/E1
Scarborough, Eng. 67/F3
Scarsdale, N.Y. 180/C1
Schaffhausen, Switz. 81/D1
Scheldt (riv.), Belg. 73/D5
Schenectady, N.Y. 161/E3
Scheveningen, Neth. 72/B1
Schleswig-Holstein (state), Ger. 70/C1
Schofield Barracks, Hawaii 129/A4
Schuylkill (riv.), Pa. 171/E3
Schwarzwald (Black) (for.), Ger. 71/C4
Schweinfurt, Ger. 71/D3
Schwerin, Ger. 70/D2
Schwyz, Switz. 81/D1
Scilly (isls.), Eng. 67/C6
Scioto (riv.), Ohio 167/E2
Scotia (sea), Antarc. 35/H8
Scotland, U.K. 66/D-2-3
Scott (isl.), Antarc. 118
Scottsbluff, Nebr. 157/B1
Scotts Bluff Nat'l Mon., Nebr. 157/B1
Scottsboro, Ala. 128/C1
Scottsdale, Ariz. 130/A1
Scranton, Pa. 171/E3
Scunthorpe, Eng. 67/F4
Scutari (lake), Europe 84/B3
Scutari (Shkodër), Alb. 84-85/B3
Sea (isls.), U.S. 142/C4
Seaford, Del. 139/F3
Seal Beach, Calif. 179/C2
Searcy, Ark. 131/B3
Searsport, Maine 151/B3
Seaside, Oreg. 169/A1
Seattle, Wash. 175/B3
Sebago (lake), Maine 151/A4
Sebha, Libya 60/D2
Sebring, Fla. 141/D3
Sedalia, Mo. 155/B2
Ségou, Mali 60/B3
Segovia, Spain 76/D2
Seguin, Texas 173/D3
Seine (riv.), France 74/D1
Sekondi, Ghana 60/B4
Selkirk, Man. 189/F4
Selma, Ala. 128/B3
Semarang, Indon. 113/J2
Semeru (mt.), Malaysia 113/K2
Semey, Kazak. 90/D3
Seminole, Okla. 168/D3
Sendai, Japan 107/F3
Seneca (lake), N.Y. 160/C3
Senegal 60/A3
Senegal (riv.), Africa 60/A3
Sennar, Sudan 61/F3
Seoul (cap.), S. Korea 106/B3
Sepik (riv.), Papua N.G. 112/B6
Sept-Îles, Que. 43/K5
Sequoia Nat'l Pk., Calif. 133/D3
Serbia (rep.) Yugo. 84/C2
Seremban, Malaysia 111/C7
Serov, Russia 90/D3
Serowe, Bots. 63/E7
Serpents Mouth (str.) 55/T
Serpukhov, Russia 89/E4
Sétif, Alg. 60/C1
Setúbal, Port. 76/B3
Sevastopol', Ukraine 89/D6
Severn (riv.), U.K. 67/E5

Severnaya Zemlya (isls.), Russia 91/F1
Severodvinsk, Russia 88/E2
Sevier (riv.), Utah 174/B3
Seville, Spain 76/C4
Seward, Alaska 129/B2
Seward (pen.), Alaska 129/A1
Seychelles 93/E6
Seyhan (riv.), Turkey 97/F4
Seymour, Ind. 145/B3
Sfax, Tun. 60/D1
'sGravenhage (The Hague) (cap.), Neth. 72/D3
Shaanxi (prov.), China 104/D2
Shaba, Congo, Rep. of the, see Katanga
Shahjahanpur, India 102/D3
Shaker Hts., Ohio 167/F4
Shakhty, Russia 89/F5
Shamokin, Pa. 171/D3
Shan (plat.), Burma 110/B2
Shandong (Shantung) (prov.), China 105/E2
Shanghai, China 105/F2
Shannon (riv.), Ire. 67/B4
Shantou, China 105/E3
Shanxi (Shansi) (prov.), China 105/E2
Shari (riv.), Africa 61/D4
Sharon, Pa. 170/A3
Shasta (lake), Calif. 132/B1
Shawinigan, Que. 185/D3
Shawnee, Okla. 168/B3
Sheboygan, Wis. 176/C4
Sheffield, Eng. 67/F4
Shelby, Mont. 156/A2
Shelby, N.C. 162/C2
Shelbyville, Ind. 145/C3
Shelbyville, Tenn. 148/C4
Shellbrook, Sask. 188/B2
Shelton, Conn. 136/B3
Shenandoah, Pa. 171/E3
Shenandoah Nat'l Pk., Va. 139/D3
Shensi, China, see Shaanxi
Shenyang, China 105/F1
Sherbrooke, Que. 185/E4
Sheridan, Wyo. 177/A2
Sherman, Texas 173/E1
's Hertogenbosch, Neth. 72/F4
Sherwood Park, Alta. 191/F1
Shetland (isls.), Scot. 66/G1
Sheyenne (riv.), N. Dak. 164/B3
Shijiazhuang, China 105/E2
Shikoku (isl.), Japan 106/D4
Shikotan (isl.), Japan 107/G2
Shiloh Nat'l Mem. Pk., Tenn. 148/B4
Shimizu, Japan 107/E4
Shimonoseki, Japan 106/C4
Shippegan, N. Br. 182/C1
Shiraz, Iran 101/H6
Shively, Ky. 149/E5
Shizuoka, Japan 107/E4
Shkodër, Alb. 84-85/B3
Sholapur, India 102/C3
Shorewood, Wis. 176/B1
Shoshone (riv.), Wyo. 177/A3
Shreveport, La. 150/A1
Shrewsbury, Eng. 67/E4
Shumen, Bulg. 84/D3
Shushtar, Iran 101/A4
Shymkent, Kazak. 90/D3
Sialkot, Pak. 102/C1
Sian, China, see Xi'an
Šiauliai, Lith. 88/B3
Siberia (reg.), Russia 90-91/D-H2
Siberut (isl.), Indon. 112/B6
Sibiu, Rom. 84/C2
Sibley Prov. Pk., Ont. 187/D1
Sibuyan (sea), Phil. 108/D4

Sichuan (prov.), China 104/D2
Sicily (isl.), Italy 79/DE6
Sidi Bel Abbès, Alg. 60/B1
Sidon, Leb., see Saida
Sidra (gulf), Africa 61/D1
Siedlce, Pol. 87/F2
Siegen, Ger. 71/C3
Siena, Italy 78/C3
Sierra Leone 60/A4
Sierra Nevada (mts.), U.S. 44/C3
Sierra Vista, Ariz. 130/C4
Sikasso, Mali 60/B3
Sikeston, Mo. 155/C4
Si Kiang, China, see Xi Jiang
Silver Bay, Minn. 153/C2
Silver City, N. Mex. 135/F2
Silver Spring, Md. 139/D1
Silverton, Colo. 134/C2
Simbirsk, Russia 89/G4
Simcoe, Ont. 186/C4
Simcoe (lake), Ont. 186/C3
Simferopol', Ukraine 89/D6
Simi Valley, Calif. 179/A1
Simla, India 102/C1
Simplon (tunnel), Europe 80/D2
Simpson (des.), Austr. 114/C3
Sinai (pen.), Egypt 94/C4
Singapore 111/E6
Singapore (cap.), Sing. 111/E6
Sinkiang, China, see Xinjiang Uygur Zizhiqu
Sint-Niklaas, Belg. 73/C5
Sinŭiju, N. Korea 106/B2
Sion, Switz. 80/C2
Sioux City, Iowa 146/A1
Sioux Falls, S. Dak. 165/E4
Siracusa (Syracuse), Italy 79/E6
Sirdaryo (riv.), Asia 90/D3
Siret (riv.), Rom. 84/D2
Sitka, Alaska 129/C4
Sitka Nat'l Hist. Pk., Alaska 129/C2
Sittard, Neth. 73/G5
Sittwe, Burma 110/A2
Sivas, Turkey 97/G3
Siwa (oasis), Egypt 94/B4
Skagerrak (str.), Europe 69/B3
Skagit (riv.), Wash. 175/A3
Skeena (riv.), Br. Col. 190/A2
Skien, Nor. 69/B3
Skikda, Alg. 60/C1
Skokie, Ill. 178/B1
Skopje (cap.), Macedonia 85/C3
Skowhegan, Maine 151/A3
Skye (isl.), Scot. 66/C2
Slave Lake, Alta. 191/D2
Sleeping Bear Dunes Nat'l Lakeshore, Mich. 152/A3
Slidell, La. 150/A4
Sligo, Ire. 67/B3
Slovakia 83/D2
Slovenia 84/A2
Słupsk, Pol. 86/C1
Smithers, Br. Col. 190/A2
Smiths Falls, Ont. 187/E2
Smoky (riv.), Alt. 191/D2
Smoky Hill (riv.), Kans. 147/B2
Smolensk, Russia 89/D4
Smyrna, Del. 139/F2
Smyrna, Ga. 142/B1
Smyrna, see Izmir
Snake (riv.), U.S. 44/D2
Snoqualmie (pass), Wash. 175/B3
Snowdon (mt.), Wales 67/E4
Sochi, Russia 89/E6
Society (isls.), Fr. Poly. 117/L7
Socorro, N. Mex. 135/E2
Socotra (isl.), Yemen 95/G7
Södertälje, Swed. 69/D3
Sofia (cap.), Bulg. 84/C3
Sognafjord (fjord), Nor. 69/A2

Sohâg, Egypt 94/C4
Sokhumi, Georgia 89/F6
Sokoto, Nigeria 60/C3
Solomon Islands 116/G6
Solothurn, Switz. 80/C1
Solway (firth), U.K. 67/E3
Somalia 61/G4
Somerset (isl.), Berm. 51/G3
Somerset, Ky. 149/D3
Somerset (isl.), N.W.T. 42/G1
Somerville, Mass. 137/F4
Somme (riv.), France 74/D2
Songhua Jiang (riv.), China 105/F1
Songkhla, Thai. 111/C6
Sonora, Texas 172/C2
Soochow, China, see Suzhou
Sorel, Que. 43/K7
Sorocaba, Braz. 59/E5
Sorrento, Italy 79/E4
Sosnowiec, Pol. 86/B4
Soufrière (vol.), Guad. 55/H5
Souris, Man. 189/D4
Souris (riv.), N. Amer. 164/B2, 189/D4
Souris, P.E.I. 183/E2
Sousse, Tun. 60/D1
South (isl.), N.Z. 115/F4
South Africa 63/E7-8
South America 56-59
Southampton, Eng. 67/F5
Southampton, N.Y. 160/C4
South Atlantic Ocean 35/J7
South Australia (state), Austr. 114/C3
S. Baymouth, Ont. 186/B2
S. Bend, Ind. 145/B1
South Carolina (state), U.S. 162-163
South China (sea), Asia 93/H5
South Dakota (state), U.S. 165
S. Elgin, Ill. 178/A2
Southend-on-Sea, Eng. 67/G5
Southern Alps (mts.), N.Z. 115/F4
Southern Pines, N.C. 163/D2
S. Euclid, Ohio 167/G5
Southfield, Mich. 178/B4
S. Gate, Calif. 179/B2
South Georgia (isl.), Antarc. 35/H8
South Korea 106/C3
S. Lake Tahoe, Calif. 132/C2
South Orkney (isls.), Antarc. 118
South Platte (riv.), U.S. 157/C1
South Pole 118
Southport, Eng. 66/F1
S. Portland, Maine 151/A4
S. San Francisco, Calif. 133/E1
South Sandwich (isl.), Antarc. 35/J8
South Saskatchewan (riv.), Can. 188/B3
South Shetland (isls.), Antarc. 118
S. Shields, Eng. 66/F3
S. Sioux City, Nebr. 157/A4
S. St. Paul, Minn. 153/C1
Spa, Belg. 73/G7
Spain 76-77
Spandau, Ger. 70/E2
Spanish Fork, Utah 174/B3
Spanish Town, Jam. 53/V10
Sparks, Nev. 132/B2
Sparrows Point, Md. 139/F2
Sparta, Greece 85/C4
Spartanburg, S.C. 162/B2
Spassk-Dal'niy, Russia 91/G3
Spearfish, S. Dak. 165/E1
Spencer (gulf), Austr. 114/C4
Spey (riv.), Scot. 66/E2
Spirit Lake, Iowa 146/A1
Spirit River, Alta. 190/C1

Index

Spitsbergen (isl.), Nor. 68/A1
Split, Croatia 84/B3
Spokane, Wash. 175/B4
Spratly (isl.) 112/E4
Spree (riv.), Ger. 70/F3
Springdale, Ark. 131/A1
Springfield (cap.), Ill. 144/B3
Springfield, Mass. 136/E2
Springfield, Mo. 155/C2
Springfield, Ohio 166/C1
Springfield, Oreg. 169/B2
Springfield, Tenn. 148/C2
Springfield, Vt. 158/B3
Spring Hill, Fla. 140/C2
Springhill, N.S. 183/D3
Springville, Utah 174/B3
Spruce Grove, Alta. 191/E1
Spruce Knob Nat'l Rec. Area, W.
  Va. 138/C3
Squamish, Br. Col. 190/B4
Squaw (valley), Calif. 132/C2
Sri Lanka 102/D4
Srinagar, India 102/C1
Stafford, Eng. 67/E4
Stalingrad, Russia see Volgograd
Stamford, Conn. 136/A4
Stanley (cap.), Falkland Is. 59/D8
Stanley (Boyoma) (falls), Congo,
  Rep. of the 63/E5
Stanovoy (range), Rus. 91/G3
Stara Zagora, Bulg. 84/D3
Starkville, Miss. 154/C2
State College, Pa. 170/C3
Staten (isl.), Arg., see Estados
Staten Island (borough), N.Y.
  180/A3
Statesboro, Ga. 142/C3
Statesville, N.C. 162/C2
Statue of Liberty Nat'l Mon., U.S.
  180/B2
Staunton, Va. 139/D3
Stavanger, Nor. 69/A3
Stavropol', Russia 89/F5
Steamboat Springs, Colo. 134/A2
Stephenville, Newf. 183/E1
Stephenville, Texas 173/D2
Sterling, Colo. 134/A4
Sterling, Ill. 144/B1
Sterling Hts., Mich. 178/C3
Sterlitamak, Russia 89/J4
Stettin, Pol., see Szczecin
Stettler, Alta. 191/E3
Steubenville, Ohio 166/C4
Stevens Point, Wis. 176/B3
Stewart (isl.), N.Z. 115/F4
Steyr, Austria 82/C2
Stillwater, Okla. 168/A3
Stirling, Scot. 66/B1
Stockholm (cap.), Swed. 69/D3
Stockport, Eng. 66/G2
Stockton, Calif. 132/C2
Stockton (plat.), Texas 172/C2
Stockton-on-Tees, Eng. 67/F3
Stoke-on-Trent, Eng. 67/F4
Stones River Nat'l Battlfld., Tenn.
  148/C2
Stornoway, Scot. 66/C1
Storrs, Conn. 136/C2
Stoughton, Mass. 137/E2
Stowe, Vt. 158/A2
Strabane, N. Ire. 67/C1
Strasbourg, France 74/G3
Stratford, Conn. 136/B3
Stratford, Ont. 186/B3
Stromboli (isl.), Italy 79/E5
Strongsville, Ohio 167/F3
Stroudsburg, Pa. 171/F4
Stuart, Fla. 141/D4
Sturbridge, Mass. 136/C2
Sturgeon Bay, Wis. 176/C3
Sturgeon Falls, Ont. 186/C1

Sturgis, S. Dak. 165/E1
Stuttgart, Ark. 131/B3
Stuttgart, Ger. 71/C4
Subic (bay), Phil. 108/B3
Subotica, Yugo. 84/B2
Sucre (cap.), Bol. 56/C4
Sudan 61/E-F5
Sudan (reg.), Africa 60-61/B-F3
Sudbury, Ont. 186/B1
Sudd (swamp), Sudan 61/F4
Sudeten (mts.), Europe 82/C1
Suez, Egypt 94/C4
Suez (canal), Egypt 94/C3
Suez (gulf), Egypt 94/C4
Suffolk, Va. 139/E3
Suir (riv.), Ire. 67/C4
Suita, Japan 107/E4
Sukabumi, Indon. 113/H2
Sukkur, Pak. 102/B2
Sula (isls.), Indon. 113/H6
Sulaimaniya, Iraq 100/D3
Sulawesi (Celebes) (isl.), Indon.
  113/G6
Sulphur, La. 150/C1
Sulu (sea), Asia 113/G4
Sulu (arch.), Phil. 113/G4
Sumatra (isl.), Indon. 112/B-C5-6
Sumba (isl.), Indon. 113/F7
Sumbawa (isl.), Indon.
  112-113/F7
Sumter, S.C. 162/C3
Sumy, Ukraine 89/D4
Sunbury, Pa. 171/D3
Sun City, Ariz. 130/B3
Sunda (str.), Indon. 112/C7
Sunderland, Eng. 66/F3
Sundsvall, Swed. 69/C2
Sungari, China, see Songhua
  Jiang
Sunnyvale, Calif. 133/F1
Sunrise, Fla. 141/D1
Sunset Crater Nat'l Mon., Ariz.
  130/B3
Sun Valley, Idaho 143/B3
Suo (sea), Japan 106/C4
Superior (lake), N. Amer. 40/K5
Superior, Wis. 176/A2
Sur, Leb. 96/F6
Surabaya, Indon. 113/K2
Surakarta, Indon. 113/J2
Surat, India 102/C2
Surgut, Russia 90/D2
Surigao (str.), Phil. 109/E6
Suriname 57/D2
Surrey, Br. Col. 190/B1
Susquehanna (riv.), U.S. 171/D4
Sutlej (riv.), India 102/C1
Suva (cap.), Fiji 116/H7
Suwalki, Pol. 87/F1
Suwannee (riv.), U.S. 140/B2
Suzhou, China 105/F2
Svalbard (isls.), Nor. 68/A1
Sverdrup (isls.), N.W.T. 40/H2
Svobodnyy, Russia 91/G3
Swakopmund, Namibia 62/D7
Swan (Santanilla) (isls.), Hond.
  48/C1
Swan River, Man. 189/D3
Swansea, Wales 67/D5
Swarthmore, Pa. 171/D2
Swatow, China, see Shantou
Swaziland 63/F7
Sweden 68-69
Sweetwater, Texas 172/C2
Sweetwater (riv.), Wyo. 177/B3
Swift Current, Sask. 184/B6
Swilly, Lough (inlet), Ire. 66/C3
Swindon, Eng. 67/F5
Switzerland 80-81
Sydney, Austr. 115/E4
Sydney, N.S. 183/F2

Syktyvkar, Russia 88/H2
Sylacauga, Ala. 128/B2
Sylt (isl.), Ger. 70/C1
Syracuse, Italy 79/E6
Syracuse, N.Y. 161/D3
Syria 97/G-H5
Syrian (des.), Asia 100/B4
Syzran', Russia 89/G4
Szczecin, Pol. 86/B2
Szechwan, China, see Sichuan
Szeged, Hung. 83/E3
Székesfehérvár, Hung. 83/D3
Szolnok, Hung. 83/E3
Szombathely, Hung. 82/D3

T

Taber, Alta. 191/F4
Table Rock (lake), Mo. 155/C2
Tabora, Tanz. 63/F5
Tabriz, Iran 100/D2
Tabuaeran (isl.), Kiribati 117/L5
Tacloban, Phil. 109/E5
Tacna, Peru 56/B4
Tacoma, Wash. 175/C1
Tadmor, Syria 97/H5
Taebaek (mt.), S. Korea 106/C3
Taedong (riv.), N. Korea 106/C4
Taegu, S. Korea 106/C4
Taejón, S. Korea 106/B3
Taganrog, Russia 89/E5
Tagus (Tajos) (riv.), Europe 76/B3
Tahiti (isl.), Fr. Poly. 117/L7
Tahoe (lake), U.S. 132/C2
Tahoua, Niger 60/C3
Taichung, Taiwan 105/F3
Taif, S. Arabia 94/E5
Tainan, Taiwan 105/F3
Taipei (cap.), Taiwan 105/F3
Taitao (pen.), Chile 58/B7
Taiwan (isl.), Taiwan 105/F3
Taiwan (str.), Asia 105/E3
Taiyuan, China 105/E2
Ta'izz, Yemen 94/E7
Tajikistan 90/A4
Takamatsu, Japan 106/D4
Takaoka, Japan 106/E3
Takasaki, Japan 107/F3
Takatsuki, Japan 107/E4
Takoma Park, Md. 139/D1
Takoradi, Ghana 60/B4
Talca, Chile 58/B6
Talcahuano, Chile 58/B6
Taldyqorghan, Kazak. 90/D3
Talladega, Ala. 128/C2
Tallahassee (cap.), Fla. 140/A1
Tallinn (cap.), Est. 88/C3
Tamale, Ghana 60/B4
Tamanrasset, Alg. 60/C2
Tamaqua, Pa. 171/E3
Tamatave, Madag., see
  Toamasina
Tambov, Russia 89/F4
Tampa, Fla. 140/C3
Tampa (bay), Fla. 140/C1
Tampere, Fin. 69/D2
Tampico, Mex. 47/F3
Tamworth, Austr. 115/E4
Tana (lake), Eth. 61/F3
Tana (riv.), Kenya 63/G5
Tandil, Arg. 58/D6
Tanega (isl.), Japan 107/H2
Tanezrouft (des.), Africa 60/B2
Tanga, Tanz. 63/F5
Tanganyika (lake), Africa 63/F5
Tangier, Mor. 60/B1
Tangshan, China 105/E2
Tanimbar (isls.), Indon. 113/J7
Tanjungkarang, Indon. 112/D7
Tanta, Egypt 94/C3
Tanzania 63/F5

Taos, N. Mex. 134/C3
Tapachula, Mex. 47/G5
Tapajós (riv.), Braz. 57/D3
Tar (riv.), N.C. 163/D1
Tarabulus, Leb. 97/F5
Tarakan, Indon. 113/F5
Taranto, Italy 79/F4
Tarawa (atoll), Kiribati 116/H5
Tarhuna, Libya 60/D1
Tarija, Bol. 58/C5
Tarim He (riv.), China 104/B1
Tarnów, Pol. 87/E4
Tarpon Sprs., Fla. 140/C2
Tarragona, Spain 77/G2
Tarrasa, Spain 77/G2
Tarsus, Turkey 96/F4
Tartu, Russia 88/C3
Tartus, Syria 97/F5
Tashkent (cap.), Uzbek. 90/D3
Tasman (sea), Pacific 116/F9
Tasmania (state), Austr. 115/D5
Tata, Hung. 83/D3
Tatar (str.), Russia 91/H3
Tatra, High (mts.), Europe 83/E2
Taunton, Eng. 67/E5
Taunton, Mass. 137/E2
Taunus (range), Ger. 71/C3
Taurus (mts.), Turkey 96/DE4
Tavoy, Burma 111/B4
Tawi Tawi (isl.), Phil. 109/C8
Tay (firth), Scot. 66/E2
Taylor, Nebr. 157/B3
Taymyr (pen.), Russia 91/E2
Tbilisi (cap.) Georgia 89/F6
Teaneck, N.J. 180/B1
Tegal, Indon. 113/H2
Tegucigalpa (cap.), Hond. 48/C2
Tehran (cap.), Iran 101/G3
Tehuantepec, Mex. 47/F5
Tejo (Tagus) (riv.), Port. 76/B3
Tel Aviv-Jaffa, Isr. 99/B3
Tela, Hond. 48/C2
Tema, Ghana 60/C4
Temirtaū, Kazak. 90/D3
Tempe, Ariz. 130/A1
Temple, Texas 173/G7
Temuco, Chile 58/B6
Tenerife (isl.), Spain 76/B4
Tennessee (state), U.S. 148-149
Tennessee (riv.), U.S. 45/J3
Ten Thousand (isls.), Fla. 141/E3
Tepic, Mexico 46/D4
Teresina, Braz. 57/E3
Terni, Italy 78/D3
Ternopil, Ukraine 89/C5
Terrace, Br. Col. 190/A2
Terra Nova Nat'l Pk., Newf.
  183/F1
Terrebonne (bay), La. 150/C3
Terre Haute, Ind. 145/A3
Tete, Moz. 63/F6
Tétouan, Mor. 60/C1
Tetovo, Macedonia 84/C3
Texarkana, Ark. 131/C1
Texarkana, Texas 173/F1
Texas (state), U.S. 172-173
Texas City, Texas 173/F3
Texel (isl.), Neth. 72/E1
Texoma (lake), U.S. 168/C3,
  173/E1
Thailand 110/C3
Thames (riv.), Eng. 67/G5
Thames (riv.), Ont. 186/B4
Thanjavur, India 102/C3
Thásos (isl.), Greece 85/D3
The Dalles, Oreg. 169/A3
Thedford, Nebr. 157/B2
The Hague (cap.), Neth. 72/D3
Theodore Roosevelt (lake), Ariz.
  130/B3

Theodore Roosevelt Nat'l Pk.,
  N. Dak. 164/BC1
The Pas, Man. 189/D2
Thermopolis, Wyo. 177/B3
Thessaloníki, Greece 85/D3
Thetford Mines, Que. 185/E4
Thibodaux, La. 150/C3
Thiès, Sen. 60/A3
Thika, Kenya 63/F5
Thimphu (cap.), Bhutan 103/E2
Thionville, France 74/G3
Thira (isl.), Greece 85/D4
Thívai (Thebes), Greece 85/C4
Thomasville, Ga. 142/A4
Thomasville, N.C. 162/C2
Thompson (riv.), Br. Col. 190/C3
Thompson, Man. 189/E1
Thompsonville, Conn. 136/C2
Thon Buri, Thai. 111/C4
Thornton, Colo. 178/A4
Thorold, Ont. 187/F4
Thule Air Base, Greenl. 40/L2
Thun, Switz. 80/C2
Thunder Bay, Ont. 188/D1
Thuringia (state), Ger. 70/D3
Thurrock, Eng. 67/G5
Thurso, Scot. 66/E1
Tian (Tien) Shan (mts.), China
  104/A1
Tianjin, China 105/E2
Tiber (riv.), Italy 78/D3
Tiberias, Isr. 98/C2
Tibesti (mts.), Chad 60/B2
Tibet (reg.), China 104/B2
Ticonderoga, N.Y. 161/F2
Tientsin, China, see Tianjin
Tierra del Fuego (isl.), S. Amer.
  58/C8
Tiête (riv.), Braz. 59/E5
Tiffin, Ohio 166/B2
Tifton, Ga. 142/B4
Tigris (riv.), Asia 94/E2
Tihama (reg.), Asia 94/D-E5-6
Tijuana, Mex. 46/A1
Tilburg, Neth. 73/F5
Tilbury, Ont. 186/A4
Timaru, N.Z. 115/F4
Timbuktu, Mali 60/B3
Timişoara, Rom. 84/C2
Timmins, Ont. 187/F1
Timor (isl.), Indon. 113/H7
Timpanogos Cave Nat'l Mon., Utah
  174/B2
Tinian (isl.), N. Marianas 116/E4
Tinley Park, Ill. 178/B3
Tippecanoe (riv.), Ind. 145/B2
Tipperary, Ire. 67/B4
Tiranë (Tirana) (cap.), Albania
  85/B3
Tîrgoviște, Rom. 84/D2
Tîrgu Mureș, Rom. 84/D2
Tiruchchirappalli, India 102/C3
Tirunelveli, India 102/C4
Tisza (riv.), Hung. 83/F3
Titicaca (lake), S. Amer. 56/C4
Titusville, Fla. 140/C4
Titusville, Pa. 170/B2
Tiverton, R.I. 137/E2
Tivoli, Italy 78/D4
Tlemcen, Alg. 60/B1
Toamasina, Madag. 63/G6
Tobago (isl.), Trin. & Tob. 51/G5,
  55/U

Tokelau 116/J6
Tokushima, Japan 106/D4
Tokyo (cap.), Japan 107/E4
Toledo, Ohio 166/A2
Toledo, Spain 76/D3
Toledo Bend (res.), U.S. 150/A1
Toliara, Madag. 63/G7
Tolima (mt.), Col. 56/B2
Toluca, Mex. 46/E4
Tomakomai, Japan 107/F2
Tombigbee (riv.), U.S. 154/C2
Tombouctou, Mali, see Timbuktu
Tombstone, Ariz. 130/C4
Toms River, N.J. 159/C3
Tomsk, Russia 90/E3
Tonawanda, N.Y. 160/B3
Tonga 117/J8
Tongareva (atoll), Cook Is. 117/L6
Tongatapu (isl.), Tonga 117/J8
Tongue (riv.), U.S. 156/C4
Tonkin (gulf), Asia 110/D3
Tonle Sap (lake), Camb. 111/C4
Tooele, Utah 174/B2
Toowoomba, Austr. 115/E3
Topeka (cap.), Kans. 147/B3
Torbay, Eng. 67/E5
Torino, Italy see Turin
Tornio (riv.), Europe 68/D1
Toronto (cap.), Ont. 187/F3
Torquay, Eng., see Torbay
Torrance, Calif. 133/F3
Torrens (lake), Austr. 114/C4
Torreón, Mex. 46/D3
Torres (str.), 116/E7
Torrington, Conn. 136/B2
Tortola (isl.), V.I. (Br.) 54/F
Tortué (Tortuga) (isl.), Haiti 52/P6
Toruń, Pol. 86/D2
Totowa, N.J. 180/A1
Tottori, Japan 106/D3
Touggourt, Alg. 60/C1
Toulon, France 75/F6
Toulouse, France 75/D6
Tourcoing, France 74/E2
Tournai, Belg. 73/B6
Tours, France 74/D4
Townsville, Austr. 115/D2
Towson, Md. 139/F1
Toyama, Japan 106/E3
Toyohashi, Japan 106/E4
Toyonaka, Japan 107/E4
Trabzon, Turkey 97/H2
Tracy, Que. 185/D4
Trafalgar (cape), Spain 76/C4
Trail, Br. Col. 191/D4
Tralee, Ire. 67/B4
Transkei, S. Africa 63/E7
Transvaal (prov.), S. Africa 63/E7
Transylvanian Alps (mts.), Rom.
  84/D2
Traverse City, Mich. 152/B3
Treasure Island, Fla. 140/F5
Trent (riv.), Eng. 67/F4
Trentino-Adige (reg.), Italy 78/C1
Trento, Italy 78/C1
Trenton (cap.), N.J. 159/B2
Trenton, Ont. 187/D3
Trier, Ger. 71/B4
Trieste, Italy 78/D2
Trincomalee, Sri Lanka 102/D4
Trinidad, Bol. 56/C4
Trinidad, Colo. 134/C3
Trinidad (isl.), Trin. & Tob. 51/G5,
  55/T
Trinidad and Tobago 51/G5
Trinity (riv.), Calif. 132/B1
Trinity (riv.), Texas 173/E2
Tripoli (Tarabulus), Leb. 97/F5
Tripoli (cap.), Libya 60/D1
Tripolitania (reg.), Libya 60/B1-2
Tristan da Cunha (isl.), St. Helena
  35/J7

Index

Trivandrum, India 102/C4
Trobriand (isls.), Papua N.G. 112/C7
Trois Rivières, Que. 185/D4
Tromso, Nor. 68/D1
Trondheim, Nor. 68/B2
Troy, Ala. 128/C3
Troy, N.Y. 161/F3
Troyes, France 74/F3
Trujillo, Peru 56/B3
Trujillo, Spain 76/D3
Truk (isls.), Micronesia 116/F5
Truro, N.S. 183/D3
Tsinan, China, see Jinan
Tsinghai, China, see Qinghai
Tsingtao, China, see Qingdao
Tsu (isl.), Japan 106/C4
Tsugaru (str.), Japan 107/E2
Tsumeb, Namibia 63/D6
Tuamotu (arch.), Fr. Poly. 117/M7
Tübingen, Ger. 71/C4
Tubuai (isls.), see Austral (isls.)
Tucson, Ariz. 130/B4
Tucumán, San Miguel de, Arg. 58/C3
Tucumcari, N. Mex. 135/D3
Tula, Russia 89/E4
Tulare, Calif. 133/D2
Tulkarm, West Bank 98/C13
Tullahoma, Tenn. 148/C4
Tullamore, Ire. 67/C4
Tulsa, Okla. 168/A4
Tumacacori Nat'l Hist. Pk., Ariz. 130/B4
Tumen (riv.), Asia 106/C2
Tunis (cap.), Tun. 60/D1
Tunisia 60/C1
Tupelo, Miss. 154/C1
Tupelo Nat'l Battlfld., Miss.154/C1
Turin, Italy 78/A2
Turkana (lake), Africa 61/F4
Turkey 96-97
Turkmenistan 90/C4
Turks & Caicos Is. 50-51/D-E2
Turku, Fin. 69/D2
Turlock, Calif. 132/C2
Turneffe (isls.), Belize 48/C1
Turnhout, Belg. 72/E5
Tuscaloosa, Ala. 128/A2
Tuscany (reg.), Italy 78/C3
Tuskegee, Ala. 128/C3
Tuticorin, India 102/C4
Tutuila (isl.), Amer. Samoa 117/J7
Tuvalu 116/H6
Tuz (lake), Turkey 96/E3
Tuzigoot Nat'l Mon., Ariz. 130/B3
Tver', Russia 88/E3
Twin Falls, Idaho 143/B4
Two Harbors, Minn. 153/C3
Two Rivers, Wis. 176/C3
Tychy, Poland 86/B4
Tyler, Texas 173/F2
Tyre (Sur), Leb. 96/F6
Tyrone, Pa. 170/E4
Tyrrhenian (sea), Italy 79/C-D4-5
Tyumen, Russia 90/D3

U

Ubangi (riv.), Africa 63/D4
Ube, Japan 106/C4
Uberaba, Braz. 57/E4
Uberlândia, Braz. 57/E4
Ucayali (riv.), Peru 56/B3
Uchiura (bay), Japan 107/F2
Udaypur, India 102/C2
Udine, Italy 78/D1
Udon Thani, Thai. 110/C3
Uele (riv.), Congo, Rep. of the 61/E4

Ufa, Russia 89/J4
Uganda 61/F4
Uijeongbu, S. Africa 63/E8
Uijiji, Tanz. 63/F5
Ujjain, India 102/C2
Újpest, Hung. 83/E3
Ujung Pandang, Indon. 113/F7
Ukhta, Russia 90/C2
Ukraine 89/E5
Ulaanbaatar (cap.), Mong. 104/D1
Ulan-Bator (cap.), Mong. 104/D1
Ulan-Ude, Russia 91/F3
Ulithi (isl.), Micronesia 116/D4
Ullŭng (isl.), S. Korea 106/C4
Ulm, Ger. 71/C4
Ulsan, S. Korea 106/C4
Umbria (reg.), Italy 78/D3
Umeå, Swed. 68/D2
Umpqua (riv.), Oreg. 169/B2
Umtata, S. Africa 63/E8
Ungava (bay), Que. 43/K4
Union, N.J. 180/A2
Union City, Calif. 133/F1
Union City, N.J. 180/B2
Union City, Tenn. 148/B3
Uniontown, Pa. 170/A4
United Arab Emirates 95/G5
United Kingdom 66-67
United States of America 44-45, 126-127
University City, Mo. 155/A4
University Park, Texas 172/C4
Upland, Calif. 179/A3
Upper Darby, Pa. 171/E1
Upper Klamath (lake), Oreg. 169/C2
Upper Red (lake), Minn. 153/B2
Upper Volta, see Burkina Faso
Uppsala, Swed. 69/C3
Urabá (gulf), Col. 56/B2
Ural (mts.), Asia 90/C3
Ural (riv.) 90/C3
Urawa, Japan 107/H2
Urbana, Ill. 144/C2
Urbandale, Iowa 146/B2
Urfa, Turkey 97/H4
Urganch, Uzbek. 90/D3
Urmia, Iran 100/D2
Urmia (lake), Iran 100/D2
Uruapan, Mex. 46/E4
Uruguay 59/D5
Uruguay (riv.), S. Amer. 59/D5
Urümqi (Urumchi), China 104/B1
Ushuaia, Arg. 58/C8
Üsküdar, Turkey 96/D6
Usol'ye-Sibirskoye, Russia 91/F3
Ussuri Wusuli (riv.), Asia 105/G1
Ussuriysk, Russia 91/F4
Ústí nad Labem, Czech Rep. 82/C1
Utah (state), U.S. 174
Utah (lake), Utah 174/B3
Utica, N.Y. 161/E3
Utrecht, Neth. 72/C3
Utsunomiya, Japan 107/F3
Uvalde, Texas 173/D3
Uxmal (ruins), Mex. 47/H4
Uzbekistan 90/D3

V

Vaal (riv.), S. Africa 63/E7
Vaasa, Fin. 68/D2
Vacaville, Calif. 132/C1
Vadodara, India, see Baroda
Vaduz (cap.), Liechtenstein 81/E1
Vail, Colo. 134/B2
Valais (canton), Switz. 80/C2

Valdés (pen.), Arg. 58/C7
Valdez, Alaska 129/B2
Valdivia, Chile 58/B6
Val-d'Or, Que. 184/B2
Valdosta, Ga. 142/B4
Valence, France 75/F5
Valencia, Spain 77/F3
Valencia, Ven. 56/C2
Valenciennes, France 74/E2
Valentine, Nebr. 157/A2
Valera, Ven. 56/B2
Valladolid, Spain 76/D2
Valledupar, Col. 56/B1
Vallejo, Calif. 133/D1
Valletta (cap.), Malta 79/E7
Valley City, N. Dak. 164/C4
Valley Stream, N.Y. 180/C2
Valleyview, Alta. 191/D2
Valparaiso, Chile 58/B4
Valparaiso, Ind. 145/A1
Van, Turkey 97/K3
Van Buren, Ark. 131/B1
Vancouver, Br. Col. 190/A1
Vancouver (isl.), Br. Col. 42/D6
Vancouver, Wash. 175/C2
Vandalia, Ill. 144/B3
Vanderhoof, Br. Col. 190/B2
Vänern (lake), Swed. 68/C3
Vanier, Ont. 186/A1
Vanua Levu (isl.), Fiji 116/J7
Vanuatu 116/G7
Varanasi, India 102/D2
Varangerfjord (fjord), Nor. 68/F
Vardar (riv.), Europe 85/C3
Varna, Bulg. 84/E3
Vashon (isl.), Wash. 175/C4
Västerås, Swed. 69/C3
Vatican City 78/D4
Vättern (lake), Swed. 69/C3
Vaupés (riv.), S. Am. 56/C3
Vegreville, Alta. 191/F2
Velikiye Luki, Russia 88/D3
Vellore, India 102/C3
Veneto (reg.), Italy 78/C2
Venezuela 56/C2
Venezuela (gulf), Ven. 56/B1
Venice, Fla. 141/D3
Venice (Venezia), Italy 78/C2
Ventura, Calif. 133/E2
Veracruz, Mex. 47/F4
Verde (cape), Sen. 60/A3
Verdun, France 74/F3
Vereeniging, S. Africa 63/E7
Verkhoyansk (range), Russia 91/G2
Vermillion, S. Dak. 165/F4
Vermont (state), U.S. 158
Vernal, Utah 174/C2
Vernon, Br. Col. 190/C4
Vero Beach, Fla. 141/C4
Verona, Italy 78/C2
Versailles, France 74/A2
Vestfjord (fjord), Nor. 68/C1
Vesuvius (vol.), Italy 79/E4
Veszprém, Hung. 83/E3
Vevey, Switz. 80/B2
Vicenza, Italy 78/C2
Vichy, France 75/E4
Vicksburg, Miss. 154/A3
Victoria (falls), Africa 63/E6
Victoria (lake), Africa 63/F5
Victoria (state), Austr. 115/D4
Victoria (cap.), Br. Col. 190/B4
Victoria (cap.), Hong Kong 105/E3
Victoria (isl.), N.W.T. 42/E1
Victoria, Texas 173/E3
Victoria Beach, Man. 189/D3
Victoriaville, Que. 185/E4
Vidalia, Ga. 142/B3

Viedma, Arg. 58/C7
Vienna (Wien) (cap.), Austria 82/D2
Vientiane (cap.), Laos 110/C3
Vieques (isl.), P. Rico 54/E1
Vietnam 110/D3
Vigo, Spain 76/B1
Vijayawada, India 102/C3
Villach, Austria 82/B3
Villahermosa, Mex. 47/G5
Villa Park, Ill. 178/A2
Villavicencio, Col. 56/B2
Vilnius (cap.), Lith. 89/C4
Viña del Mar, Chile 58/B6
Vinalhaven (isl.), Maine 151/B4
Vincennes, Ind. 145/A4
Vindhya (range) India 102/C2
Vineland, N.J. 159/B4
Vinita, Okla 168/A4
Vinnytsya, Ukraine 89/C5
Vinson Massif (mt.), Antarc. 118
Virden, Man. 189/D4
Virginia (state), U.S. 138-139
Virginia, Minn. 153/C2
Virginia Beach, Va. 138/B1
Virginia City, Mont. 156/C4
Virginia City, Nev. 132/B2
Virgin Is. (Br.) 51/H1, 54/F
Virgin Is. (U.S.) 51/H1, 54/F, G
Virgin Is. Nat'l Pk., V.I. (U.S.) 54/F
Visakhapatnam, India 102/D3
Visalia, Calif. 133/D2
Visayan (sea), Phil. 109/D5
Vista, Calif. 133/F3
Vistula (riv.), Pol. 87/D2
Vitsyebsk, Belarus 88/D3
Viti Levu (isl.), Fiji 116/H7
Vitória, Braz. 59/F5
Vitoria, Spain 77/E1
Vladikavkaz, Russia 89/F6
Vladimir, Russia 88/F3
Vladivostok, Russia 91/G3
Vlorë, Alb. 85/B3
Vltava (Moldau) (riv.), Czech Rep. 82/C2
Vohimena (cape), Madag. 63/G7
Vojvodina (aut. rep.) Yugo. 84/B2
Volcano (isls.), Japan 107/G3
Volga (riv.), Russia 89/G5
Volgograd, Russia 89/F5
Vologda, Russia 88/E3
Vólos, Greece 85/C4
Volta (lake), Ghana 60/B4
Volta (riv.), Ghana 60/C4
Volta Redonda, Braz. 59/E5
Volturno (riv.), Italy 79/E4
Vorkuta, Russia 88/K1
Voronezh, Russia 89/E4
Vosges (mts.), France 74/G3
Voyageurs Nat'l Pk., Minn. 153/C2
Vyatka, Russia 88/G3

W

Wabash, Ind. 145/B2
Wabash (riv.), U.S. 144/C3, 145/A3
Waco, Texas 173/E2
Waddenzee (sound), Neth. 72/F1
Wad Medani, Sudan 61/F3
Wahiawa, Hawaii 129/A4
Wahpeton, N. Dak. 164/C4
Wailuku, Hawaii 129/C3
Wainwright, Alta. 191/F2
Waipahu, Hawaii 129/A4
Wakayama, Japan 106/D4
Wake (isl.), Pacific 116/G4
Wakefield, Eng. 67/F4

Wake Forest, N.C. 163/D1
Walbrzych, Pol. 86/C3
Walcheren (isl.), Neth. 73/B5
Wales, U.K. 67/E4
Wall, S. Dak. 165/E1
Wallaceburg, Ont. 186/A4
Wallasey, Eng. 66/F2
Walla Walla, Wash. 175/C4
Wallingford, Conn. 136/B3
Wallis & Futuna 117/J7
Walnut Canyon Nat'l Mon., Ariz. 130/B3
Walnut Creek, Calif. 133/E1
Walsall, Eng. 67/F4
Waltham, Mass. 137/F4
Walvis Bay, Namibia 62/D7
Wapakoneta, Ohio 166/C1
Warangal, India 102/C3
Warren, Mich. 178/C3
Warren, Ohio 166/B4
Warren, Pa. 170/B2
Warrington, Eng. 66/G2
Warrnambool, Austral. 115/D4
Warsaw (cap.), Pol. 87/E2
Warta, Pol. 86/B2
Warwick, R.I. 137/D3
Wash, The (bay), Eng. 67/G4
Washington (mt.), N.H. 158/C2
Washington, N.C. 163/E2
Washington, Pa. 170/A4
Washington, D.C. (cap.), U.S. 139/D1
Washington (state), U.S. 175
Waterbury, Conn. 136/B3
Waterbury, Vt. 136/A2
Waterford, Ire. 67/C4
Waterloo, Belg. 73/D6
Waterloo, Iowa 146/B3
Waterloo, Ont. 187/D4
Waterton-Glacier Int'l Peace Pk., N. Amer. 156/A4
Waterton Lakes Nat'l Pk., Alta. 191/E4
Watertown, Conn. 136/A3
Watertown, N.Y. 161/D2
Watertown, S. Dak. 165/D4
Watertown, Wis. 176/C4
Waterville, Maine 151/B3
Watford, Eng. 67/B5
Watkins Glen, N.Y. 160/C3
Watling (isl.), see San Salvador (isl.)
Watsonville, Calif. 133/D1
Watts Barr (lake), Tenn. 149/D4
Wau, Sudan 61/E4
Waukegan, Ill. 178/B1
Waukesha, Wis. 176/A1
Wausau, Wis. 176/B3
Wawatosa, Wis. 176/A1
Waxahachie, Texas 173/E2
Waycross, Ga. 142/B4
Waynesboro, Va. 139/D3
Weatherford, Okla. 168/B2
Webster, N.Y. 160/C1
Weddell (sea), Antarc. 118
Weimar, Ger. 71/D3
Weirton, W. Va. 138/C1
Weiser, Idaho 143/A3
Welkom, S. Africa 63/E7
Welland, Ont. 187/F4
Wellington (isl.), Chile 58/B7
Wellington (cap.), N.Z. 115/F4
Wellsboro, Pa. 171/D2
Wels, Austria 82/B2
Wenatchee, Wash. 175/B3
Wendover, Utah 174/A2
Wenzhou, China 105/F3
Weser (riv.), Ger. 70/C2
Weslaco, Texas 173/D4
W. Allis, Wis. 176/A1
West Bank 98-99/C3

W. Bend, Wis. 176/C4
Westbrook, Maine 151/A4
W. Chester, Pa. 171/E4
W. Covina, Calif. 179/D3
W. Des Moines, Iowa 146/B2
Westerly, R.I. 137/D3
Western Australia (state), Austr. 114/B3
Western Sahara 60/A2
Westerville, Maine 151/B3
Westerville, Ohio 166/C3
W. Fargo, N. Dak. 164/C4
Westfield, Mass. 136/B2
W. Hartford, Conn. 136/B2
W. Haven, Conn. 136/B3
W. Helena, Ark. 131/B3
West Indies 50-51
W. Jordan, Utah 174/C2
W. Lafayette, Ind. 145/A2
Westland, Mich. 178/B4
W. Memphis, Ark. 131/B3
W. Mifflin, Pa. 170/A1
Westminster, Calif. 179/C2
Westminster, Colo. 178/A4
Westminster, Eng. 67/B5
W. Monroe, La. 150/A2
Westmount, Que. 184/B1
W. Palm Bch., Fla. 141/D4
W. Point, Miss. 154/C2
Westport, Conn. 136/A3
W. Seneca, N.Y. 160/B1
W. Springfield, Mass. 136/B2
W. Valley City, Utah 174/C1
W. Vancouver, Br. Col. 190/A1
West Virginia (state), U.S. 138-139
W. Warwick, R.I. 137/D3
Westwego, La. 150/B4
Wetar (isl.), Indon. 113/H7
Wetaskiwin, Alta. 191/E2
Wewak, Papua N.G. 112/B6
Wexford, Ire. 67/C4
Weyburn, Sask. 188/C4
Whalsay (isl.), Scot. 66/G1
Whangarei, N.Z. 115/F3
Wheat Ridge, Colo. 178/A4
Wheeling, Ill. 178/A1
Wheeling, W. Va. 138/C2
Whiskeytown-Shasta-Trinity Nat'l Rec. Area, Calif. 132/A1
Whitby, Ont. 187/F3
White (riv.), Ind. 145/A4
White (mts.), N.H. 158/B3
White (sea), Russia 88/E1
White Bear Lake, Minn. 153/C1
Whitecourt, Alta. 191/E2
Whitefish, Mont. 156/A1
Whitefish Bay, Wis. 176/B1
Whitehorse (cap.), Yukon 42/C3
White Mtns. Nat'l Rec. Area, Alaska 129/B1
White Nile (riv.), Africa 61/F4
White Plains, N.Y. 180/C1
White River Junction, Vt. 158/B3
White Rock, Br. Col. 190/B1
White Sands Nat'l Mon., N. Mex. 135/F2
White Sulphur Sprs., W. Va. 138/C3
Whitewater, Wis. 176/C4
Whitney (mt.), Calif. 133/D3
Whittier, Calif. 179/B2
Whyalla, Austr. 114/C4
Wichita, Kans. 147/C3
Wichita Falls, Texas 173?¹
Wicklow, Ire. 67/C4
Wien, see Vienna
Wiener Neustadt, Austria 82/C3
Wiesbaden, Ger. 71/B3
Wigan, Eng. 66/G2
Wight (isl.), Eng 67/F5

Index

Wildwood, N.J. 159/B4
Wilhelmshaven, Ger. 70/B2
Wilkes-Barre, Pa. 171/E3
Wilkinsburg, Pa. 170/B1
Willamette (riv.), Oreg. 169/B2
Willapa (bay), Wash. 175/C1
Willemstad (cap.), Neth. Ant. 51/E4
William H. Taft Nat'l Hist. Site,
  Ohio 167/F1
Williamsburg, Va. 139/E4
Williams Lake, Br. Col. 190/C3
Williamsport, Pa. 171/D3
Williamstown, Mass. 136/B1
Willimantic, Conn. 136/C2
Williston (lake), Br. Col. 190/B1
Williston, N. Dak. 164/B1
Wilmar, Minn. 153/B4
Wilmette, Ill. 178/B1
Wilmington, Del. 139/F2
Wilmington, N.C. 163/E2
Wilson, N.C. 163/E2
Winchester, Eng. 67/F5
Winchester, Ky. 149/E2
Winchester, Va. 139/D2
Wind (riv.), Wyo. 177/B3
Wind Cave Nat'l Pk., S. Dak.
  165/E1
Windhoek (cap.), Namibia 63/D7
Windsor, Conn. 136/B2
Windsor, Ont. 186/B4
Windward (isls.), W. Indies 51/G4
Winfield, Kans. 147/F3
Winkler, Man. 189/E4
Winnebago (lake), Wis. 176/C4
Winnemucca, Nev. 132/A1
Winner, S. Dak. 165/F3
Winnetka, Ill. 178/B1
Winnibigoshish (lake), Minn.
  153/B2
Winnipeg (cap.), Man. 189/F4
Winnipeg (lake), Man. 189/E2
Winnipegosis (lake), Man. 189/D2
Winnipesaukee (lake), N.H.
  158/C3
Winona, Minn. 153/C4
Winooski, Vt. 158/A2
Winslow, Ariz. 130/C3
Winston-Salem, N.C. 163/E4
Winter Haven, Fla. 140/C3
Winter Park, Fla. 140/C3
Winterthur, Switz. 81/D1
Wiscasset, Maine 151/B4
Wisconsin (riv.), Wis. 176/B4
Wisconsin (state), U.S. 176
Wisconsin Dells, Wis. 176/B3
Wisconsin Rapids, Wis. 176/B3
Wittenberg, Ger. 70/E3
Wloclawek, Pol. 87/D2
Woburn, Mass. 137/F4
Woking, Eng. 67/B6
Wolfsburg, Ger. 70/D2
Wollongong, Austr. 115/E4
Wolverhampton, Eng. 67/E4
Wŏnju, S. Korea 106/C3
Wŏnsan, N. Korea 106/B3
Woodbridge, N.J. 180/B3
Woodbridge, Ont. 187/E3
Woodland, Calif. 132/C1
Woods, Lake of the (lake),
  N. Amer. 153/B2, 186/C1
Woods Hole, Mass. 137/F4
Woodstock, N. Br. 182/B2
Woodstock, Ont. 186/B4
Woodward, Okla. 148/A2
Woonsocket, R.I. 137/D2
Wooster, Ohio 166/B3
Worcester, Eng. 67/F4
Worcester, Mass. 136/C2
Worcester, S. Africa 63/D8
Worland, Wyo. 177/A3
World 34-35

Worms, Ger. 71/C4
Worthing, Eng. 67/F5
Worthington, Minn. 153/A4
Wrangel (isl.), Russia 91/K2
Wrangell, Alaska 129/C2
Wrangell-St. Elias Nat'l Pk.,
  Alaska 129/B2
Wrexham, Wales 67/E4
Wright Brothers Nat'l Mem., N.C.
  163/F1
Wrightsville Bch., N.C. 163/E3
Wroclaw, Pol. 86/C3
Wuhan, China 105/E2
Wuhu, China 105/E2
Wupatki Nat'l Mon., Ariz. 130/B2
Wuppertal, Ger. 70/B3
Würzburg, Ger. 71/D4
Wusuli Jiang, China, see Ussuri
Wuxi, China 105/F2
Wyoming, Mich. 152/B4
Wyoming (state), U.S. 177

X

Xankändi, Azer. 89/G7
Xenia, Ohio 167/D1
Xiamen, China 105/E3
Xi'an, China 105/D2
Xiangtan, China 105/E3
Xingu (riv.), Braz. 57/D3
Xining, China 104/D2
Xinjiang Uygur Zizhiqu (aut. reg.),
  China 104/B1
Xinxiang, China 105/E2
Xizang (aut. reg.), China 104/B2
Xuzhou, China 105/E2

Y

Yablonovyy (range), Russia 91/F3
Yakutsk, Russia 91/G2
Yalu (riv.), Asia 106/B2
Yamagata, Japan 107/F3
Yambol, Bulg. 84/D3
Yamoussoukro (cap.), Côte
  d'Ivoire 61/B4
Yanbo, S. Arabia, see Yenbo
Yakima, Wash. 175/C3
Yangtze (Chang Jiang) (riv.),
  China 105/E2
Yankton, S. Dak. 165/F4
Yantai, China 105/F2
Yao, Japan 107/E4
Yaoundé (cap.), Camb. 60/D4
Yap (isl.), Micronesia 116/D5
Yarmouth, Mass. 137/F2
Yarmouth, N.S. 182/B4
Yarmuk (riv.), Asia 98/D2
Yaroslavl', Russia 88/E3
Yazd, Iran 101/J5
Yazoo (riv.), Miss. 154/B2
Yazoo City, Miss. 154/A2
Yekaterinburg, Russia 90/D3
Yelets, Russia 89/E4
Yellow (Huang He) (riv.), China
  105/E2
Yellow (sea), Asia 105/F2
Yellowknife (cap.), N.W.T. 42/E3
Yellowstone (riv.), U.S. 156/B4
Yellowstone Nat'l Pk., U.S.
  177/A4
Yemen 94/D6
Yenbo, S. Arabia 94/D5
Yenisey (riv.), Russia 90/E3
Yerevan (cap.), Armenia 89/F6
Yerington, Nev. 132/C2
Yichang, China 105/E2
Yinchuan, China 104/D2
Yogyakarta, Indon. 113/J2

Yoho Nat'l Pk., Br. Col. 191/D3
Yokkaichi, Japan 106/E4
Yokohama, Japan 107/E4
Yokosuka, Japan 107/E4
Yonkers, N.Y. 180/B1
Yorba Linda, Calif. 179/C3
York (cape), Austr. 115/D2
York, Eng. 67/F3
York, Nebr. 157/B3
York, Pa. 171/D4
Yorkton, Sask. 189/D3
Yorktown, Va. 139/E4
Yosemite Nat'l Pk., Calif. 132/C2
Yoshkar-Ola, Russia 88/G3
Youghal, Ire. 67/B5
Youghiogheny (riv.), U.S. 170/A4
Youngstown, Ohio 166/B4
Ypres (Ieper), Belg. 73/A6
Ysyk-Köl (lake), Kyrgyz. 90/D3
Yucatán (pen.), Mex. 47/H4
Yugoslavia 84/B2
Yukon (terr.), Can. 42/C3
Yukon (riv.), N. Amer. 40/C3
Yuma, Ariz. 130/A4
Yumen, China 104/C2
Yunnan (prov.), China 104/D3
Yuzhno-Sakhalinsk, Russia 91/H3

Z

Zaandam, Neth. 72/E3
Zabrze, Pol. 86/A4
Zacapa, Guat. 48/B2
Zacatecas, Mex. 46/D3
Zagreb (cap.), Croatia 84/A2
Zagros (mts.), Iran 100/E4
Zahedan, Iran 101/M6
Zahle, Leb. 97/G6
Zákinthos (Zante) (isl.), Greece
  85/C4
Zalaegerszeg, Hung. 82/D3
Zambezi (riv.), Africa 63/E6
Zambia 63/E6
Zamboanga, Phil. 109/C7
Zanesville, Ohio 166/C3
Zanjan, Iran 100/F2
Zanzibar (is.), Tanz. 63/F5
Zaporizhzhya, Ukraine 89/E5
Zaragoza, Spain, see Saragossa
Zaria, Nigeria 60/C3
Zarqa, see Ez Zarqa
Zawia, Libya 60/D1
Zefat, Isr. 98/C2
Zermatt, Switz. 80/C2
Zhambyl, Kazak. 90/D3
Zhangjiakou, China 105/E1
Zhejiang (prov.), China 105/E3
Zhengzhou, China 105/E2
Zhezqazghan, Kazak. 90/D3
Zhytomyr, Ukraine 89/C4
Zibo, China 105/E2
Zielona Gora, Pol. 86/B3
Zigong, China 104/D3
Ziguinchor, Sen. 60/A3
Žilina, Slovakia 83/E2
Zimbabwe 63/E-F6
Zinder, Niger 60/C3
Zion, Ill. 144/C1
Zion Nat'l Pk., Utah 174/A4
Zlatoust, Russia 90/D3
Zlín, Czech Rep. 83/D2
Zomba, Malawi 63/F6
Zonguldak, Turkey 96/D2
Zrenjanin, Yugo. 84/C2
Zuni, N. Mex. 135/A2
Zug, Switz. 81/D1
Zugspitze (mt.), Europe 71/D5
Zürich, Switz. 81/D1
Zwickau, Ger. 71/E3
Zwolle, Neth. 72/H3